COLUMBIA GORGE GETAWAYS

12 WEEKEND ADVENTURES, FROM TOWNS TO TRAILS

Laura O. Foster

Towns to Trails
Portland, Oregon

Photographs by the author unless otherwise noted.
Maps by Matthew Hampton of Cascade Cartography, LLC
Editing by Jenefer Angell of Passionfruit Projects
Book design by Brad Smith and Etah Chen of Hot Pepper Studios

Published in 2016 by Towns to Trails Media
www.townstotrails.com
www.gorgegetaways.com

Printed in the United States of America

Library of Congress Cataloging-in-Publication Data

ISBN 978-0-9971082-0-0

On Dog Mountain. *Courtesy Kate McPherson*

TABLE OF CONTENTS

01 FOREWORD

03 ABOUT THE COLUMBIA RIVER GORGE NATIONAL SCENIC AREA

06 HOW TO USE THIS BOOK

12 GORGE HIGHLIGHTS TOUR IN ONE TO FIVE DAYS

14 GORGE OVERVIEW MAPS

TOUR 1

22 WASHOUGAL AND CAPE HORN, WASHINGTON
◆ woolen mill touring and shopping ◆ exploring a very long beach
◆ flat biking to two rivers and downtown restaurants ◆ hiking to waterfalls and clifftops

TOUR 2

36 NORTH BONNEVILLE, BEACON ROCK STATE PARK AND BONNEVILLE HOT SPRINGS RESORT, WASHINGTON
◆ soaking and swimming in hot spring pools ◆ exploring a river island and its stories ◆ biking flat trails ◆ hiking up a pillar or to waterfalls

TOUR 3

52 STEVENSON AND SKAMANIA LODGE, WASHINGTON
◆urban exploring to river, waterfall and brewpub ◆ luxuriating at a forest spa resort
◆ festival-going at a scenic cove ◆ biking along and across the river

TOUR 4

66 CARSON AND THE GIFFORD PINCHOT NATIONAL FOREST, WASHINGTON
◆ escaping to an ancient forest overnight ◆ soaking in hot springs
◆ seeing timber country ◆ hiking to waterfalls and mountain tops

TOUR 5

80 WHITE SALMON, BINGEN, CATHERINE CREEK AND COYOTE WALL, WASHINGTON
◆ rafting the White Salmon ◆ exploring dam relics ◆ walking to restaurants from a downtown inn ◆ experiencing two premier gorge hikes

TOUR 6

98 LYLE, MARYHILL AND GOLDENDALE OBSERVATORY STATE PARK, WASHINGTON
◆ star-gazing ◆ exploring Maryhill Museum and other Sam Hill wonders
◆ road-tripping through high prairie scenery ◆ spotting bald eagles
◆ biking part or all of the Klickitat Trail

TOUR 7

114 LYLE AND COLUMBIA HILLS STATE PARK, WASHINGTON
♦ taking a petroglyph tour ♦ wine-touring ♦ following scenic backroads ♦ hiking through wildflowers and old ranch equipment

TOUR 8

126 THE DALLES AND DESCHUTES RIVER STATE RECREATION AREA, OREGON
♦ discovering 10,000 years of history ♦ biking river to bluff in The Dalles ♦ wine-tasting, exploring and shopping in a historic downtown ♦ jet-boating or biking at the Deschutes

TOUR 9

148 MOSIER, THE HISTORIC COLUMBIA RIVER HIGHWAY AND ROWENA CREST, OREGON
♦ picking cherries ♦ car-free biking to Hood River through twin tunnels
♦ town-to-trail hiking to a waterfall and Mosier Plateau
♦ scenic highway touring to vineyards, overlooks and beaches

TOUR 10

164 HOOD RIVER, OREGON
♦ taking a lesson in standup paddling or windsurfing ♦ shopping and eating downtown ♦ urban biking to beer, beach and bluff ♦ scenic touring to food, wine, waterfalls and museums

TOUR 11

194 CASCADE LOCKS AND THE HISTORIC COLUMBIA RIVER HIGHWAY STATE TRAIL, OREGON
♦ biking to waterfalls, overlooks and sturgeon ♦ learning about the Cascades of the Columbia and the locks that tamed them ♦ relaxing in brewpubs and galleries ♦ discovering Eagle Creek waterfalls and spawning salmon

TOUR 12

214 TROUTDALE AND WATERFALLS ALONG THE HISTORIC COLUMBIA RIVER HIGHWAY, OREGON
♦ biking or driving to waterfalls and viewpoints ♦ exploring a converted county poor farm ♦ urban trekking to shops, Sandy River beaches, restaurants, museums and galleries

236 APPENDIX A
Festivals and events by month

243 APPENDIX B
Outfitters, guides, lessons, cruises, excursions and online resources

253 APPENDIX C
Buying local fish

254 ACKNOWLEDGMENTS

255 INDEX

From the Historic Columbia River Highway State Trail

FOREWORD

As the executive director of a nonprofit organization that works to protect the Columbia River Gorge, I am often asked why I have stayed in my job for nearly two decades. The answer lies in what Laura Foster unveils in this book: the Columbia Gorge is a place you never fully "discover" and every excursion in the gorge reinforces that this place is much more than a pretty face.

As one of our nation's only National Scenic Areas, the gorge's landscapes are both majestic and sublime. Driving past waterfalls on Oregon's Historic Columbia River Highway, tasting cherries or wine grown on volcanic slopes, or hiking on quiet trails (yes, there are many, as this book demonstrates), your senses are overtaken as if a master painter with a full assortment of colors and textures has added never-seen variations of sunlight, clouds and rain to his palette.

For many visitors who know only of the gorge's signature attractions, their impression of the gorge is powerful but superficial. A quick photo here, a short walk there. Opportunities lost. Laura takes you beyond the selfies and popular hikes to the bounties and back stories of the gorge's towns and natural areas. With this set of 12 vacations, you can delve into the secrets of the gorge's beaches, back roads, historic downtowns, trails, shopping, dining, dams and museums.

As you read this book and choose your next Columbia Gorge adventure, remember that you are standing on the shoulders of those who fought to protect this place from the commercialism that has overrun many beautiful areas of our country. Remember that you are a guest in the backyard of 70,000 local residents. Remember that endangered species and wildflowers that exist nowhere else in the world are sharing their home with you.

Welcome to one of America's great treasures.

Executive Director
Friends of the Columbia Gorge

To learn more about Friends' guided hikes, membership opportunities, advocacy and conservation work, visit **gorgefriends.org.**

From Cape Horn, looking east

COLUMBIA RIVER GORGE NATIONAL SCENIC AREA

In 1986, the Columbia River Gorge was designated by President Ronald Reagan and the United States Congress as the country's second National Scenic Area.* The gorge, which forms part of the border between Oregon and Washington, carves a deep passage through the Cascade Mountains of the Pacific Northwest. Deep in the gorge, waterfalls drop off cliffs up to 600 feet high. Above the river, snow-capped volcanoes frame the gorge's towns, orchards, vineyards and vistas.

Like a national park

The Columbia River Gorge is like a national park but in many ways even better, with its historic riverfront towns full of restaurants, galleries and stores; its gorge-grown food, beer, wine and cider; and its many ways to play, from standup paddling to bike touring to windsurfing. And when you're lifting your face up to the mist at a waterfall or looking down at the vista from atop a peak, it's easy to see why the gorge has been protected as a National Scenic Area.

The king of roads

A century ago, when the nation was in the midst of improving its roadways, builders in the Pacific Northwest realized that the gorge would be an epic setting for a masterpiece of road engineering. The result is Oregon's Historic Columbia River Highway, dedicated in 1916. It's one of the most scenic journeys you'll ever take: the highway curves into waterfall-splashed dells, loops in graceful figure eights from cliff to river, and swoops over canyons atop elegant arched bridges. Even before the road was finished, in 1915 the U.S. Secretary of Agriculture created the nation's first "scenic reserve" along its route.

Completed in the early 1920s, the narrow Columbia River Highway was soon superseded by a bigger, less curvy and more level route through the gorge, now called Interstate 84, which stays close to the water. Today, with through-traffic diverted to the interstate, the old highway on the hill is ideal for driving slowly, stopping often

---

* California's Mono Basin National Forest Scenic Area was the first, in 1984.

and enjoying the journey. Long stretches are open only to bikes and pedestrians.

Geologic forces

Violent floods created the landscapes of today's gorge. During the last Ice Age (12,000 to 18,000 years ago) glaciers periodically dammed the Clark Fork River in western Montana. Behind each dam, an enormous lake formed. Episodically, perhaps every 40 to 140 years, the ice dam melted or was breached. When that happened, the water burst forth, raging down the valley of the Columbia River westward to the Pacific Ocean. Geologists estimate the floodwaters flowed as fast as 65 mph and in the narrow gorge reached depths of 1,000 feet. As they scoured every inch of land in their path, the waters collected trees, boulders, ice chunks, soil, sand and gravel, battering the Columbia's valley into a vertical steepness. After 40 to 60 such flood events, tributary creeks that once flowed gently into the river now dropped straight off cliffs hundreds of feet high, creating the stunning scenery of the Columbia River Gorge.

Native Americans

Native Americans found the gorge to be a hospitable homeland. Salmon and other fish were abundant, the climate mild, and the river a transportation route for commerce and gathering sustenance. Humans have lived in the gorge for over 10,000 years. At sites in the eastern gorge, the river narrowed into basalt-lined chutes, fish were concentrated, and vast settlements and markets arose.

The Indians' economy and way of life changed with the arrival of the first nonnative trappers and traders in the late 1700s who carried diseases that ultimately decimated entire populations. By the 1850s, when Euro-American settlement had begun in earnest in the Pacific Northwest, native people in the gorge were not in a strong position to resist the U.S. government's pressure to sign treaties. In 1855 they surrendered their lands in exchange for perpetual rights to historic fishing and food gathering sites. These treaty tribes are the Umatilla, Nez Perce, Yakama and Warm Springs. Tribal fishers still fish in traditional ways with dip nets and drift nets. As they have for millennia, their fishing platforms, or scaffolds, hang off cliffs along the river, especially at historic fishing and food gathering sites such as the Cascades of the Columbia (at Cascade Locks, Oregon, and Bonneville Dam) or near the mouth of the Klickitat River, a Columbia tributary. Many historic fishing sites, such as the Long Narrows and Celilo Falls east of The Dalles, are now underwater, flooded by twentieth century dams. In-lieu fishing sites, several of which are seen in this book, are reserved for tribal fishers to replace fishing grounds inundated by rising water behind the dams.

Settlement and economic change

Beginning in the 1840s, early settlers logged the forests and fished the river, and lumber mills and salmon canneries were once common Columbia River industries. They were the economic engines that created good jobs and thriving small towns along the river—the towns you'll explore with this book. As the resource-based economies evolved over the last century, and especially since the 1980s, gorge towns began to focus on other economic engines. The transition began in earnest with the naming of the gorge as a National Scenic Area, new restrictions on harvesting timber, and the gorge's emergence as a world-famous windsurfing destination.

Today, the economies of gorge towns are eclectic. Drones are manufactured, wine grapes are grown and wine bottled, orchard crops are exported, timber is harvested, sporting equipment is designed and manufactured, beer is brewed and bottled, and Google servers hum.

A national treasure

The Columbia River Gorge is not a park preserved in its natural, unchanged state, but a fascinating corridor of scenic beauty, outdoor recreation, superb food and drink, and vibrant towns. If you live in the Portland region, you're lucky to be close enough to enjoy the gorge often, and in every season.

HOW TO
USE THIS BOOK

When you're planning a vacation—even a short weekend getaway—the Internet offers many options. The problem is, they're buried in a galaxy of websites. The amount of info to sort through can be as stressful as a day on deadline.

12 vacations, ready to go, in one book

This book solves that problem for you. With 12 complete two- to three-day itineraries for a range of gorge destinations, it's like having a personal tour guide waiting for you in your glove box. *Columbia Gorge Getaways* makes it easy for you to decide on Thursday to escape for the weekend and on Friday hit the road, fully executed plan in hand. It's the only book that wrangles all of the gorge's many enticements into one easy-to-use set of itineraries: from a wind-surfing lesson to hot spring–soaking, from biking scenic streets to lifting a pint of local IPA, from museum-going to wine-tasting, from waterfall-touring to river swimming.

Use the book in late winter to head east to the sunny, flower-sprouting bluffs of the eastern gorge. Use it in spring to combine a tour of blooming cherry and apple orchards with other gorge adventures. Use it in summer to build a weekend of hiking and urban exploring around a windsurfing or blues festival. Use it in fall to tour wineries at harvest and follow the call of back roads through high deserts and prairies.

It's what to do with out of town guests

When you have visitors who come to the Northwest eager to see all the beautiful sites they've read about in the *New York Times*, hand them this book, wave goodbye and know they'll come back from the gorge excited, happy and perhaps ready to move here themselves.

Each chapter, or tour, covers one gorge town (in a few tours it's two or three towns), from the lush green west end of the gorge to the brilliantly arid east end. For each tour, you'll find out what to see and do—indoors and outdoors, active and relaxing—and where to eat, drink and sleep. The highlights tour condenses the best of the gorge into a one to five day experience.

What to bring, when to come

You'll also get tips on whether to call ahead to make reservations for

an outing, lesson or adventure, and what you might want to bring—
like bikes, swimsuits or a cooler for hauling home a fresh-caught
salmon. And always, bring binoculars. Bald eagles, despite not being
rare anymore, are still an awesome sight, and they're common in the
gorge. The tours also tell you the best times of year to visit, and how
long it takes to get there from the Portland area (specifically, from the
I-84/I-5 interchange).

Appendix A describes gorge festivals and events by month. A
festival makes a great fulcrum on which to build a getaway adventure.
Appendix B lists whom to call if you want a lesson, a guide, a rental or
an excursion—from aerial tours to windsurfing. Appendix C tells you
where to buy freshly caught fish from a tribal fisher.

Boldface text in the tours denotes places or businesses that are
listed, with details, at the end of the tour or in Appendix B.

Here are a few things to know about the gorge:

Climate and weather

From Washougal, Washington, and Troutdale, Oregon, on the west
end to the mid-gorge, at about Stevenson and Carson, Washington,
and Cascade Locks, Oregon, the climate is maritime: influenced by the
Pacific Ocean. That means mild temperatures in winter and plentiful
rain from fall through spring. Summers are reliably dry, as they are
throughout the Portland region. In winter it can freeze (and waterfalls
are spectacular when it does—head out to see them if roads are safe),
but freezing temperatures do not persist long.

From mid-gorge to the east end—Hood River, Oregon, and
White Salmon, Washington, to The Dalles, Oregon, and Goldendale,
Washington—the climate and landscapes change dramatically and
amazingly: annual rainfall plummets, and Douglas fir and western red
cedar forests are replaced by Ponderosa pine and Oregon white oak.
The land is often bare, or barely covered with soil, leaving the gorge's
geologic story on splendidly naked display, with layers of volcanic flows
sliced in cross section by Ice Age floods. Winter can be very cold in
the eastern gorge: the climate is more continental, with the relatively
warmer air off the Pacific Ocean blocked by the Cascade Mountains.

Generally, spring can come as early as late January to the eastern
gorge. And that brings out the wildflowers, which will fill your heart
and your memory card. Various species of flowers roll out their beauty
until about late May. So early to late spring is ideal for the eastern gorge,
which coincides nicely with the Portland area's rainy season—just

about the point when you find that grey skies have truly lost their charm, the gorge is starting to heat up, and you can escape there. Spring and into summer are also great for rafting the tributary rivers.

Summer is when the west winds blow and the mid-gorge celebrates with windsurfing festivals and events. Hood River especially is a joyful place to visit if you like to bike, hike, swim or otherwise be in or near the water. Lots of gear rentals and lessons make this the place to try a new water sport. The restaurant choices fill several pages of this book. I love open-water swimming so the book lists good swimming holes and sandy beaches. Water temps are brisk, with 70 degrees about the top limit, but in summer the dry warm air makes swimming pure pleasure, surrounded as you are by cliffs or waterfalls.

Fall is brilliant, with maples turning yellow and vineyards and orchards in the mid and eastern gorge glowing orange through mid-November or so. Winds are often calm then and the gorge is a more peaceful, contemplative place than in summer.

Waterfalls are spectacular in winter and early spring when they're roaring with seasonal run-off. The rainy season is a good time to visit deep woods and waterfalls on the west end, where the rain and peace create a green sanctuary and nearby hot springs or brewpubs warm you afterward.

Seasonality and business hours

In the tours, hours listed for stores, restaurants, wineries and museums are high season unless otherwise indicated. Even in summer, Monday and Tuesday are often quiet days in gorge towns, with many venues closed. If you're coming in the off season, expect that hours may be different, or call ahead if it's vital that something be open before you make the trip.

Passes you may need

Not all sites in the gorge require passes. Below are passes you may need and where they're required. In case you get to a site without a pass, carry $5 and $10 bills so you can buy one at a trailhead.

Discover Pass

This pass gives access to state recreation lands in Washington, including state parks, popular water access sites (such as along the Washougal River) and other natural or wildlife areas.

In 2016, annual passes are $30 and can be shared between two vehicles. Day passes are $10. The fine for not having one is $99, reduced to $59 if you show proof you've purchased one within 15 days of your fine. Buy a pass online at discoverpass.wa.gov or at various stores in the gorge. See discoverpass.wa.gov for a list of stores by county. Washington's gorge counties are, west to east: Clark, Skamania and Klickitat. Beacon Rock State Park is the only fee site in the gorge with an automated pay station. Washington has many free days for visiting state parks. Find this year's list at discoverpass.wa.gov.

Northwest Forest Pass

This pass is issued by the U.S. Forest Service as a day or e-pass ($5) or annual pass ($30). It's good in both Oregon and Washington for Forest Service–managed day use sites such as the Bridge of the Gods, Eagle Creek and Dog Mountain trailheads. The Interagency Annual Pass and some other passes work too. For sites where the pass is required within the Columbia River Gorge National Scenic Area see fs.usda.gov. The pass is good for the vehicle and all passengers.

Buy the day, annual and e-pass at discovernw.org. In the gorge you can buy a pass from the Columbia River Gorge National Scenic Area offices, 902 Wasco Ave., Suite B, Hood River.

Oregon State Parks Pass

Oregon has hundreds of state parks. A few charge a fee, including Rooster Rock, Viento and Mayer state parks, plus Benson State Recreation Area and the Mark O. Hatfield trailheads at the Hood River to Mosier segment of the Historic Columbia River Highway State Trail.

Buy a $5 day use pass at the sites named above or from REI in Portland or Hillsboro, Plaid Pantry in Troutdale (246 W Columbia River Highway), Vista House, Shortt Supply (116 Oak St., Hood River) and Bi-Mart (3300 Sixth St., The Dalles.) Or buy the $30 annual pass by calling 800-551-6949. Join the Oregon State Parks Foundation and receive a free pass.

Major gorge roads

I-84 is the freeway on the Oregon side that runs east to west on or near the river level. It's speedy and scenic but you'll have to drive so fast you'll miss a lot. Construction on it began in the 1930s, when transportation planners realized the windy and narrow Columbia River Highway—which was built between 1913 and 1922—could not handle increasing traffic loads and vehicle sizes. From the 1930s onward, improvements to the interstate highway led to today's four lanes of 65-mph traffic.

Oregon's Historic Columbia River Highway originally ran 73 miles from Troutdale to The Dalles. It was dedicated in 1916 and attracted worldwide attention for its beauty. After the freeway came online, parts of this scenic road were abandoned or destroyed. Since 1987, Oregon Department of Transportation has been reviving and restoring those sections. Learn about the work at oregon.gov/odot/hwy/hcrh. The book takes you on all drivable segments, called the Historic Columbia River Highway, and on non-motorized segments, called the Historic Columbia River Highway State Trail. The highway was designed to showcase waterfalls, scenic viewpoints and the land's sinuous curves. On drivable sections the speed limit is low, so you can enjoy the journey and stop often.

Washington has a gem in its SR 14, a mostly two-lane road that hugs the banks of the Columbia for 180 miles from Vancouver eastward. Speeds are efficient, up to 55 mph, but not knuckle-whitening. The views are incredible, plus it doesn't bypass the towns, so you can easily stop for coffee or a meal. Older, curvy sections have been superseded in places with straightaways built out over the water. Those older sections, featured in several scenic tours in the book, were part of the road when it had another name, the Evergreen Highway. Old Highway 8 is another of those scenic road sections the book takes you on.

Alternatives to driving

From Portland's Union Station, you can take **Amtrak's Empire Builder** train to the gorge, with stops in Bingen and Wishram, Washington. However, if you bring your bike, you're met with fairly inhospitable biking conditions on SR 14, which is the only option for east-west travel in many spots on the Washington side. It's narrow, fast and curvy with no shoulder. Contact **Mt. Adams Transportation Services**; its buses connect to Amtrak in Bingen and Wishram and can get you to White Salmon or Hood River where good biking roads await you. See Appendix B's "Public transportation, buses" for other providers who'll get you where you're going in the gorge, with or without a bike.

On the Oregon side, east-west biking on the Historic Columbia River Highway is superb except for one stretch where bikers have to use the shoulder of I-84 for about 10 miles between Wyeth and the west end of Hood River (exits 51 to 62). Not advised. From exit 62 eastward you can bike Hood River streets to the Historic Columbia River Highway and take that beautiful road all the way to The Dalles.

Alternatively, you can put your bike on a boat in Portland (see page 209), get off in Cascade Locks and start biking. You can also take TriMet to Troutdale and begin biking at the west end of the historic highway.

Taxes on goods and lodging

Oregon

No sales tax on anything. Lodging, or occupancy, taxes range in gorge locales from 8 percent in Cascade Locks to slightly over 13 percent in Troutdale.

Washington

There's no tax on groceries in Washington. Sales tax on other items in gorge locales ranges from 7 percent in Klickitat County to 8.4 percent in Clark County. Ask when you're making a purchase: retailers aren't required to but may give you a sales tax exemption if you live in states and Canadian provinces or territories that have 0 to 3 percent sales tax: Alaska, Colorado, Delaware, Montana, New Hampshire, Oregon, Alberta, Northwest Territories, Nunavut and Yukon Territory. You just have to show a valid driver's license or other official identification. The tax exemption does not apply to restaurant food and drink, lodging or marijuana.

Lodging tax in Washington (which includes the sales tax) ranges in gorge locales from 9 percent in parts of Skamania and Klickitat counties to 10.4 percent in Clark County.

GORGE HIGHLIGHTS TOUR
IN ONE TO FIVE DAYS

If you're visiting the Portland-Vancouver region for just a few days or want to show your visitors the best of the Columbia River Gorge, this condensed itinerary showcases the highlights. Do all of the days, for a five-day tour, or pick a day or two for a shorter tour. All locations are within 100 miles of Portland.

Use the Index for more information on sites named here. Skip activities if you want, and peruse the relevant tours for other sites and activities that might be of interest to you.

From April through October, if you want a guided petroglyph tour at Columbia Hills State Park on Day 3, call ahead to reserve at 509-439-9032. If you want to raft the White Salmon River on Day 4, make advance arrangements. See Appendix B.

Oregon, west end
Portland to Hood River: 62 miles

Tours 10, 11 and 12 cover these sites, plus where to stay, shop and eat.

- From Portland, drive east on I-84 to exit 22, Corbett, which will lead you uphill to the Historic Columbia River Highway, a National Historic Landmark. Stop for your first big gorge view at Crown Point and learn about the gorge at its jewel-like visitor center, Vista House, where you can get coffee and snacks.

- From Crown Point, continue east on the historic highway. You'll pass many waterfalls: enjoy them from roadside viewpoints or via short hikes. At Multnomah Falls, Oregon's number one tourist attraction, hike to the bridge at the base of the upper falls. Have lunch in the historic stone lodge. Reserve a table at 503-695-2376 during the summer.

- From Multnomah Falls, drive east on I-84. Go 9 miles and exit at Bonneville Dam, exit 40. See Herman the giant sturgeon, and maybe take a dam tour or feed fish in hatchery ponds. Call the dam's fish count hotline: 541-374-4011. (It also tells the river's temperature at the dam.) If the number of fish passing through the fish ladders is high, watch at the underwater viewing station. In September and October, stop at Eagle Creek (exit 41 eastbound only) to watch salmon spawn.

The elements at their finest, Vista House

Looking west from Hood River's Ruthton County Park (just off I-84 exit 62), April

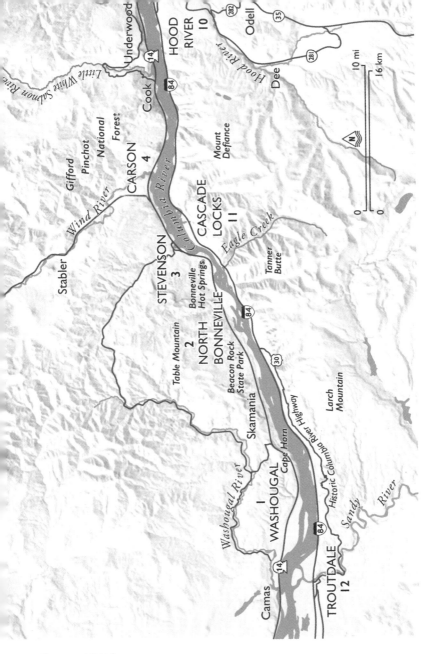

Little White Salmon River

Underwood

HOOD RIVER 10

Odell

35

282

14

Hood River

Cook

281

Dee

84

Gifford Pinchot National Forest

CARSON 4

Columbia River

Mount Defiance

N

10 mi
16 km

0

Wind River

Stabler

STEVENSON 3

CASCADE LOCKS 11

Eagle Creek

Bonneville Hot Springs

Tanner Butte

Table Mountain 2

NORTH BONNEVILLE

84

Beacon Rock State Park

30

Skamania

Larch Mountain

Washougal River

Cape Horn

Historic Columbia River Highway

Camas

WASHOUGAL 1

14

84

TROUTDALE 12

Sandy River

George, west end

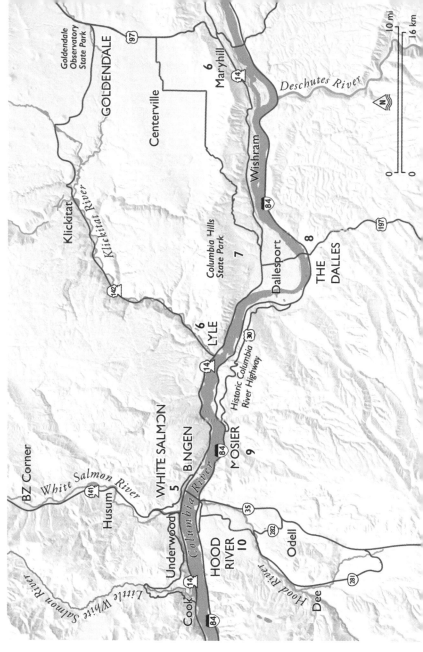

George, east end

- From Bonneville Dam or Eagle Creek, drive east on I-84 and take exit 44, Cascade Locks. Drive east on the main street, WaNaPa, a short ways, then turn left on Portage Road and into Cascade Locks Marine Park. Here, see the historic locks, the Bridge of the Gods and views of the Bonneville Landslide on the Washington side. Eat at Thunder Island Brewing above the locks. Back on WaNaPa, shop at galleries and buy canned or smoked salmon at Brigham Fish Market, owned by a Native American family.
- From Cascade Locks, continue east on I-84 to Hood River, exits 62 to 64. Eat at a brewpub and spend the night downtown, on the waterfront or at a working orchard (page 191 for options).

Oregon, east end
Hood River to The Dalles: 22 miles

Tours 8, 9 and 10 cover these sites, plus where to stay, shop and eat.

- After breakfast in Hood River (page 185 for options), drive the Hood River Fruit Loop (hoodriverfruitloop.com or the similar, but shorter scenic drive on page 173), and stop at wineries, orchards, farm stands and the Western Antique Aeroplane and Automobile Museum.
- Back in Hood River after your morning excursion, shop for local art, outdoor clothing or gifts downtown and eat lunch. Page 185 lists options on the waterfront, downtown or in the Heights.
- In the afternoon, leave Hood River and drive I-84 east to exit 69, which leads into the heart of tiny Mosier. From there, drive east on an extremely beautiful section of the Historic Columbia River Highway past vineyards, orchards and viewpoints. Take in the spectacular views at the Rowena Crest Overlook.
- From Rowena Crest, continue east on the historic highway into The Dalles, stopping at the west end of town at the Columbia Gorge Discovery Center and Museum for an hour or so of learning about the gorge.
- From the museum, drive east into downtown (via I-84 exit 85 or continuing on the old highway). Stay at The Dalles Inn and walk to dinner at the Baldwin Saloon or Clock Tower Ales.

Looking north from Rowena Crest overlook at the mouth of the Klickitat River, June

Hood River's Western Antique Aeroplane and Automobile Museum

Oregon and Washington, east end
The Dalles to Maryhill Museum of Art: 21 miles
Maryhill Museum of Art to White Salmon:
34 miles

Tours 6, 7 and 8 cover these sites, plus where to stay, shop and eat.

- After breakfast in The Dalles (page 145 for options), drive east on I-84 and take exit 87 north to cross the Columbia River on U.S. 197. In Washington now, drive east on SR 14 through country scoured bare by the Missoula Floods to the fantastical Maryhill Museum of Art. Inside are treasures. Spend an hour or two, and then have lunch at Loïe's: The Museum Cafe.
- Maryhill Museum is the furthest east you'll go; after finishing up there, drive west on SR 14 about 1 mile for wine-tasting with big views at Maryhill Winery. Enjoy live music on the terrace from 1 to 5 p.m. weekends from Memorial Day into September.
- Continue west on SR 14 about 14 miles to Columbia Hills State Park. At its riverfront, see petroglyphs at one of the Columbia's longest-inhabited sites. If you have time, do the park's Crawford Oaks hike. In spring, wildflowers carpet the slopes. For a look at the eastern gorge's ranching past, see the old equipment and ranch house at the park's Dalles Mountain Ranch.
- Continue west on SR 14 10 miles to Lyle and stop at the Klickitat Trail or at Balfour-Klickitat Day Use Area for a stroll along the bluffs in an area frequented (especially in winter) by bald eagles.
- Drive west on SR 14 another 11 miles to White Salmon. Have dinner at Everybody's Brewing or Henni's Kitchen and Bar and spend the night at the Inn of the White Salmon. If you have energy and daylight left, stretch your legs with the town walkabout on page 82.

Washington, middle and west end
White Salmon to Skamania Lodge: 25 miles

Tours 3, 4 and 5 cover these sites, plus where to stay, shop and eat.

- Wake up in White Salmon and head out for your raft trip on the White Salmon River, the gorge's most rafted whitewater river. If rafting's not your thing, call Northwestern Lake Riding Stables for a horseback ride, or take a hike at Coyote Wall or Catherine Creek. Afterward, have lunch in White Salmon or Bingen (page 95 for options).
- From Bingen, drive 5 miles west on SR 14 to the Spring Creek National Fish Hatchery on the Columbia. Take a tour, enjoy

Maryhill Museum of Art, May

Balsamroot at Dalles Mountain Ranch in Columbia Hills State Park, April

stupendous views and watch windsurfers if the west wind is blowing.

- In the afternoon, continue west on especially scenic stretches of SR 14 to Stevenson's Skamania Lodge. Settle into this luxurious resort and have dinner in the dining room, bar, or outside on the patio overlooking the gorge cliffs.

Windsurfers, from Spring Creek National Fish Hatchery, April

Washington, west end
Skamania Lodge to Portland via SR 14: 54 miles

DAY
5

Tours 1 and 2 cover these sites, plus where to stay, shop and eat.

- Wake up at Skamania Lodge and enjoy the excellent pool before you check out. Then drive west 9 miles on SR 14 to Beacon Rock State Park. Walk the path-of-many-switchbacks to the top of the 848-ft peak (elevation gain: 680 feet) and enjoy views up and down the gorge. If you've got more energy, do another one of the park's shorter hikes to waterfalls or along the river.
- From Beacon Rock, drive 15 miles west on SR 14 and get out your camera for a flat and beautiful walk at Steigerwald Lake National Wildlife Refuge.
- Stop in Washougal for a late lunch downtown at Our Bar or Amnesia Brewing, allowing time to spend an hour shopping at Pendleton Woolen Mills before its 5 p.m. close.
- From Washougal, drive back to the Portland-Vancouver area.

Eating outside, overlooking gorge cliffs, at Skamania Lodge

WASHOUGAL AND CAPE HORN

WASHINGTON

At the far west end of the gorge, Washougal's got one of the gorge's best beaches—Cottonwood Beach at Captain William Clark Park—plus the wonderful Pendleton Woolen Mills and superb downtown eating and drinking spots.

A summer overnight in Washougal feels like the easiest, best vacation you've had in a long time. In just 23 miles and 29 minutes from downtown Portland you can hike along a river or atop cliffs, swim, explore a wildlife refuge, shop at a woolen mill outlet store, and have a burger at a bar called the Big Foot Inn.

A hot-weather weekend is ideal for this getaway, but other seasons when the weather is fine are excellent too, and you're more likely to have the beach to yourself. I like visiting Washougal any time, and especially when the Pendleton outlet store is having a sale. The biking is low-stress here, so even if you're not an avid urban biker, the ride on the flat Dike Trail and city streets is relaxing and pleasant.

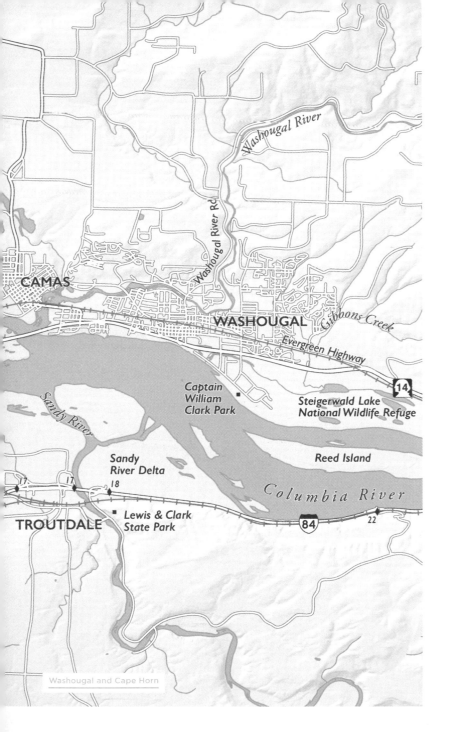

Washougal River

Washougal River Rd

CAMAS

WASHOUGAL

Gibbons Creek

Evergreen Highway

14

Captain
William
Clark Park

Steigerwald Lake
National Wildlife Refuge

Sandy River

Sandy
River Delta

Reed Island

17

17

18

Columbia River

TROUTDALE

Lewis & Clark
State Park

84

22

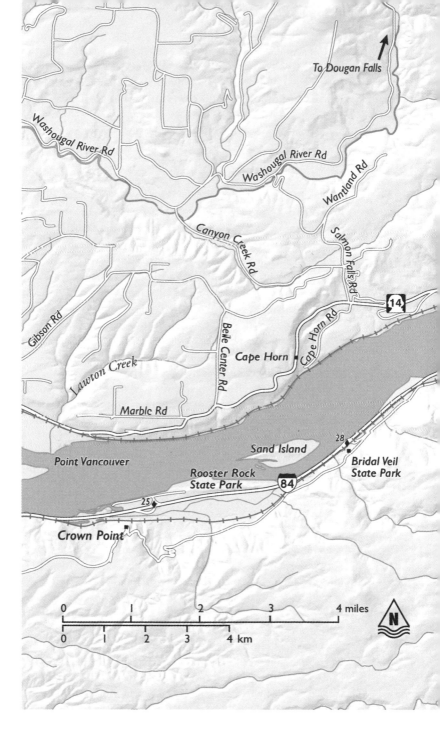

To Dougan Falls

Washougal River Rd

Washougal River Rd

Wantland Rd

Canyon Creek Rd

Salmon Falls Rd

14

Gibson Rd

Belle Center Rd

Cape Horn

Cape Horn Rd

Lawton Creek

Marble Rd

Point Vancouver

Sand Island

28

Bridal Veil
State Park

Rooster Rock
State Park

84

25

Crown Point

| 0 | | 1 | | 2 | | 3 | | 4 miles |

| 0 | 1 | 2 | 3 | 4 km |

N

You may want to bring bikes, bike locks (a cable lock works better than a U-lock on the Dike Trail if you want to hike at Steigerwald Lake National Wildlife Refuge), swimsuits and a Discover Pass. If you want to rent a standup paddleboard on Day 2, reserve at Sweetwater SUP Rentals.

Download a map of the Cape Horn Trail at capehorntrail.org.

Adventure 1
Hiking Cape Horn

If you bring your bike, drop it off at Washougal's **Best Western Plus Parkersville** (your home for the night) so you won't have to leave it in or on your car at the Cape Horn trailhead.

From the Best Western, head east on SR 14. Pass Mount Pleasant Iris Farm at Marble Road. A National Display Garden for Japanese iris, it sits on the flanks of a Boring Lava dome, one of 32 shield volcanoes and cinder cones west of the Cascade Mountains. Stop to visit during bloom time in May.

Continue east on SR 14 to one of the gorge's most photographed views atop Cape Horn. The narrow Cape Horn Overlook pullout on SR 14 offers an easy-access, stunning view that helps you get the lay of the land for the Cape Horn hike you're about to do. The overlook is near where road crews blasted a level road base out of the vertical cliff. They used too much dynamite and a more-than-anticipated hail of rock cascaded down onto the lowlands you can see from here. Below you, the peaceful road winding along a green field is Cape Horn Road, which once led to a boat landing on the Columbia. On the full Cape Horn Trail loop, described next, you walk up that road near the end of the hike.

To hike the Cape Horn Trail, continue east on SR 14 and turn left on Salmon Falls Road, then right immediately into a Park and Ride lot. Park and walk across Salmon Falls Road to the trailhead. Here, enter the upper part of the Cape Horn Trail loop. This trail section is open year-round, for a 5-mile out-and-back hike to an overlook. The full 7.7-mile loop, which takes you out to the cliffs above the river and down to their base along Cape Horn Road, is open July 16 to January 30. The rest of the year it's closed to protect nesting peregrine falcons. See gorgefriends.org and capehorntrail.org.

One area along the upper trail loop was subdivided as residential lots in 1983, before the gorge was named a National Scenic Area and land protections put in place. A Portlander, Nancy Russell, who later founded Friends of the Columbia Gorge, bought 12 of the undeveloped

16 lots in order to preserve them. Later, other land conservation groups purchased two of the remaining four undeveloped lots. In 2006, Friends bought the last two lots: one that had a home on it, and another undeveloped lot. Friends had the home demolished; the site is now the Nancy Russell Overlook

Adventure 2
Waterfall splashing and river floating

After the hike, drive this scenic route to waterfalls and swimming holes: From the Park and Ride at Salmon Falls Road and SR 14, drive north on Salmon Falls 3 miles and turn right on Washougal River Road. Follow it 5 miles to the end of the pavement, to Dougan Falls on the Washougal River. Dougan Creek Falls is here too. Both have good swimming holes.

Afterward, return to Washougal River Road and drive back to the intersection with Salmon Falls Road. Keep right to stay on Washougal River Road. At Canyon Creek Road, stock up on snacks at **Washougal River Mercantile**. On the drive downriver into Washougal, find good swimming holes around mileposts 4 and 3 on Washougal River Road. Some sites require a Discover Pass.

Adventure 3
Eating, drinking and sleeping on the river

Check into your room at the **Best Western Plus Parkersville** on the river near the new-in-2015 Washougal Waterfront Park, built in part on the site of the Hambleton Lumber mill that closed in 2010. From the Best Western, walk to happy hour (3 to 6 p.m.) at the **Puffin Cafe**. It's floating on the river just west of the hotel at the Port of Camas-Washougal's marina.

From the Best Western, drive or bike 1.4 flat miles on quiet streets into downtown to **Amnesia Brewing** or **Hearth Restaurant**: go north on Second Street/Port Street, turn right on C Street, turn right on Ninth Street, then left on B Street, which turns into Main Street after crossing Washougal River Road.

Adventure 1
Biking to beaches, a wildlife refuge, a woolen mill and restaurants

DAY
2

You can also walk this approximately 7-mile flat route. Check out of your room, bike into town and have breakfast and coffee at **OurBar**. From there, bike to the route's start: the parking lot at the end of

Durgan Street, just past **Two Rivers Heritage Museum**. Head toward **Pendleton Woolen Mills**, turn right on Pendleton Way, and pass through the pedestrian/bike tunnel under SR 14. Basalt petroglyphs here are student-made replicas of rock art in the gorge, much of which was lost when Columbia River dams inundated ancient sites of human occupation. The tunnel opens up to Steamboat Landing Park. Though today only pilings remain, in the 1880s this was Washougal Landing, where steamboats met passengers and goods were loaded. Head east on the Dike Trail. It's tightly packed gravel and runs 3.5 miles one way atop a dike built in 1966, which turned river bottomlands that flooded annually into industrial sites. Interpretive signs offer great info along the way. On clear days, Mount Hood is your constant companion.

On the Dike Trail at 32nd Street a large parking area testifies to the popularity of Captain William Clark Park, a wild ribbon of woods and beaches here. In 1806, the Lewis and Clark expedition camped here for seven days during their two-year exploration of the Pacific Northwest for President Thomas Jefferson. At Recognition Plaza, replica concrete canoes lie scattered about as if the explorers will be back in just a moment. From the plaza, head to the river on the Provision Camp Trail for scenic walking and swimming at Cottonwood Beach. Lock your bike at the rack here if you want to swim and hike around. The expedition camped on the beach and hunted game for provisions while Clark scouted the mouth of the Willamette River. Lower river levels from late summer to fall expose up to 2 miles of beach. You'll feel like you're in the wilderness.

After exploring the Provision Camp Trail and beach, come back to the Dike Trail and go east another 2.1 miles as the trail leads into Steigerwald Lake National Wildlife Refuge. After years as a pasture for cattle owned by Portland's Steigerwald Dairy, this land was slated to become a repository for spent nuclear fuel. Instead, after intense battles in the 1980s, nearly 1,000 acres were preserved. Towering cottonwoods, Gibbons Creek and seasonal lakes attract flocks of migrating birds. It's a photographer's dream.

While in the refuge, enjoy views on the Dike Trail of the cliffs below Oregon's Crown Point and Vista House, plus Reed Island State Park in the river. William and Myrtle Reed settled on it in 1890 with their five boys, who rowed daily to the Oregon shore, then walked 1.5 miles uphill to school in Corbett. The great flood of 1894 forced the family off the island. They moved permanently to Corbett.

Within the refuge, the 2.8-mile Gibbons Creek Wildlife Art Trail (open May 1 to September 30) intersects the Dike Trail. Other than the Dike Trail, bikes and leashed dogs are not permitted in the refuge. So if you want to explore the interior of the refuge, stash your bike or lock it to the gate at the Art Trail. Back on the Dike Trail, you can bike east to a fence and private land just west of Point Vancouver. Of this place Washington Irving wrote in 1836: "This point is said to present one of the most beautiful scenes on the Columbia; a lovely meadow, with a silver sheet of limpid water in the center, enlivened by wild-fowl, a range of hills crowned by forests, while the prospect

Replica canoes, circa 1805

is closed by Mount Hood."

When you're ready to come back into town, retrace your route on the Dike Trail. Take the first trail off the dike west of Recognition Plaza; it leads to 27th Street—a short, shoulderless, 25-mph road through farm pastures and industrial sites. In a former cow pasture is the Stevenson Off-Leash Dog Park at Main and 27th.

From 27th, turn left on Main Street and pass pretty old homes, then right on 24th, right on G and left on 25th to Hathaway Park, Washougal's first park. Dedicated in 1910, it sits along a riffling section of the Washougal River. Even on a hot day when Cottonwood Beach was busy, the vibe was sleepy here. A small beach offers a chance to dip into the river next to a non-motorized boat ramp for kayakers and drift boats.

From the park, return to Main Street and head west. At 20th is C. F. Burkheimer Fly Rod Company, where custom and stock rods

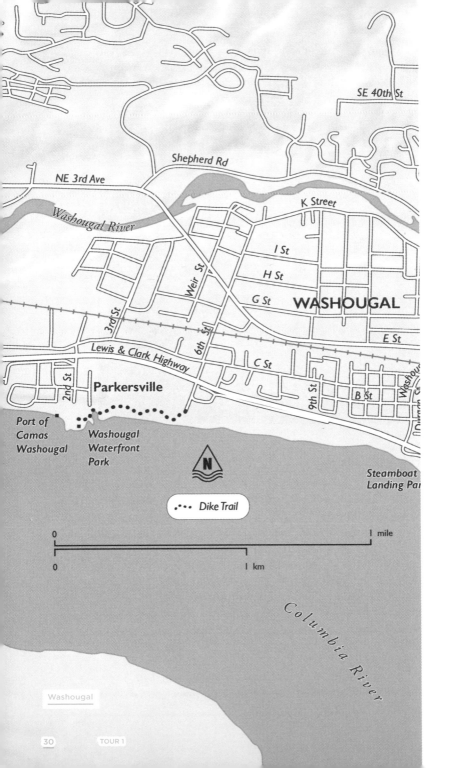

SE 40th St

Shepherd Rd

NE 3rd Ave

Washougal River

K Street

I St

H St

Weir St

G St

WASHOUGAL

3rd St

E St

6th St

Lewis & Clark Highway

C St

2nd St

Parkersville

9th St

B St

Port of
Camas
Washougal

Washougal
Waterfront
Park

N

Steamboat
Landing Par

•••• Dike Trail

0   1 mile

0   1 km

Columbia River

Washougal

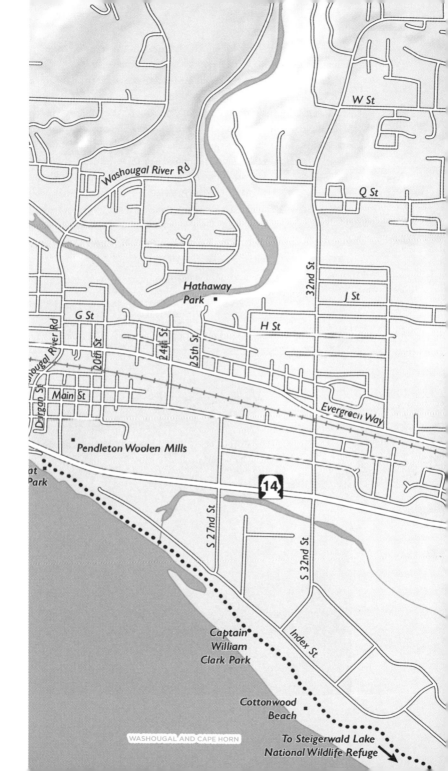

W St

Washougal River Rd

Q St

32nd St

J St

Hathaway
Park

G St

H St

24th St

25th St

Washougal River Rd

20th St

Dirgan St

Main St

Evergreen Way

Pendleton Woolen Mills

at
Park

[14]

S 27th St

S 32nd St

Captain
William
Clark Park

Index St

Cottonwood
Beach

To Steigerwald Lake
National Wildlife Refuge

are manufactured. Stop for lunch at **Amnesia Brewing** on Main or go on to **Big Foot Inn**, which is close to the woolen mill. At Main and 17th (now Pendleton Way), residents used to get water from the town pump in the middle of the intersection.

From Main, turn left on Pendleton Way. Stop at **Pendleton Woolen Mills** for a tour or shopping at the outlet. The company was founded in 1889 in Salem, Oregon, by an English weaver, Thomas Kay. In 1909, his grandsons, named Bishop, reopened a defunct mill in Pendleton, Oregon. Three years later they opened this mill. Today, Pendleton Woolen Mills is still owned by the Bishop family. Listen for the wail of the mill's steam whistle calling employees to work. The brass bell atop the red-brick boiler building was cast in 1865 at Paul Revere's foundry in Boston. If the **Two Rivers Heritage Museum** is open, stop in for a visit. Afterward bike to your car.

Portal to beauty

Adventure 2
Standup paddle boarding, kayaking or fishing

DAY
2

Just west of Washougal is Camas. From its Heritage Park you can paddle Lacamas Lake in a kayak or on a board rented from Sweetwater SUP Rentals. See Appendix B.

Or hire an expert guide to take you fishing for walleye, sturgeon, salmon or steelhead. People have fished the Columbia for over 10,000 years. Both of these guides have over 25 years' experience: Steve's Guided Adventures, 360-609-1902, or Dave Maroon's Fishing Adventures, 503-750-3319.

Eat and Drink in Washougal

Amnesia Brewing. Portland transplants craft local beer and fare; try the pulled pork with fresh cut slaw. Ages 21 and older. Saturday and Sunday noon to 9 p.m.; Monday and Tuesday 3 to 9 p.m.; Wednesday 11 a.m. to 9 p.m.; Thursday and Friday 11 a.m. to 10 p.m. 1834 Main St. 360-335-1008

Big Foot Inn. Classic bar with pool table and good food within sight of Pendleton Woolen Mills. Daily 6 a.m. to 2 a.m. 105 Pendleton Way. 360-835-2826

Hearth Restaurant. Wood-oven bistro. Tuesday to Saturday 4 to 9 p.m. Pendleton Way and A Street. 360-210-7028

OurBar. Great coffee, breakfast and hearty sandwiches plus beer and wine, run by two veterans of the culinary world. Wednesday to Sunday 8 a.m. to 3 p.m. 1887 E Main St. 360-954-5141

Puffin Cafe. On the docks at the Port of Camas-Washougal; Caribbean food and drink. Winter: daily 11 a.m. to 7 p.m. Spring and fall: to 8 p.m. Summer: to 9 p.m. 14 South A St. 360-335-1522

Washougal River Mercantile. Grocery basics. Monday to Friday 7 a.m. to 8 p.m.; Saturday and Sunday 8 a.m. to 8 p.m. 4232 Canyon Creek Road. 360-837-3470

Shop in Washougal

Pendleton Woolen Mills. Tour this century-old mill and find deals in the outlet store on blankets and clothes, including that American classic, the plaid outdoorsman shirt. Store: Monday to Friday 8 a.m. to 5 p.m.; Saturday 9 a.m. to 5 p.m.; Sunday 11 a.m. to 5 p.m. 2 Pendleton Way. Call 360-835-1118 for tour hours.

Discover and Learn in Washougal

Two Rivers Heritage Museum. Tuesday to Saturday 11 a.m. to 3 p.m. 1 Durgan St. 360-835-8742

Stay in Washougal

Best Western Plus Parkersville Inn and Suites. On the river next to the developing Washougal Waterfront Park. Get a riverside room for the view and to avoid SR 14 noise. 121 S Second St. 360-835-9292 [$$$]

TreeSong Nature Awareness and Retreat Center.
Nature programs in a wooded Washougal River setting, plus kid summer camps and adult group and personal nature retreats. 41 Tree-ific Drive. 360-837-8733 [$$$$]

Camp in Washougal

Port of Camas-Washougal. RV camping (no tents) near marina. No hookups. Memorial Day to Labor Day: weekdays only. Labor Day to Memorial Day: seven days a week. 24 South A St. 360-835-2196. [$]

Lodging Cost Key			
$	$$	$$$	$$$$
<$50	$51 to $99	$100 to $200	>$200

NORTH BONNEVILLE, BEACON ROCK STATE PARK AND BONNEVILLE HOT SPRINGS

WASHINGTON

This sleepy stretch of the gorge contains treasures: Beacon Rock, Hamilton Mountain and Bonneville Hot Springs. Here, the great Bonneville Landslide that came down from Table Mountain squeezed the Columbia into a narrow channel, leaving behind sheer cliffs, waterfalls and a broad flat area—the slide's runout—that makes for easy-going biking.

This west end of the gorge is good for four-season exploring: it doesn't get too hot in summer, and in other seasons on clear days it's equally good for hiking and biking. I like to come in winter to the hot springs, which are especially soothing after a day hiking in the cool air.

You may want to bring bikes, bike locks and a Discover Pass. Trails are paved, except in places on Hamilton Island, where hybrid tires work fine.

Adventure 1
Hiking the trails of Beacon Rock State Park

Leave early in the day and drive scenic SR 14 to your first stop. If it's November to January, on your drive east on SR 14, watch tundra swans feeding on wapato at Franz Lake National Wildlife Refuge (MP 31.5). The highway pullout overlooks 552 acres, one of the few Columbia River bottomlands not separated from the river by a dike or other structure. Chuck Williams, Cascade Indian and an early proponent of gorge land protections, wrote about his great-grandmother Kalliah who lived on this land until her death in 1906:

. . . .

"My great grandma . . . known as Indian Mary . . . was born down on our family land that's now part of Franz Lake National Wildlife Refuge. Since she was an Indian, she couldn't legally own land. She had got a contract with the government to take the mail around the Cascades [the rapids]. She would meet the boat on her horse, and take the mail around. When these whites were trying to steal her land from her, she went to [the Indian agent in Vancouver]. He got a bill through Congress, signed by Grover Cleveland, that held her land in trust. We held it for decades."

. . . .

The land became a refuge in 1990.

Stop for snacks in Skamania at the **Skamania General Store** or breakfast at its **Beacon Rock Cafe**, which starts serving at 7 a.m. From there head slightly further east on SR 14 to Beacon Rock State Park for one big hike, Hamilton Mountain, or a trio of fun shorter hikes that offer the best of the gorge: waterfalls, amazing views and a walk through the gorge's most volatile geologic story. Discover Pass required. Hikes in the park, listed from hardest to easiest:

Hamilton Mountain

An ultimate gorge hike. Gorgefriends.org says it best: "Waterfalls, cliffs, deep forests, and stunning views," including Hardy and Rodney falls. 7.5 miles. 2,100 feet of elevation gain. From SR 14, opposite Beacon Rock, drive uphill on the road to the campground. Turn right into the first parking area, to the trailhead. From May to early October, the WET bus stops on weekends at this trailhead. See gorgefriends.org or oregonhikers.org.

Beacon Rock

This is one not to miss: a spectacular basalt pillar on the river's edge. The 0.85-mile path climbs 680 feet to the top; it was built by Henry Biddle (1862–1928), a geologist and engineer. He bought the land in 1915 and hired crews to create the 4-foot-wide trail with 52 switchbacks. In 1931 the Army Corps of Engineers wanted to purchase the 848-foot pillar from Biddle's heirs, dynamite it to chunks, and use the rock to build a jetty at the mouth of the Columbia River. Instead, the heirs donated Beacon Rock and surrounding land to the state, making it Washington's first state park in the gorge. Park on SR 14 at MP 35 at the base of the rock. From May to early October, the **WET bus** stops on weekends at this trailhead.

Hardy Falls and Rodney Falls

Great for kids: two waterfalls in a 2.5-mile out-and-back walk with 440 feet of elevation gain. Start at the Hamilton Mountain trailhead, described above.

Doetsch Ranch meadows

For an easy walk, take the 1-mile accessible trail through a riverside meadow that was pasture for the Doetsch Ranch from 1920 to 1987. From the serenity of the meadow, look up at Beacon Rock. During the epic Missoula Floods that carved the gorge, its top was beneath 200 feet of water.

From SR 14, west of Beacon Rock itself, turn on Doetsch Ranch Road, park and follow the path into and around the meadow. From here you can also walk to the boat ramp near the base of Beacon Rock. Across the channel is Pierce Island, preserved as a natural area in 1984 when it was at risk of becoming a dumpsite for dredge spoils. Covered in a forest of black cottonwood, willow and ash, the island ranges from 130 to 200 acres depending on water levels.

Adventure 2
Soaking at Bonneville Hot Springs

DAY
1

From Beacon Rock State Park, drive east on SR 14. Opposite the Beacon Rock Golf Course entrance in North Bonneville, turn left onto a section of the old gorge highway, here called Evergreen Drive. If you're so inclined, buy pot at The Cannabis Corner, 420 Evergreen Drive, the first government-owned marijuana store in the nation. Pick up a map of North Bonneville trails here; it will come in handy on Day 2. Continue east on Evergreen and Cascade Drive to Bonneville Hot

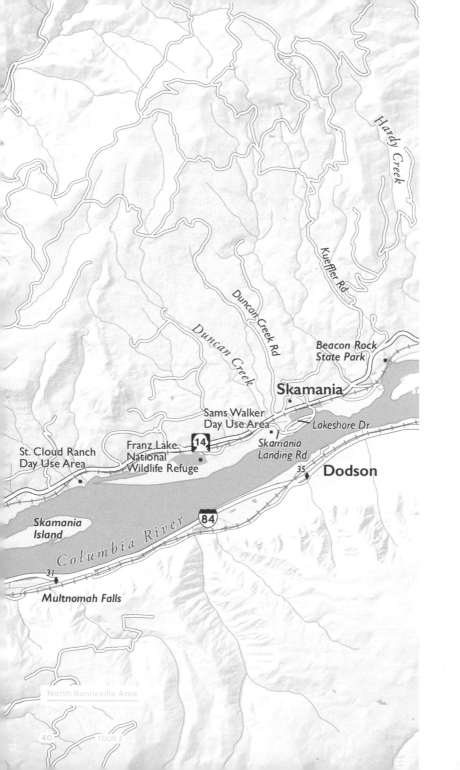

Hardy Creek

Kueffler Rd

Duncan Creek Rd

Duncan Creek

Beacon Rock
State Park

Skamania

Sams Walker
Day Use Area

Lakeshore Dr

St. Cloud Ranch
Day Use Area

Franz Lake
National
Wildlife Refuge

14

Skamania
Landing Rd

35

Dodson

84

*Skamania
Island*

Columbia River

31

Multnomah Falls

North Bonneville Area

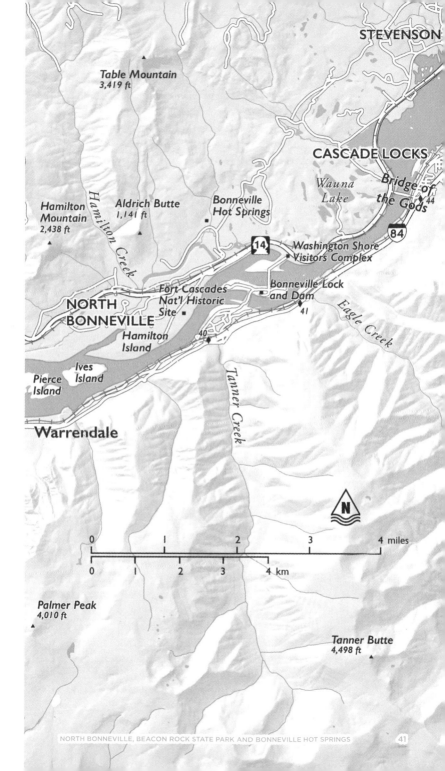

STEVENSON

Table Mountain
3,419 ft

CASCADE LOCKS

Wauna
Lake

Bridge of
the Gods
44

84

Hamilton
Mountain
2,438 ft

Aldrich Butte
1,141 ft

Bonneville
Hot Springs

Hamilton Creek

14

Washington Shore
Visitors Complex

NORTH
BONNEVILLE

Fort Cascades
Nat'l Historic
Site

Bonneville Lock
and Dam
41

Eagle Creek

Hamilton
Island

40

Ives
Island

Tanner Creek

Pierce
Island

Warrendale

N

| 0 | | 1 | | 2 | | 3 | | 4 miles |

| 0 | 1 | 2 | 3 | | 4 km |

Palmer Peak
4,010 ft

Tanner Butte
4,498 ft

Springs Resort and Spa. Check into your room, get a mineral bath and wrap, facial, massage or foot rejuvenation. Or just soak your hike-tired bones. Staying elsewhere? You can still partake of this relaxation smorgasbord, although I recommend sleeping here—there's nothing like sliding up to bed right after a long soak. The sauna and hot tubs—indoors and out—are good places to chat with other gorge visitors. The 88-degree F, 25-meter indoor swimming pool is sparkling clean and hard to leave. Have dinner at the resort's Pacific Crest Dining Room.

DAY 2

Adventure 1
Hiking a butte or biking to the river

Have breakfast at the **Clubhouse Grill** at the Beacon Rock Golf Course and ponder your day's options:

Hiking Aldrich Butte

If you want another hike, Aldrich Butte is a lesser-known peak within the great Bonneville Landslide mass, and a lot easier than the Table Mountain and Hamilton Mountain hikes that take you to the cliffs above the landslide. This one starts just beyond the hot springs and lifts you via an old roadbed to sweeping views of the dam, river and Oregon's peaks. 3.2 miles round trip with 1,070 feet of elevation gain. At the top, the U.S. Army commandeered a fire lookout during WWII and installed guns to defend Bonneville Dam from attack. See oregonhikers.org.

Biking North Bonneville's trails

If you've had enough hiking, this easy bike loop offers a relaxing jaunt out to the river. The route's not strenuous: paved, light-traffic roads or flat, car-free trails with interesting stops along the way.

Start at Bonneville Hot Springs and get on the paved Greenleaf Trail, heading south. It's easy to miss this first turn: from the paved trail, turn right on Shady Oaks Lane, left on Lakeside Way, right on Lookin Lane, and left onto the trail. Stop at the bench overlooking lovely Greenleaf Slough, a former channel of the Columbia River. Keep on the trail; stop at Cascade Cemetery. Graves date from the late 1880s from the town of Cascades, which washed away in the great flood of 1894. You'll see its former location at the Fort Cascades National Historic Site later in the route. In the cemetery, a headstone marked *Ankutty Tillikum Musem* (Here lie the ancient ones) marks the grave of Native Americans originally interred on nearby Bradford Island. When that island was selected in the 1930s as the site of Bonneville

ANKUTTY
TILLIKUM
MUSEM

At Cascade Cemetery

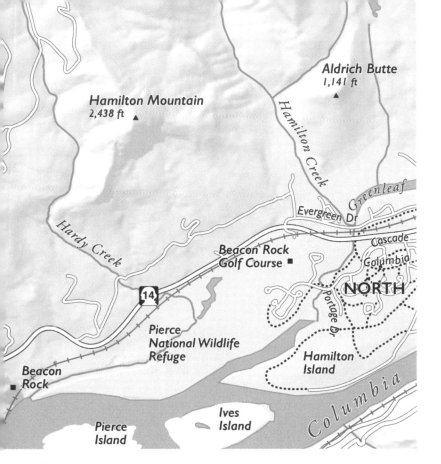

Aldrich Butte
1,141 ft ▲

Hamilton Mountain
2,438 ft ▲

Hamilton Creek

Greenleaf

Evergreen Dr

Cascade

Hardy Creek

Beacon Rock
Golf Course ■

Columbia

NORTH

14

Portage Dr

Pierce
National Wildlife
Refuge

Hamilton
Island

Beacon
■ Rock

Columbia

Ives
Island

Pierce
Island

Trails of North Bonneville

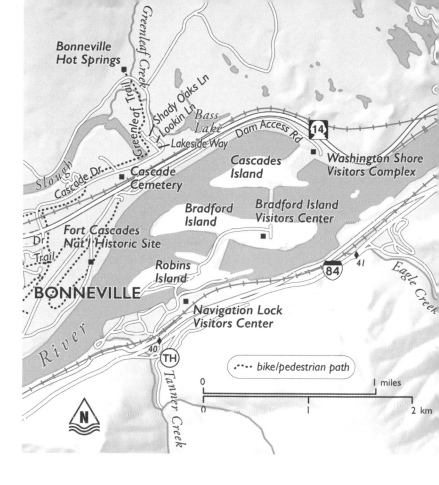

Bonneville Hot Springs

Greenleaf Creek

Greenleaf Trail

Shady Oaks Ln
Lookin Ln
Bass Lake
Lakeside Way
Dam Access Rd
14

Slough

Cascade Dr.
Cascade Cemetery

Cascades Island

Washington Shore Visitors Complex

Bradford Island

Bradford Island Visitors Center

Dr.
Fort Cascades Nat'l Historic Site
Trail

Robins Island

BONNEVILLE

Navigation Lock Visitors Center

84
41

Eagle Creek

River

40
TH

Tanner Creek

···· bike/pedestrian path

0   1 miles

0   1   2 km

N

Dam, remains were removed and placed here.

From the cemetery, stay west on the Greenleaf Trail to Hamilton Creek. At the creek, turn left, following the trail along the creek's east bank. Cross under SR 14 and keep south and west on trails. The goal: to get to the river. You're now in the heart of North Bonneville. Today's community of about 1,000 residents is the second version of the town. The first was established on the Columbia in 1933 to house workers building Bonneville Dam. In 1978 the town had to be relocated because it was in the construction path of the dam's second powerhouse.

Look for signs to the Strawberry Island Trail, and more specifically for the intersection of Cascade and Portage drives, at a retirement home. Go south on Portage to its end at a ball field. Here hike or bike out to Hamilton Island, called Strawberry Island by Lewis and Clark.

Today's Hamilton Island consists of meadows atop a man-made hill—rock deposited during construction of Bonneville Dam's second powerhouse in the 1970s. Along with the increase in elevation, the island became a peninsula after fill connected it to the Washington shore. From the trailhead at the ball field, you can take trails left, right or straight up onto the hill. The middle, uphill, path leads to the island's peak and a set of benches to enjoy the wonderful sky views framed by the gorge walls. The top of the island also offers a great vantage point of the Bonneville Landslide mass. If you take the right trail at the ball field, you'll end up at the scenic tip of Hamilton Island, overlooking Ives Island. Hamilton Creek comes in on the right. You can wade or walk dry land out to Ives at low water. Beaches and swimming are fine on its north side. Audubon Washington recommends this area for excellent birding.

Don't go back the way you came; instead, after exploring, head riverward and east via a paved road, gravel single-track or forested single-track trails. Keep the river on your right and you'll end up at **Fort Cascades National Historic Site**. Go to its parking lot and pick up an interpretive brochure, and walk or bike the 1.5-mile forested loop. You'll cover land inhabited by Indians, the town of Cascades (1850–1894), an Army fort, and a fish cannery. For thousands of years, until white settlement, portage trails around the Columbia's rapids were controlled by Native Americans. In 1855 the U.S. Army claimed this land and built Fort Cascades, one of several forts it used to control the portage route. Indians burned the fort to the ground in 1856, in what the Army calls the Cascades Massacre. The rebuilt fort was abandoned in 1861. (See the grave of Norman Palmer, killed during the massacre, on the Trail of the Gods walk, page 59.) The townsite was abandoned after the great flood of 1894 washed all the buildings away.

To return to the start, from the Fort Cascades parking area, ride east to Dam Access Road. Pass under SR 14, turn right on Cascade Drive and return to Bonneville Hot Springs.

If the Army Corps of Engineers allowed bikes to ride past the guard station at **Bonneville Lock and Dam**, you could extend the ride to a few more interesting sites. But they don't. So once you've returned to Bonneville Hot Springs and are back in your car, drive back to Dam Access Road, proceed through the guard station, park, and take a guided tour of the dam's second powerhouse, built in 1981. The first, completed in 1938, is at the Bonneville Lock and Dam Historic Site on the Oregon side; see Tour 11. On the tour, look down at the dam's generators. In summer and fall, watch salmon swim upstream through viewing windows. And don't miss a hidden gorge gem: drive to the end of the parking area, then keep going past a fence. The roadway leads to a little-used parking area, with trails to views of the river, dam and Native American fishing platforms.

Adventure 2
Walking the preservation-development divide

DAY
2

On the way back to Portland take a short, flat walk to two gorge locales that starkly illustrate a contentious issue: gorge preservation versus development. The first stop is Sams Walker Day Use/Picnic Area. From SR 14, turn on Skamania Landing Road at MP 32.8. Within 0.25 mile, park at Sams Walker. Northwest Forest Pass required.

In 1983, the Trust for Public Land bought this swath of riverfront from a developer who planned a residential subdivision. Today it's a patchwork of fields, river viewpoints, and oak and cedar forests. Its 1.1-mile Forest Service trail traverses land inhabited for millennia and farmed beginning in the 19th century. It's a gorgeous walk far from highway sounds, with stops and picnic benches at overlooks. When you turn inland you'll pass craggy Oregon white oaks (also known as Garry oaks, especially outside of Oregon). Their age suggests they were here when Indians burned shrubs and tree seedlings to promote growth of the oaks, whose acorns were a food source, and to create open meadows favored by deer and other game. The trail also winds through a grove of Western red cedar.

The second half of this walk, Skamania Landing, is the rare riverfront subdivision in the gorge. After the gorge became a National Scenic Area in 1986, such development was prohibited outside of 13 defined urban areas.

From Sams Walker, begin a 1.5-mile stroll through the neighborhood by walking east on Skamania Landing Road. At a Y, go right, to pass homes fronting on the Columbia. Come to a one-lane bridge over Duncan Creek and return to the start via Lakeshore Drive, where homes front on the flooded lower reaches of Duncan Creek.

After the walk, drive west on SR 14 and stop for a quick walk at the riverfront St. Cloud Ranch Day Use/Picnic Area (MP 30). In 1909, it was the estate of Paul and Florence Vial. They built a home, tennis courts, swimming pool and boat dock, and planted gardens and an orchard, naming it after the Paris suburb where they honeymooned in 1903. The Trust for Public Land purchased the property and later sold it to the U.S. Forest Service. Trail 4410 meanders 1 mile through an orchard of Spitzenberg and Newtown Pippin apples—all that remains of the Vials' riverfront home. Cuttings from these trees grow at the Washington State University Vancouver Heritage Orchard. Enjoy views of Oregon's Oneonta Gorge and Multnomah Falls. When river levels are low, you can walk the rocky beach here. Northwest Forest Pass required.

From St. Cloud Ranch, drive SR 14 west to Vancouver.

Eat and Drink in Skamania and North Bonneville

Clubhouse Grill. At Beacon Rock Golf Course. Breakfast, sandwiches and burgers. Weekends 7 a.m. to 7 p.m.; weekdays 8 a.m. to 7 p.m. 102 Grenia Road, North Bonneville. 509-427-5730

Pacific Crest Dining Room. At Bonneville Hot Springs Resort and Spa. Daily: breakfast 7:30 to 10:30 a.m., lunch 11:30 a.m. to 2:30 p.m., dinner 5 to 9 p.m. Also at the resort: Pacific Crest Lounge for ages 21 and older: Sunday to Thursday 2 to 9:30 p.m.; Friday and Saturday 2 to 11 p.m. 1252 E Cascade Drive, North Bonneville. 509-427-7767

Skamania General Store. Before you hike or bike, stop here and fill your pack, or eat breakfast and lunch at its Beacon Rock Cafe—great fries and lamb burgers. Daily 6 a.m. to 10 p.m. Cafe: 7 a.m. until after lunch. SR 14 and Woodard Creek Road, Skamania. 509-427-4820

Shop in North Bonneville

The Cannabis Corner. Local growers represented. Cash only. Daily 10 a.m. to 7 p.m. 420 Evergreen Drive, North Bonneville. 509-427-4393

Discover and Learn in North Bonneville

Bonneville Lock and Dam Washington Shore Visitors Complex. Powerhouse tours September to early June: Saturday and Sunday 10 a.m., 1:30 and 3:30 p.m. Call to confirm times. Other months: daily tours. At the end of Dam Access Road (MP 37 off SR 14), North Bonneville. Daily 9 a.m. to 5 p.m. 509-427-4281. nwp.usace.army.mil

Fort Cascades National Historic Site. An outdoor museum you walk or bike through, with interpretive info at specific stops. Follow signs from Dam Access Road (MP 37 off SR 14), North Bonneville. nwp.usace.army.mil

Stay in North Bonneville

Bonneville Hot Springs Resort and Spa. Though the resort hides its charms behind an unwelcoming exterior, inside is a swimmer's dream: a warm 25-meter pool, with indoor and outdoor hot tubs, a full-service, friendly spa and cozy, clean rooms. A site used by Native Americans for thousands of years, it's been a mineral waters spa since the 1880s. 1252 E Cascade Drive, North Bonneville. Call 866-459-1678 or visit the website for day use and treatment rates. [$$$ to $$$$]

Camp in and around North Bonneville

Beacon Rock State Park. The park's year-round Woodard Creek Campground for RVs is pretty but adjacent to the noise of SR 14. A seasonal campground best for tents, about a mile uphill from SR 14, gets you away from road noise. Group camping sites with shelters and kitchen also available. At the park's boat moorage are two tent sites. All sites first come, first served. [$]

Lewis and Clark Campground and RV Park. If you like old-timey RV and mobile home parks in a scenic setting, this place is for you. Friendly and on a creek. The club room is full of old logging equipment. 355 Evergreen Drive, North Bonneville. 509-427-5559 [$]

Lodging Cost Key			
$	$$	$$$	$$$$
<$50	$51 to $99	$100 to $200	>$200

Bonneville Hot Springs Resort

Two uses of the river: Native American fishing platforms, and Bonneville Dam

TOUR
3

STEVENSON AND SKAMANIA LODGE

WASHINGTON

Escape the big city with this getaway in a small town that offers everything from great food and beer to an excellent museum and resort. Stevenson is 45 miles from Portland, and is easy to sightsee by bike on (mostly) level paved paths that connect Skamania Lodge with the waterfront, downtown, hiking trails and Washington's premier gorge history museum. Streets in this town of 1,500 people offer a wonderful break from Portland's traffic buzz. You could do this entire getaway on a bike, leaving your car sitting quietly in its parking space.

Come during one of Stevenson's many festivals that celebrate beer, timber, wind or the blues. (See Appendix A.)

You may want to bring bikes, bike locks and a Discover Pass.

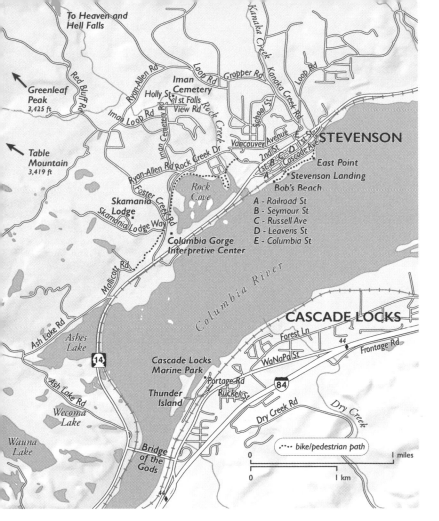

To Heaven and
Hell Falls

Kanaka Creek

Greenleaf
Peak
3,425 ft

Table
Mountain
3,419 ft

Red Bluff Rd

Ryan-Allen Rd

Iman Loop Rd

Loop Rd

Gropper Rd

Kanaka Creek Rd

Loop Rd

Iman
Cemetery

Holly St

Iman Cemetery Rd

1st Falls
View Rd

Rock Creek

Scheel St

Vancouver Avenue

E

STEVENSON

Ryan-Allen Rd

Rock Creek Dr

2nd St

1st St

B

C

D

1st St

Cascade Ave

East Point

A

Stevenson Landing

Foster Creek Rd

Rock
Cove

Bob's Beach

A - Railroad St
B - Seymour St
C - Russell Ave
D - Leavens St
E - Columbia St

Skamania
Lodge

Skamania Lodge Way

Columbia Gorge
Interpretive Center

Columbia River

Mallicott Rd

CASCADE LOCKS

Forest Ln

44

Frontage Rd

Ash Lake Rd

Ashes
Lake

WaNaPa St

Cascade Locks
Marine Park

14

84

Ash Lake Rd

Thunder
Island

Portage Rd

Ruckel St

Wecoma
Lake

Dry Creek Rd

Dry Creek

Wauna
Lake

Bridge
of the
Gods

····· bike/pedestrian path

0   1 miles

0   1 km

44

Stevenson and Cascade Locks

Adventure 1
Biking or walking to a waterfall, beaches, lunch and shops

Drive from Portland via I-84 to SR 14, in slightly less than an hour. Get to Stevenson by midmorning and park in the far reaches of the lot at the **Columbia Gorge Interpretive Center Museum** on Rock Creek Drive. If you're staying at Skamania Lodge, you can borrow bikes. With stops to eat lunch and explore, give yourself a few hours by bike or four or so hours on foot. It's about 6.5 miles.

Start at the museum grounds. (A visit inside is on the next day's itinerary.) From the museum entrance road, go left on Rock Creek Drive, then right on the gentle uphill of Foster Creek Road, then right on Ryan-Allen Road.

From Ryan-Allen, go left on Iman Cemetery Road. It's steep for 0.3 mile—the only steep place on the route—then turn right on First Falls View Road, and left on Holly Street to Iman Cemetery. Walk to the back fence. People kept cutting a hole in the fence to get to the waterfall view, so the cemetery installed an unlocked gate. It leads to a forested bluff. Be careful: No fencing separates you from high cliffs being eaten away by a mini-Niagara, the spectacular, 40-foot Upper Rock Creek Falls. Winter and spring flows are best; by late summer,

Hidden waterfall behind a cemetery fence

Left to right: The landslide head scarps of Table Mountain, Red Bluffs and Greenleaf Peak, from Oregon

the falls don't cover the entire bluff face but are still beautiful. Best viewing is when trees are leafless. Explore the short trails along the bluff, respecting no trespassing signs, then return to the cemetery.

From the cemetery, backtrack to Iman Cemetery Road. Go left on it then right on Iman Loop Road. Stop at this intersection and, for fantastic views, go left about 0.1 mile to a roadside pullout where you can see, left to right, 3,419-foot Table Mountain and the Red Bluffs that connect it with 3,425-foot Greenleaf Peak. Their vertical faces are head scarps—cliffs caused by landslides, in this case within the Cascade Landslide Complex. One lobe of this immense complex was the Bonneville Landslide. Approximately 400 years ago this slide pushed the Columbia River toward the Oregon shore, and for a time completely dammed it, giving rise to the legend of the Bridge of the Gods and the name of the current bridge, seen later in the tour. Slides still happen: in the winter of 2007–08, 3 to 5 acres slid off Greenleaf Peak.

After enjoying the view, return to the Ryan-Allen and Iman Loop intersection and go northeast on Ryan-Allen. Cross Rock Creek on a bridge. At a stop sign, curve right on Loop Road then immediately left on Gropper Road. Though bike lanes are absent, traffic is light. At Wind River Middle School and Stevenson High, check out the petrified tree fenced off next to the road.

From Gropper, turn right to head downhill on Kanaka Creek Road. "Kanaka" is a sometimes derogatorily used term for Native Hawaiians. Many Hawaiians came to work at Fort Vancouver and its outlying posts when the fort was run by the Hudson's Bay Company from the 1820s to 1840s. Here it refers to a family who had settled along the creek, cutting wood for delivery to The Dalles.

From Kanaka Creek Road, turn right on School Street and pass good-looking homes. From School Street, go left at Vancouver Avenue. Pass the Skamania County Courthouse with its nicely signed public restroom and the Courthouse Annex with its petroglyph. The elegant mid-century library is worth a stop for its design, its huge oak out front and the sculpture by famous Portland artist Lee Kelly that hangs outside.

From Vancouver Avenue, turn right at the library on Columbia and then left on Second so that you're heading east on the road's south side; go past a hardware store and cross a westbound entrance to First Street. Next, come to an eastbound exit from First Street. At the top of this exit road, go right on a relatively unimproved road—Cascade Avenue—that is much more interesting here than the typical road. It heads downhill, goes under railroad tracks, and has a couple of scenic crossings of Kanaka Creek until it ends at the Columbia River. Trails lead left a short ways and to Pebble Beach, a nice place to swim.

Investigate the shoreline, keeping on the riverside path wherever you can or on Cascade Avenue when the path peters out. Pass East Point, where kiteboarders and boaters launch. Come back to this beach in July for the **Bridge of the Gods Kiteboarding Festival**.

At the foot of Russell Avenue is Stevenson Landing, where cruise ships dock and steamboats used to. It also used to be the Washington terminus of the ferry that was replaced by the Bridge of the Gods in 1926. To its west is oak-shaded Bob's Beach, a park and windsurfing launch site.

From Stevenson Landing, go north on Russell, turn right on First, then left on Leavens Street, which ends at Second, Stevenson's main street. Turn left. The **Skamania County Courthouse** is on the right, an International-style midcentury gem. It's open to visitors, so go inside for a look at the main corridor lined with historic photographs.

Have lunch at one of many options downtown. Afterward, go west on Second; just beyond Seymour Street, veer right on Rock Creek Drive, which used to be called County Road, serving as the Evergreen Highway's route through Stevenson. Later, the current, less curvy route of SR 14 was built atop a straight line of fill placed across the cove.

On Rock Creek Drive, turn left on a path marked with rock columns leading to a pedestrian bridge over Rock Creek. (If you pass the Rock Creek Terrace Apartments, you just missed it.) The path leads to the Skamania County Fairgrounds, located along a cove that used to be the Rock Creek Delta. Beginning in the 1860s the land here was logged and lumber milled at Felix Iman's mill. Stumps of old cedars can still be seen near the playground: old growth western red cedars are rot-resistant and their stumps can last centuries. Later the land was a dairy. Look for two lines of tall poplars, a common windbreak on farms. In 1938, river levels rose above the new Bonneville Dam, flooding this creek delta and turning it into an island-dotted cove.

Rock Cove had to be dredged in 2007 when the Piper Road Landslide deposited a million cubic yards of debris into the creek bed. In winter and spring Rock Cove is noisy with waterfowl. In summer, it's busy with festivals.

Follow the bike/pedestrian path around the cove, passing interesting interpretive signs. At a point nearest the Columbia, look up—you can see **Skamania Lodge**, situated within the landslide mass that slid from the mountains above. The path/sidewalk rejoins Rock Creek Drive and continues west. Follow it back to the museum and the start.

Adventure 2
Flying through trees or biking a mythical bridge

DAY
1

Ziplining in the woods

Fly through the trees on Skamania Lodge's Zip Line Tour. About $100 for two and a half hours. zipnskamania.com

Biking or walking the Trail of the Gods

If you'd rather keep your feet on the ground or on the pedals, take the paved trail that connects Stevenson to old roads that offer practically car-free biking all the way to the Bridge of the Gods. From there you can cross the Columbia into Oregon. This set of roads and paths is called the Trail of the Gods. It's about 3.5 miles one way from the Columbia Gorge Interpretive Center Museum to Cascade Locks Marine Park.

Start in Stevenson by heading west on Rock Creek Drive. At its intersection with Skamania Lodge Way, take the paved path on the uphill side of Rock Creek Drive and follow it west to Mallicott Road. Go left on Mallicott, then right on quiet, little-used Ash Lake Road, which winds around Ashes Lake. Like Rock Cove, the lake is a creek valley inundated when river levels rose behind Bonneville Dam. Ash Lake Road used to be part of the route of the old Evergreen Highway.

From Ash Lake Road, carefully cross SR 14 to a wide paved area on the road's south side. Head west. Just before the bridge is a parking area; look left for a short path to the grave of Norman Palmer, who was killed by Native Americans at the Cascades Massacre of 1856.

From the grave, continue to the Bridge of the Gods. Built in 1926 for Model T–size cars and trucks, the bridge has the human scale seen today only on pedestrian bridges. I recommend walking your bike across: you'll better enjoy views of the river and Native American fishing scaffolds. Plus it's safer to walk because the deck is grated, the railings low and the wind can whip. The bridge doesn't have sidewalks but traffic is limited to 15 mph and since the bridge is part of the 2,650-mile Pacific Crest Trail, bikers and hikers are just as welcome as autos. Bikers and walkers pay 50 cents to cross, and cars $1. Pay on the Cascade Locks side. The bridge spans the river at its narrowest point, so it's a short crossing.

The first bridge at this location was created by the Bonneville Landslide, possibly after a massive earthquake around 1700 which caused the south slope of Washington's Table Mountain to collapse into the river. This natural dam and its eventual erosion gave rise to the Native American legend the bridge is named for. See portofcascadelocks.org for a longer version of the story. Today, upstream of the bridge at low water, you can see remnant rocks from that slide. These rocks were part of the great Cascades of the Columbia, where the river dropped 26 feet in a mile and picked its way through islands, rocky channels and boulders. Ancient Indian portage paths around the rapids were widened into portage roads, then replaced first by a steam portage rail line, and later by the railroad and locks. Upstream are excellent views of the Cascade Locks, which operated from 1896 to 1938 when they were inundated by rising river levels from the new Bonneville Dam.

In 1927, aviation pioneer Charles Lindbergh flew his famous "Spirit of St. Louis" plane into Portland to dedicate the Swan Island Airport. While here, he flew under the Bridge of the Gods. In 1938 the bridge was raised 44 feet and lengthened 729 feet to accommodate higher water levels created by the dam.

Once across the bridge and in Cascade Locks, reward yourself with chowder at Brigham Fish Market or a meal at Thunder Island Brewing, and mosey over to Cascade Locks Marine Park for a closer look at the hand-carved stonework still visible at the locks. (See Tour 11.) Return the same way.

DAY
2

Adventure 1
Relaxing, learning or exploring

For your second day in Stevenson, slow it down and pick one of these options.

Learning about the gorge

Immerse yourself in gorge history at the Columbia Gorge Interpretive Center Museum. See a full-sized fish wheel replica, giant steam engine, 1917 Curtiss biplane and Native American artifacts.

Exploring the backcountry and a waterfall picnic

Get picnic food at A & J Select Market and drive or, if you've got a stout tires, bike to Heaven and Hell Falls. This little gem along Rock Creek above Stevenson is a bit hard to find but worth the effort. This is the same creek you saw behind the cemetery and pooling at Rock Cove.

Get there: On Rock Creek Drive in Stevenson, turn north on Ryan-Allen Road. Follow it about 1 mile, then turn left on Red Bluff Road, which becomes Rock Creek Road. Follow this fairly good gravel road 5.8 miles, staying left at a fork about 2.5 miles in. Cross over Rock Creek at Steep Creek Falls then watch for a pullout on the left, about 0.3 mile later. A path leads 100 feet to the falls. See waterfallsnorthwest.com.

Hiking Skamania Lodge trails

Hike easy Skamania Lodge Trails open to the public, whether or not you are a guest at the lodge: Lake Loop at 1.75 miles, Creek Loop at 1.5 miles or Gorge Loop, a 1-mile fitness trail with workout stations.

Relaxing at the spa

Get a spa treatment at the Waterleaf Spa and Fitness Center in Skamania Lodge, and spend the rest of the day in the pools, sauna, hot tubs and workout rooms. A perfect rainy day retreat. You don't have to be an overnight guest to use these facilities if you book a spa treatment. 509-427-2529 or 800-221-7117.

Eat and Drink in Stevenson

Note: Highway 14 and Second Street are the same road, Stevenson's main street.

A & J Select Market. Groceries and deli. Daily 7 a.m. to 9 p.m. 265 SW Second St. 509-427-5491

Andrew's Pizza and Bakery. Pizza on homemade dough, plus flatbread sandwiches. Monday to Saturday 11 or 11:30 a.m. to 8:30 or 9 p.m. 310 SW Second St. 509-427-8008

Big River Grill. A landmark; good food and beers. Monday to Friday 11 a.m. to 9 p.m.; Saturday and Sunday 8 a.m. to 9 p.m. 192 SW Second St. 509-427-4888

Big T's Diner. Burgers. Daily 8 a.m. to 8 p.m. 73 NW First St. 509-427-0333

Cascade Dining Room. The more formal of two Skamania Lodge dining choices. (See also River Rock Restaurant.) Reservations recommended. Monday to Saturday 7 a.m. to 2 p.m. and 5 to 9 p.m.; Sunday 9 a.m. to 2 p.m. and 5 to 9 p.m. 509-427-7700

Granny's Gedunk. Big scoops of ice cream. April to October. 196 SW Second St. 509-427-4091

La Casa de Sabor. Get the special or ask for the chicken tomatillo soup. Monday to Friday 11 a.m. to 7 or 8 p.m.; Saturday 12 to 8 p.m.; Sunday 12 to 6 p.m. 47 SW Russell Ave. 509-427-5423

Little Viking Drive-In. Burgers and ice cream. Daily 11 a.m. to 10 p.m. 340 SW Highway 14. 509-427-8888

River Rock. At Skamania Lodge (see below). Less formal than the lodge's Cascade Dining Room. Eat by the fire, at the bar or on the patio. Great burgers. Monday to Thursday 11 a.m. to 10 p.m.; Friday and Saturday 11 a.m. to 11 p.m.; Sunday 7 a.m. to 10 p.m. 509-427-7700

Robbie's Coffee House. Robbie will inquire whether you're in town for business or just visiting; soon you will be chatting not just with her but other customers. Monday to Saturday 8 a.m. to 5 p.m. 350 SW Highway 14. 509-427-0154

Venus Cafe. Daily 7 a.m. to 1 p.m. 326 SW Highway 14. 509-427-2233

Walking Man Brewing. Brewing locally since 2000, with pub fare. Wednesday to Thursday 4 to 9 p.m.; Friday to Sunday 12 to 9 p.m. 240 SW First St. 509-427-5520.

Shop in Stevenson

Bloomsbury of Kanaka Creek Farm. A quartet of elegant clothing, home goods, plants and gift stores along Second Street and Russell Avenue. Monday to Saturday 10 a.m. to 5:30 p.m.; Sunday 11 a.m. to 4 p.m. 240 SW Second St., Stevenson. 509-427-4444.

Columbia Gorge Interpretive Center Museum. Gift shop with local art, crafts and history books. Daily except major holidays 9 a.m. to 5 p.m. 990 SW Rock Creek Drive. 509-427-8211.

Moon River Home and Living. Repurposed items, furniture and home goods. 350 SW Highway 14. 503-348-2385.

Tin Roof Rusted. Antiques and vintage items for home and garden. Monday to Saturday 10 a.m. to 5 p.m.; Sunday 12 to 5 p.m. 350 SW Highway 14.

Discover and Learn in Stevenson

Columbia Gorge Interpretive Center Museum. Daily except major holidays 9 a.m. to 5 p.m. 990 SW Rock Creek Drive. 509-427-8211

Skamania County Chamber of Commerce and Visitor Center. Memorial Day to Labor Day: Monday to Friday 8:30 a.m. to 5 p.m.; Saturday 9 a.m. to 5 p.m.; Sunday and holidays 10 a.m. to 4 p.m. 167 NW Second St. For other season hours: 800-989-9178

Skamania County Courthouse. Historic photos line the main corridor. Monday to Friday 8 a.m. to 5 p.m. 240 NW Vancouver Ave. 509-427-3780

Taste Wine and Spirits in Stevenson

Klickitat Canyon and Columbia Gorge Winery. Tasting room and outside deck. Weekends 12 to 6 p.m. 350 SW Highway 14.

Skunk Brothers Spirits. Local moonshine. Tasting room Tuesday to Sunday 1 to 5 p.m. 40 SW Cascade Ave., Suite 45. 360-213-3420

Stay in Stevenson

Columbia Gorge Riverside Lodge. A quartet of cozy, elegant Ponderosa pine log cabins (most with three units each) on the water in Stevenson, next to Bob's Beach. Well-equipped kitchenettes: get groceries or take-out and eat on the deck so you can savor the views outside your door. At La Frontera, the cabin nearest the river, we heard but weren't annoyed by train whistles; earplugs remained on the nightstand unused. 200 SW Cascade Ave. 509-427-5650 [$$ to $$$$]

Resort at Skamania Coves. Six vacation home rentals on the Columbia River plus 17 RV sites with full hook-ups ($). Not walkable to town but has its own swimming coves, forested paths and boat dock. One mile east of Stevenson at 45932 SR 14. 509-427-4900 [$$$$]

Rodeway Inn. Friendly service and clean rooms on Stevenson's main street for a low price. 40 Second St. 509-427-5628 [$$ to $$$]

Skamania Lodge. If you want to utterly relax, go here. 254 rooms and suites. Great for off-season months: golfing and hiking the resort's trails in the mist are all the sweeter when a 25-meter pool and fireside burger await you. Spa-like locker rooms with massage and other pampering make you hope for more rain. The Cascadian-style architecture is inspired by Mount Hood's Timberline Lodge, with local basalt and timbers recycled from an Astoria, Oregon, cannery. Don't miss framed rubbings of gorge petroglyphs, taken before dams submerged the art. The 175-acre resort and lodge were developed by Salishan, Inc., developer of Salishan Lodge on the Oregon Coast and Sunriver Resort in Central Oregon. Walk to town and the museum on pedestrian paths. 1131 SW Skamania Lodge Way. 844-432-4748 or 509-427-7700 [$$$ to $$$$]

Lodging Cost Key			
$	$$	$$$	$$$$
<$50	$51 to $99	$100 to $200	>$200

Rhododendrons at Skamania Lodge, May

TOUR
4

CARSON AND THE GIFFORD PINCHOT NATIONAL FOREST

WASHINGTON

This adventure takes you to the ancient trees of the Pacific Northwest. Here, in the Gifford Pinchot, one of the nation's oldest national forests, pioneer forester Thornton Munger established a research arboretum and studied Douglas firs beginning in the 1910s. His aim was to develop a system of sustainable and profitable forest management, as opposed to the then prevalent sense that trees represented a one-time crop to harvest. He later chaired the Committee of 50 that led to the establishment of Portland's Forest Park in 1948.

In the Gifford Pinchot, spend a night or two at the Government Mineral Springs Guard Station, a small cabin in a grove of 500-year-old firs and cedars. From there, hikes are close by and varied: through old growth forests, up a creek to a swimmable pool under Puff Falls, on a huckleberry-loaded trail to a five-volcano viewpoint, Observation Peak, and to one of the gorge's tallest waterfalls, Falls Creek Falls.

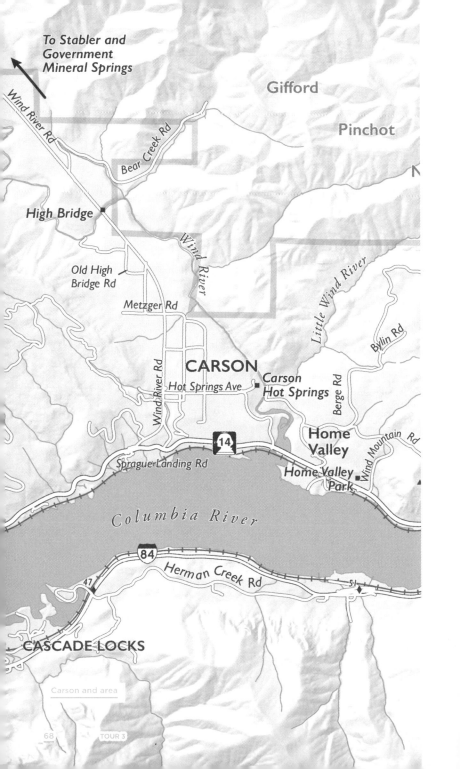

To Stabler and
Government
Mineral Springs

Wind River Rd

Gifford

Pinchot

Bear Creek Rd

High Bridge

Wind River

Old High
Bridge Rd

Little Wind River

Metzger Rd

Bylin Rd

Wind River Rd

CARSON

Carson
Hot Springs

Berge Rd

Hot Springs Ave

14

Home
Valley

Wind Mountain Rd

Sprague Landing Rd

Home Valley
Park

Columbia River

84

Herman Creek Rd

47

51

CASCADE LOCKS

Carson and area

68   TOUR 3

When you're ready to come out of the woods and back down to the Columbia River, hike Dog Mountain or soak in a century-old bathhouse at Carson Hot Springs Resort.

This is the rainiest part of the gorge—hence the giant trees. For sun and play in the creeks, late summer is best but every season has its beauty. Just come prepared for the weather and get outdoors in whatever it may be. A crackling fire in the guard station will be your reward.

Book the guard station cabin far in advance (see page 79 for details). Buy a Northwest Forest Pass. For the guard station, pack in a cooler of food and ice, water to drink and cook with (you can wash dishes with mineral spring water), and head lamps. Propane wall lanterns in the cabin are not bright enough for reading. Bring bedding and towels. Fully equipped kitchen (except a fridge). You may want to make an advance reservation to soak at Carson Hot Springs as well.

Adventure 1
Exploring the gorge's ancient forests

You can check into the guard station at 2 p.m. but leave early for a leisurely drive, and to do one of the suggested hikes beforehand.

Drive out I-84, cross the Bridge of the Gods, go east on SR 14, and grab coffee and morning sweets at **Robbie's Coffee House** in Stevenson before you hit the hinterlands. Continue east on SR 14 to Wind River Road, and then turn left to go north into Carson. Get last-minute groceries and ice at **Carson General Store**. A little further north, when crossing Metzger Road, slow down or turn right for a look at High Cascade's immense log yard, a block east off the main road. It's not a sight you'll see just anywhere. The sawmill and planer mill here produce kiln-dried and green (not dried) dimensional lumber. About half the wood milled is Douglas fir, and most of the rest is white fir, with some Ponderosa pine. The wood comes from Oregon and Washington forests, both publicly and privately owned.

About 1.5 miles north of the mill, pull over just before you get to High Bridge, the 260-foot-tall bridge over the Wind River. Park off the road and walk onto the bridge. There are no sidewalks or shoulders, but traffic is light, views of oncoming cars or trucks are good and you can move out of the way to the other side. From your perch above the treetops, gaze into a deep canyon of columnar basalt. If you want to get down to the river's edge where kayakers put in and take out, backtrack slightly on Wind River Road, then turn right (south) on Old High Bridge Road. Turn right at the next road. About 0.5 mile of gravel road leads downhill through a clear-cut and second-growth forest to a potholed staging area for boaters. Park and enjoy the show and river views.

Going north on Wind River Road, and passing Stabler you're near the former site of the Wind River Canopy Crane. From 1996 to 2011, researchers observed the tree canopy of this 500-year-old forest and published more than 250 articles on topics ranging from carbon flow to the retention of pollutants in lichens. Changing priorities led to the crane's removal in 2011 but its tower still transmits data to researchers. An old Civilian Conservation Corps work center is on Hemlock Road west of Stabler.

Continue on Wind River Road to the Government Mineral Springs area: from Stabler, drive north on Wind River Road; in 5.8 miles, come to a Y. Go straight (the left fork), which is Government Mineral Springs Road. To get to the guard station from the Y, drive 1 mile west on Government Mineral Springs Road following one-way signs. If it's too early to check in, do a hike first. Falls Creek Falls is nearby.

The one-way loop here was a Forest Service campground from the early 1900s to the 1970s. The guard station cabin was built in 1937 by the Civilian Conservation Corps as an administration base for the campground

Timber country, then and now

From the 1850s to the 1990s timber was the main economic engine in the mid-gorge, with 500-year-old logs riding flumes and trucks out of the forests to mills in almost every small community. Old growth trees were milled for lumber for local construction and export, but also cut up for steamboat fuel from the 1850s through the 1920s.

In Skamania County, home to Carson and Stevenson, 90 percent of county land is forests owned by the federal government. Those public timberlands brought living-wage jobs and tax revenues until the 1990s when new federal protections for fish, wildlife and water quality caused severe cutbacks to logging in public forests. Today only the High Cascade mill remains. In 1992, the closure of the county's largest employer, the Stevenson Co-Ply plywood mill, was offset in part by the opening of Skamania Lodge, a destination resort funded in part by the federal government as part of the new Columbia River Gorge National Scenic Area. The county began to transition from a resource-based economy to one based on services, a trajectory it continues on today.

What defines an old growth or ancient forest? According to the U.S. Forest Service's Pacific Northwest Research Station, a Pacific Northwest old growth forest has conifers (narrow-leafed, cone-bearing trees, usually evergreen) of 350 to 750 years old. The youngest old growth forests are 200 years old; the oldest 1,000 years old.

and other forest uses. Both the cabin and former campground are in a grove of ancient trees. In the 1970s, after several trees fell during windstorms, the campground was closed and the guard station cabin mothballed. Happily, it was renovated in 2002 and its Cascadian-style details, à la Timberline Lodge, restored for rentals. The current campground was built in a nearby area without big trees on land that was home to a mineral springs resort from 1910 to 1935.

Why all the activity so far from civilization? The answer: Iron Mike, a soda springs whose waters were touted as healthful. Soda springs contain large amounts of dissolved sodium salts, mostly

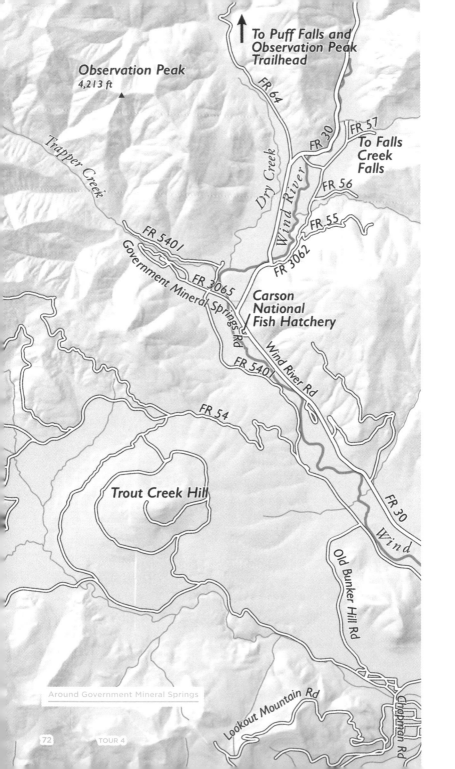

To Puff Falls and
Observation Peak
Trailhead

FR 64

Observation Peak
4,213 ft

FR 30

FR 57

To Falls
Creek
Falls

Trapper Creek

Dry Creek

Wind River

FR 56

FR 55

FR 5401

FR 3062

Government Mineral Springs Rd

FR 3065

Carson
National
Fish Hatchery

FR 5401

Wind River Rd

FR 54

Trout Creek Hill

FR 30

Wind

Old Bunker Hill Rd

Around Government Mineral Springs

Lookout Mountain Rd

Chapman Rd

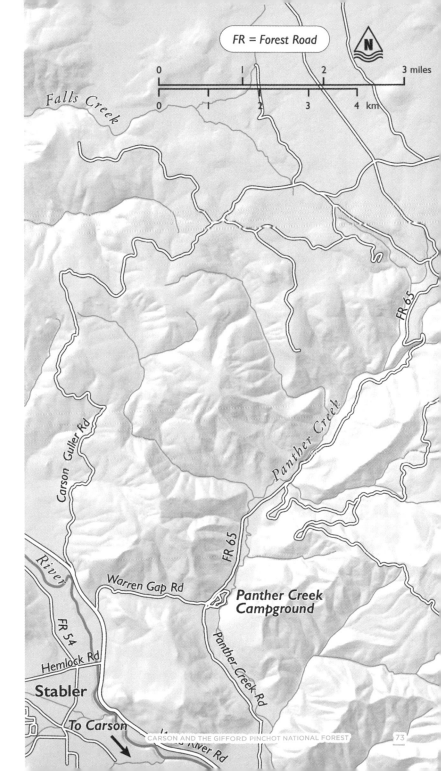

FR = Forest Road

Falls Creek

FR 65

Carson Guler Rd

River

Panther Creek

Warren Gap Rd

FR 65

Panther Creek Campground

Panther Creek Rd

FR 54

Hemlock Rd

Stabler

To Carson

River Rd

Sampling the spring water

sodium carbonate. Try the naturally CO2-charged water; the pump is near the new campground, a short walk from the guard station. The water's very hard, with 360 mg per liter of calcium, and very salty; its sodium content is 585 mg per liter. It doesn't have much hydrogen sulfide—the classic rotten-egg odor of some hot springs—so the smell is not strong. But the taste . . . yuck. The resort operated at full capacity during Prohibition, far from the prying eyes of "revenoors." It had a dance hall, bath houses, an ice cream parlor and 50 rooms to rent. It burned down in 1935.

The guard station cabin is a rarity: overnight lodging where 500-year-old firs and cedars tower above you in the front, side and back yards. The silence, with no electric appliances in the cabin or traffic from nearby roads, is rare and wonderful. Trails from the cabin lead to more big trees in the old campground, to Iron Mike, to the Trapper Creek Wilderness and to Road 5401, which is lined with summer homes along Trapper Creek.

All of these hikes are close by:

Dry Creek aka Puff Falls

Walk up a creek and end in a sunny swimming hole below a 100-foot falls. The creek bed is the sort of scene naturalists try to replicate when they restore urban streams: huge trees fallen in the stream collect debris, diverting parts of the flow into quiet deep pools. In other places water riffles shallowly over smooth rocks, and banks are shaded with overhanging branches. At the end of the walk is a perfect reward: a swim in a deep pool that catches summer's afternoon sun.

From the Y junction of Wind River and Government Mineral Springs roads, go north on Wind River Road. In 2.1 miles, the road bends right; here turn left on FR 64/Dry Creek Road. Drive 2.1 miles to a creek crossing (it flows through an enormous culvert under the road). If you see the Big Hollow Trailhead, you've gone too far. Park and walk/rock-hop upstream in the creekbed about 1 mile to the falls. An excellent swimming hole is right below the road too.

Falls Creek Falls

This is one of southern Washington's largest waterfalls, dropping 335 feet in three tiers. Don't Google for photos; let this beauty reveal itself to you from the trail.

From the Y junction of Wind River and Government Mineral Springs roads, go 0.7 mile north on Wind River Road, then right on FR 3062. At 1.1 miles keep left at a junction. Keep to the main road and at 0.9 mile, go right at FR 057, and about 0.5 mile to the Lower Falls Creek Trail 152A. It's a 1.7-mile one-way walk through sections of old growth forest to the falls. The lower part next to the creek is spectacular and the falls themselves are a fine reward. See gorgefriends.org.

Observation Peak

The hike is 5.6 miles round-trip with 1,400 feet of elevation gain, climbing through old growth Douglas fir and western hemlock. Huckleberry picking is prime in August (or mid-July in a hot summer like 2015).

On a clear day you'll have a five-volcano view atop a peak once occupied by a fire lookout. The volcanoes are part of the Cascade Volcanic Arc, a series of volcanoes about 100 miles inland from the Pacific Ocean, from California to British Columbia. The arc, in turn, is part of the Pacific Ring of Fire. South to north are mounts Jefferson, Hood, Adams, St. Helens and Rainier. St. Helens and Hood are two of the more active volcanoes in the arc. All the volcanoes seen here are the spectacular results of the collision of two tectonic plates about 50 miles off the Oregon and Washington coasts. There, in the Cascadia Subduction Zone, the oceanic Juan de Fuca plate is colliding with and diving under the continental North American plate. As the oceanic plate dives deeper below the continental plate, its leading edge melts the overlying rock, creating the volcanoes.

To get there, from the Y junction of Government Mineral Springs and Wind River roads, head north on Wind River Road. In 2.1 miles the road bends right; turn left onto Dry Creek Road/FR 64. Drive 6 miles (4 are paved; 2 are manageable, slowly, even in a low-slung Prius). Then fork left at the 6-mile mark junction onto Road 5800 (it may not be signed). Drive 2 miles, staying on the main gravel road and left at any major forks. The trailhead is on the left. Oregonhikers. org offers more info.

After the hike, come back to the cabin, light a fire and cook the food you brought. If you don't want to cook, **Backwoods Brewing Company** is 15 miles away in Carson.

Adventure 1
Choosing one or more of...

If you're staying another night at the guard station, crack open your book, play games or take another hike from the Day 1 options. If you're ready to emerge from the trees, here are things to do that cover a few different bases:

Train-spotting and a beach stop

If after a day in the woods you want someone to cook for you, the **Whistle Stop Espresso and Deli** on SR 14 in Home Valley will make you happy. Afterward, cross SR 14 to Home Valley Park. Its crescent-shaped sandy beach on the Columbia River has an awesome view of Wind Mountain. Across the river are Oregon's cliffs. If gorge trains intrigue you there's no better photographer's perch than the footbridge over the train tracks here. It's thrilling to have the train come at you and then pass directly under. The footbridge path runs from east of the Whistle Stop over the highway into Home Valley Park.

Soaking at Carson Hot Springs

For a soothing mineral water soak, wrap or massage, head to **Carson Hot Springs Resort**. Leave the smart phone in the car. In the old bathhouse, a soak in a claw foot tub followed by a tight wrap with warm linens is a wonderful tonic for hyper-connected people. A stern attendant will shush any chatter, leaving you to listen to your thoughts. A dry sauna and massage are also available.

Hiking Wind Mountain

This symmetrical peak offers a serene 3-mile out-and-back hike to good views with 1,171 feet of elevation gain. At the top are stone trenches and piles from Native American spirit quests. Stay on the trails and do not move any rocks.

From SR 14 at the east end of Home Valley, turn north on Wind Mountain Road. Drive 1.4 miles and turn right on Girl Scout Road; drive 0.2 mile to the pavement's end; park and walk the gravel road to the signed trailhead, on the right.

Hiking Dog Mountain

Thousands of hikers make a pilgrimage to this mountain each May and June to celebrate with the earth as it welcomes spring with a joyous yellow carpet of balsamroot. Up on top you won't be the first to fling out your arms and burst into "The Sound of Music." On weekends during peak bloom the vast parking lot is packed and the trail offers no solitude. Go midweek if you can. 7 miles, 2,820 feet of elevation gain on steep trails. Northwest Forest Pass required. SR 14 at MP 53, east of Home Valley. For more info see wta.org.

Adventure 1
Rafting the Wind River

DAY
3

If the season is right and you've got the rafting chops, raft the Wind River. It begins in McClellan Meadows, between mounts St. Helens and Adams. **Wet Planet Whitewater** and **River Drifters** run 11-mile rafting trips on its Class IV and V whitewater. For a mellower river, head to the White Salmon. See Appendix B for outfitter info.

Adventure 2
Squeezing in one more hike

Pick up one of the hikes you didn't already do, and then head back to Portland.

Eat and Drink in Carson (unless otherwise noted)

Backwoods Brewing Company. Tables out back overlook cows and cliffs. Local beer and cider, good pizza, sandwiches. Saturday and Sunday 11:30 a.m. to 9 p.m.; Monday to Friday 3 to 9 p.m. 1162B Wind River Road. 509-427-3412

Blue Collar Cafe. Diner food near the High Cascade mill. Get the day's special. Monday to Friday 9 a.m. to 8 p.m.; Saturday and Sunday 8 a.m. to 8 p.m. 22 Hughes Road. 509-427-4000

Carson General Store. Full grocery store and some fast food. Daily 7 a.m. to 9 p.m. Next to Backwoods Brewing. 1162 Wind River Road. 509-427-4520

Elk Ridge Clubhouse and Lounge. On the golf course at Carson Hot Springs Resort. Friendly service, mountain and golf course views, good breakfast, lunch and light dinner food. Its sports bar addresses any screen deficits your lodging might have. Sunday to Thursday 8 a.m. to 7 p.m.; Friday and Saturday to 10 p.m. 509-427-0127

Home Valley Store. Convenience store with fishing tackle, bait and fishing licenses. Monday to Saturday 6 a.m. to 8 p.m.; Sunday 7 a.m. to 7 p.m. 50151 SR 14, Home Valley. 509-427-4015

Whistle Stop Espresso and Deli. Great pastries, coffee and breakfast. Try the breakfast burrito. Daily 5 a.m. to 8 p.m. 50341 SR 14, Home Valley. 509-427-0155

Shop in Carson

Antiques Trading Post. Weekends. At Hot Springs Avenue and Wind River Road. 509-427-4766

Stay in and around Carson

Carson Hot Springs Resort. Motel-style rooms at an ancient resort. Request a Wind River room with a private hot tub on the balcony; they'll fill it with fresh mineral water before you arrive. Soak and take in views of tall firs in the canyon. You can hear the river but can't see it. Good beds, quiet rooms. 372 St. Martins Springs Road. Call 509-427-8296 for same-day or advance reservations for a soak or a room. [$$]

Carson Ridge Luxury Cabins. Ten cabins in a rustic-elegance style. 1261 Wind River Road. 877-816-7908 [$$$]

Government Mineral Springs Guard Station. Reserve this 1937 two-bedroom cabin far in advance. Two-night minimum on weekends. 15 miles north of Carson. Reserve at recreation.gov. [$$]

Rivermist Lodge. Five-room bed and breakfast on an old riverboat landing road. Sprague Landing was also the terminus of an early log flume that followed the route of Wind River Highway to the Columbia River. 212 Sprague Landing Road, Stevenson (near Carson). 509-427-4810 [$$$]

Sandhill Cottages. Wonderfully intact 1930s tourist auto court with five cottages, restored with period kitsch, most with kitchenettes. Our tourist forebears did not expect luxury, and you can experience that here. Walk to Carson Hot Springs. 932 Hot Springs Ave. 509-427-3464 [$$]

Camp in Home Valley

Home Valley Campground. County-owned park on the Columbia River. 24 forested sites for tents, cab-over campers and small RVs. No reservations, electricity or water hookups. Showers and restrooms: yes. East of the campground is a pretty forest with a short riverside trail that offers solitude. April 1 to October 31. SR 14 at MP 50. 509-427-3980 [$]

Timberlake Campground and RV Park. This private, 22-acre forested park about 3 miles above SR 14 is on land owned by the same family since the 1890s. 43 RV sites with hookups, 22 tent sites. Far from highway sounds. March 1 to October 31. 112 Bylin Road, Home Valley. 509-427-2267 [$]

Wind Mountain RV Park and Lodge. A few motel-style rooms and full-service RV campground with 30 sites. 50561 SR 14. 509-607-3409 [$ to $$]

Lodging Cost Key			
$	$$	$$$	$$$$
<$50	$51 to $99	$100 to $200	>$200

TOUR
5

WHITE SALMON, BINGEN, CATHERINE CREEK AND COYOTE WALL

WASHINGTON

When you want a weekend of bright light, gorgeous scenery, local food and drink, and outdoor action, you may think first of Hood River. Many people are less familiar with its counterparts on the Washington side, White Salmon and Bingen. This pair of towns, one high on a bluff and one on the river, are equally brilliant, with great food and drink, minus the Hood River buzz. Like Hood River, they're on the dry side of the Cascades, so when Portland is grey, there's a good chance you'll find the sun in White Salmon and Bingen.

Get there in 75 minutes from Portland via I-84 and across the Hood River Bridge, or take the slightly longer, but so-scenic drive east on SR 14. After a weekend here you may find yourself studying real estate listings and considering a significant change of life.

Spring through fall are best for rafting, horseback riding and touring wineries. Hiking at Coyote Wall and doing some forensic exploring of the old Condit Dam are spectacular any time of year, but wildflowers are best at Catherine Creek in spring.

You may want to reserve your rafting and horseback riding adventures in advance. If you want to stop at Gorge Crest Vineyards, make an appointment.

Adventure 1
Rafting and/or horseback riding

Do these activities in either order, or just do one.

Reserve a half-day raft trip on the White Salmon, one of the United States' Wild and Scenic Rivers. The river follows the route of collapsed lava tubes that carry snowmelt off Mount Adams, an active volcano. Four-hour trips through Class III and IV rapids leave at 9:30 a.m. or 1:30 and 2:30 p.m., generally April to October. Meet at the offices of the rafting companies. (See Appendix B for outfitters plus details on minimum ages and months of operation.) They'll take you to the put-in at the BZ Corner Launch Site for 8 miles on the river. Take-out is at Northwestern Park. Zoller's offers longer trips, including one to the mouth of the White Salmon through the blasted away Condit Dam site.

Complement the river time with a one- to three-hour horseback ride into the mountains, or create a customized ride at **Northwestern Lake Riding Stables**, located near Northwestern Park. Scheduled rides run April 1 through October 31, morning, afternoon and evening. Other months, rides are weather-dependent. See Appendix B.

Adventure 2
Unwinding in White Salmon

After your active day, check into the **Inn of the White Salmon**, a small, elegant and affordable hotel on Jewett Boulevard, White Salmon's main street. Before dinner, explore the town's bluff top streets with a 3.3-mile hill walk that starts at Jewett and Main. The last stop on the walk is downtown itself, where you can eat at **Everybody's Brewing** or **Henni's Kitchen and Bar** and then walk back to the inn.

From Jewett Boulevard and Main Avenue/First Avenue, turn south on First Avenue. Walk a few blocks to Oak Street, the last street before the steep bluff begins, and turn left. Walk along Oak and enjoy beautiful homes that perch above the Columbia.

From Oak at Fourth, turn right on Oak Place, a little cliff-hugging loop that offers more beautiful homes; it curves back up to Oak at Fifth.

At Fifth and Oak, go north on Fifth two blocks, then dip into the cute Wyers End pocket neighborhood: from Fifth turn right on Wyers Street, left on Fifth Place and left on Upper Wyers Street. This 2.4-acre neighborhood of cottages was built in 2009 and 2010. Residents share and care for common areas. Small is beautiful here.

At Upper Wyers and Fifth walk north on Fifth to Jewett Boulevard and turn left, then walk four blocks along it before turning right on Main. Here you get to climb for about 0.5 mile. At the city park stop at the big-enough-for-adults swings, then turn left on Spring Street, which lifts you to an even higher hill with views down the gorge and across the canyon of the White Salmon River.

From the end of Spring Street, turn left on El Camino Real, which curves into Lincoln Street as it drops you downhill and back into town. From Lincoln turn right on Garfield then left on Jewett Boulevard. The old, red building east of the Inn of the White Salmon is an 1870 springhouse. Jewett is named for A.H. and Jennie Jewett, who settled here in 1874 from Wisconsin. In the early 1900s Sam Hill (see Tour 6) wanted to purchase their Jewett Farm Resort on the bluff here (at today's E Jewett Boulevard and 10th Avenue). The sale for $80,000 was almost finalized until Sam pulled out a flask to make a toast. Instantly the deal was off: Jennie Jewett was a prohibitionist. Hill had to look further east, where he purchased 5,000-plus acres, explored in Tour 6.

End the walk at your restaurant of choice on Jewett, or go another 1.4 miles (round trip) along more scenic streets atop the bluff. Start on Jewett Boulevard and walk west. At 245 W Jewett Blvd is the Lauterbach House, built in 1904. Rudolph Lauterbach, born in Germany in 1854, came to this area in 1892; he bought forestland, cleared much of it, and in 1901 platted his land into some of the lots that are today's town. Walk west on Jewett's shoulder about 0.4 mile to Waubish Street, and enjoy the scenic 0.3-mile walk to its dead end. Along the way bluff-edge homes take in the big views; the road ends with views of the mouth of Hood River on the Oregon side of the Columbia. Retrace your steps into town, have dinner and walk back to your bed at the Inn of the White Salmon.

Adventure 1
Hiking spectacular gorge scenery

DAY
2

Have breakfast in White Salmon at **North Shore Cafe**, and then head to Bingen ("bin-jin"). Get there by driving east on Jewett Boulevard. It ends in Bingen.

Despite its small size, there are big employers in Bingen. Workers

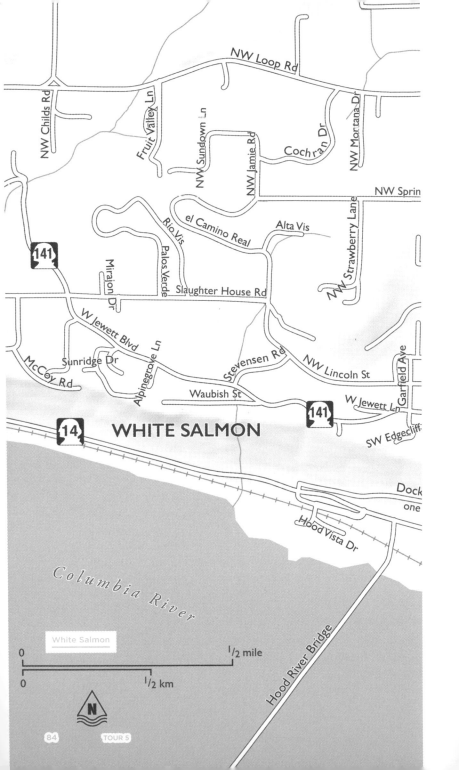

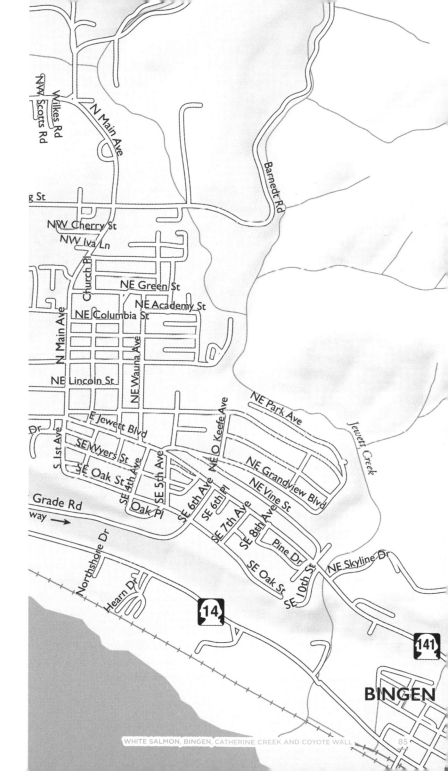

NW Scotts Rd

NW Wilkes Rd

N Main Ave

Barnedt Rd

g St

NW Cherry St

NW Iva Ln

Church Pl

NE Green St

NE Academy St

NE Columbia St

N Main Ave

NE Wauna Ave

NE Lincoln St

E Jewett Blvd

NE O Keefe Ave

NE Park Ave

Jewett Creek

Dr

S 1st Ave

SE Myers St

SE 4th Ave

SE 5th Ave

SE Oak St

Oak Pl

SE 6th Ave

SE 6th Pl

NE Grandview Blvd

NE Vine St

SE 7th Ave

SE 8th Ave

Pine Dr

NE Skyline Dr

Grade Rd

way →

Northshore Dr

Hearn Dr

SE Oak St

SE 10th St

14

141

BINGEN

commute here from the entire length of the gorge to work at SDS Lumber, manufacturer of lumber and plywood; at Insitu, Inc., maker of drones; and at Underwood Fruit, which grows, packs and ships apples, pears and cherries.

The following hike options range from easy to challenging and are best late winter to early summer for wildflower blooms. Summer can be too hot, especially midday, but fall and nice winter days are sublime too.

Coyote Wall and the Labyrinth Loop

Coyote Wall and the Syncline are two names for the same geographic feature: a huge vertical cliff created by both the faulting and horizontal folding of layers of basalt. Even though the Syncline is misnamed (it's actually an anticline), no matter: the cliff is a jaw-dropper, whether you see it from across the river or up close, as here. For more on this fascinating geologic feature, see Tour 9, where from Mosier, Oregon, you can see Coyote Wall best relative to the surrounding landscape.

One hike from the Coyote Wall Trailhead is Coyote Wall, 7.8 miles and 1,895 feet of elevation gain. You don't have to go the full way to get spectacular views from atop the cliff. Two other hikes are the Labyrinth Loop, 5.8 miles with 1,200 feet of elevation gain, and the Labyrinth Hike, 2 miles with 570 feet of gain. Find turn-by-turn directions for all three at oregonhikers.org.

To get to Coyote Wall, from Highway 141 (Jewett Boulevard) and SR 14 in Bingen drive east 3.3 miles on SR 14 to Courtney Road. Turn left then immediately right into the Coyote Wall Trailhead. Discover Pass required.

Catherine Creek

So special and scenic, this former cattle ranch was one of the first land purchases by the U.S. Forest Service in 1986 when the gorge was named a National Scenic Area.

From Highway 141 (Jewett Boulevard) and SR 14 in Bingen, drive east 4.5 miles on SR 14 to Old Highway 8. Turn left and drive 1.5 miles to the Catherine Creek Trailhead, a parking pullout on the left. The Catherine Creek Arch Loop is a 3.5-mile hike with 500 feet of elevation gain to a rock arch that is sacred to Native Americans. On the right side of the road is a parking pullout for the spectacular, 1.5-mile, near-flat Catherine Creek Universal Access Trail. Discover Pass required at both pullouts. See gorgefriends.org.

Adventure 2
Scenic touring: wine, hatcheries and windsurfers

DAY
2

After your hike, come back to Bingen for lunch. If it's open, stop by the **Gorge Heritage Museum**. Then relax for a spectacular bit of auto-touring.

From Bingen, head west on SR 14 to begin a route that'll have you hopping out of your car and snapping scores of photos. In summer, afternoon heat brings on the west wind, and that brings out windsurfers.

Your first stop is the Spring Creek National Fish Hatchery. Expert windsurfers ride the wind and waves in this stretch of the gorge from spring to early fall. (See Appendix A for July and August events that offer great spectating.) The hatchery, with its oaks and rocky crags, is a beautiful place to watch from. A Discover Pass is required for the state park section of the fish hatchery site. West winds bring large swells and windsurfers close to shore. The video "Hatchery Swell" shows the 6- to 8-foot swells (vimeo.com, by Warren Morgan). Inspired? Take windsurfing lessons in quieter waters from the many instructors in Hood River. See Appendix B.

Once known as white salmon for their paler flesh, tule fall Chinook salmon are raised at and released from the hatchery, which was established in 1901 by the Broughton Lumber Company. After Bonneville Dam raised river levels, the hatchery was rebuilt on higher ground in 1941. Pleasant riverside trails serve up huge views. The tall waterfall across the river is Wah Gwin Gwin Falls; you can bike or walk to its top in Tour 10. Fish-viewing action at the hatchery depends on the month.

- January to May. Weekends, workers feed smolts (young salmon) to be released in spring to swim downriver to the ocean. Visitor Center is open weekends.
- March. In trailers parked in the lots, workers are marking fish; open weekdays to visitors.
- June to August. No fish, but prime windsurfing-watching; picnic at tables overlooking the water.
- Late August to September. Mature fall Chinook return. The September Open House (call 509-493-1730 for the date) is a great time to bring kids.
- October to December. Weekdays, workers tend fish in the incubation buildings.

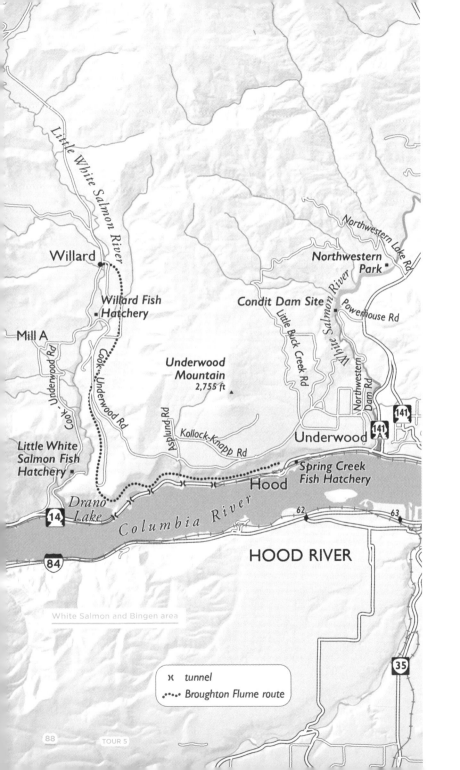

Little White Salmon River

Willard

Willard Fish
Hatchery

Mill A

Cook – Underwood Rd

Cook-Underwood Rd

Little White
Salmon Fish
Hatchery

Drano
Lake

14

84

Columbia River

Underwood
Mountain
2,755 ft

Asplund Rd

Kollock-Knapp Rd

Underwood

141
A

141

White Salmon River

Condit Dam Site

Little Buck Creek Rd

Powerhouse Rd

Northwestern
Park

Northwestern Lake Rd

Northwestern Dam Rd

Hood

Spring Creek
Fish Hatchery

62

63

HOOD RIVER

35

White Salmon and Bingen area

x   tunnel
......• Broughton Flume route

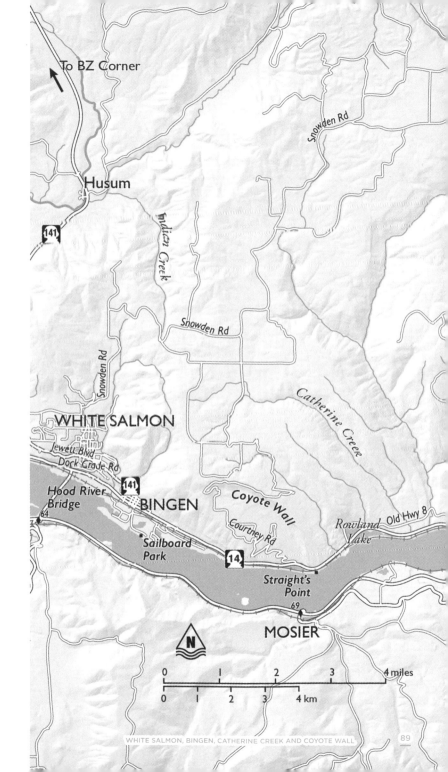

To BZ Corner

Snowden Rd

Husum

141

Indian Creek

Snowden Rd

Snowden Rd

WHITE SALMON

Catherine Creek

Jewett Blvd
Dock Grade Rd

Hood River
Bridge

141

BINGEN

Coyote Wall

Rowland
Lake

Old Hwy 8

64

Courtney Rd

14

Sailboard
Park

Straight's
Point

69

N

MOSIER

| 0 | | 1 | | 2 | | 3 | | 4 miles |
| 0 | 1 | 2 | 3 | 4 km |

Across SR 14 from the hatchery is a large complex of deteriorating buildings, the Broughton Mill. It's been closed since 1986, in part due to changing regulations for the harvest of timber, and also because the old growth trees the company milled were largely gone after a century of logging. Its owners plan to turn it into a high-end resort.

West of the hatchery, near MP 56 are Swell City and Cheap Beach, two windsurfing areas that the Columbia Gorge Windsurfing Association rates as "advanced." Here and westward, the road is passing along the flanks of Underwood Mountain, a 2,755-foot shield volcano. Early gorge road builders did not have the technology to build a road on its steep riverside slope, so they went inland; today that inland route is the Cook-Underwood Road, which you'll soon be on. By 1936 the state had blasted five tunnels through the base of the mountain, between Spring Creek National Fish Hatchery and Drano Lake. The adjacent railroad tunnels were built in the early 1900s.

Count the tunnels as you pass through; after the third one, look for a gravel road to the right just before the fourth tunnel. Turn right on the road and stop. Look up: on the hill is one of the last standing remnants of a flume that operated from 1913 to 1986. It carried rough cut lumber downhill from a Broughton mill at Willard, Washington, to the Broughton mill just seen, where it was planed into the final product. The journey took 55 minutes. The flume's water came from the Little White Salmon River. Each Friday, a worker walked the 9 miles of the flume's length on a 12-inch-wide boardwalk attached to its side to check for bad boards or leaks. At times he was up to 90 feet above the ground. A friend, Hal Broughton, told me of walking the flume and riding it occasionally as a young man, a commitment that once made could not be undone.

Come back to SR 14, turn right, cross over Drano Lake and immediately turn right onto the road to the Little White Salmon National Fish Hatchery, one of the gorge's most scenically sited hatcheries. When it opened in 1896, commercial fishing had already decimated salmon runs, just fifty years after Euro-American settlement. Nine million salmon are raised here each year.

The hatchery is about 1 mile up the river from SR 14. Stop at the Visitor Center to see salmon in tanks, held here until they are ready for human-induced spawning, and a viewing platform where you can see salmon jump. Picnic tables make excellent spots to stop and watch the salmon run up the river in fall.

Even if the hatchery is closed, the route leading to it is a destination itself, with its Native American fishing scaffolds on Drano Lake and beautiful cliffs as the land narrows into the river's gorge. Before Bonneville Dam was built, the shallow, gravel-filled mouth of the Little White Salmon was an important fishing site for tribes. An accessible fishing path and platform let you get down to the water.

The hatchery is open daily, 7:30 a.m. to 4 p.m. Salmon-viewing varies with the month and season.

- Mid-April. See Spring Chinook salmon smolts (young salmon) get released to begin their journey to the ocean.
- May and June. Watch spring Chinook return.
- Early July. Watch the release of upriver bright Chinook salmon smolts.
- Mid-July to mid-August. Watch human induced spawning on Tuesdays. Call 509-538-2755 for this year's dates.
- Late August to mid-November. Walk along the river to see Chinook and coho salmon return to spawn (naturally, with no human intervention) between the upper and lower parts of the hatchery.
- September. Watch Native Americans fishing from scaffolds with long-handled dip nets.

Native American fishing scaffolds

After the hatchery visit, return to driving west on SR 14 and take the first right onto Cook-Underwood Road, the original road around Underwood Mountain. Climb the canyon of the Little White Salmon. At Jessup Road, take a left to look at the pretty logging community of Mill A, once a Broughton Lumber company town. Its tiny school has just a few dozen students.

Back on Cook-Underwood Road, keep driving north. Just past

the Willard National Fish Hatchery a bridge crosses the Little White Salmon. Cross, then park at one of two pullouts. The north side pullout has a trail that leads easily to the river under the bridge: scenic, though not as good as the south side trail, which is sketchier but with excellent riverside views. This river has been called the most challenging whitewater river on the West Coast, and until the 1990s no one ran it. Only the most expert kayakers run it now, and it has claimed a few lives. You don't want to fall in here, so use your judgment about hiking down the steep trails.

From the Little White Salmon, begin to head back out to the rim of the gorge, passing orchards and vineyards. Just beyond Asplund Road a pullout offers an incredible view: Mount Hood, Oregon's cliffs, the Hood River Valley and the Columbia Gorge. Just past milepost 10 another pullout gives a great vantage, down the face of the cliff to the Broughton Mill and the Spring Creek hatchery. Wine-tasting is by appointment only at **Gorge Crest Vineyards**, 341 Kollock-Knapp Road. Further on is **AniChe Cellars**, 71 Little Buck Creek Road; visit its vineyard, picnic area and tasting room.

Beyond about milepost 13 is the community of Underwood. Its Chris-Zada Cemetery (on Cooper Avenue, off Cook-Underwood Road) is a lovely stop for a stroll. If you want another short and interesting walk, turn left off Cook-Underwood Road onto Northwestern Dam Road; drive to its dead end, park and walk an old road to where you can see remnants of the Condit Dam site. (See this tour's Day 3 adventure for more on the dam.) Back on Cook-Underwood Road, at the bottom of the hill just before you reach SR 14, pass an in-lieu fishing site reserved for Native Americans. At the junction is **White Salmon Vineyard Wine Tasting Room and Cafe**.

To return to White Salmon, go left on SR 14, cross the White Salmon River and take the first left, the intriguing, one-way Dock Grade Road, which climbs the bluff up to White Salmon.

Adventure 3
Sleeping in an old inn or schoolhouse

Stay another night at the **Inn of the White Salmon** and try a different restaurant this night, or eat in Bingen and stay in the **Columbia River Gorge Hostel**, a Depression-era schoolhouse where you can stay in a bunk or private room. Afterward wander out to Bingen's Sailboard Park. Its big lawn has grand views up the gorge. It's also a landing site for paragliders who drift down from the cliffs above. Want to try it? See Appendix B.

Adventure 1
Scenic driving to a blasted dam and a rafting viewpoint

Before you take the fast route back to Portland, do some sleuthing and sight-seeing of local history, past and present, plus incredible views of Class V whitewater.

First: a look at the Condit Dam site. This dam on the White Salmon River was part of the nation's twentieth-century love affair with dam building, when just about every river and creek was harnessed for power, irrigation or recreation. It was dynamited in 2011. For fascinating videos of the dam's destruction and the river's immediate response see whitesalmontimelapse.wordpress.com.

To get there: In White Salmon, drive west on Jewett/Highway 141, which bends to the north. At the boundary for the Columbia River Gorge National Scenic Area, turn left on Powerhouse Road and drive a short way to the pavement's end at a wide spot in the road. Here, the dam was built where basalt ledges had channeled the river into a narrow slot. Salmon fought their way up this river for millennia but from 1913 to 2011 the dam blocked them from upstream spawning grounds. The fish, amazingly, returned as soon as the dam disappeared. Look upstream to cliffs that used to be underwater. New trees have been planted. The flat bench upriver from the parking pullout was a temporary road used to haul chunks of the dam away until the final bits were exploded with dynamite. Past the pullout, keep driving another 1 mile (or, for better views, walk it) to the now-desolate concrete powerhouse in the river. Beyond it a fork in the road leads past homes once used by dam workers, and the road turns into a footpath to the same abandoned bridge you saw if you walked past the dead end of Northwestern Dam Road on Day 2. Some people dream of the bridge being rehabbed and the two roads connected.

Back on Highway 141, for more forensic sightseeing, drive about a mile north of Powerhouse Road to Northwestern Lake Road and turn left. Drive across the river to Northwestern Park. This used to be Northwestern Lake when the dam existed. Today it's got a sort of mysterious look to it. It used to be the end point of raft trips. No longer. Some trips now run all the way to the mouth of the White Salmon.

For the whitewater: From the park, keep north about 2 more miles on Highway 141 to Husum Falls in Husum. It's a Class V, 10-foot drop, just east of Highway 141. Some rafts portage; some go over. From the river bridge, you can watch. Just a tad further north on Highway 141, at about milepost 12.5, the BZ Corner Launch gives excellent viewing

of rafters and kayakers who run the river year-round. At the launch, descend the 0.1-mile trail to the White Salmon to watch the action. The trail is lined with parallel steel rails for rafts to slide on. A 0.25-mile spur trail leads upriver, offering more views of the canyon and a waterfall.

Come back down Highway 141 and, not far south of Powerhouse Road, veer right on Alternate SR 141. It follows the White Salmon down to SR 14. Turn left on SR 14, then right to get on the Hood River Bridge. From it drive I-84 west back to the Portland area.

Eat and Drink in White Salmon

Everybody's Brewing. Big view of Mount Hood. Fabulous vegetarian burrito and beer. Good service and classic rock on the speakers. Sunday to Thursday 11:30 a.m. to 9:30 p.m.; Friday and Saturday 11:30 a.m. to 10:30 p.m. 151 E Jewett Blvd. 509-637-2774

Feast Market and Delicatessen. Groceries, meats and sandwiches from local sources. Monday to Saturday 9 a.m. to 8 p.m.; Sunday 10 a.m. to 7 p.m. 320 E Jewett Blvd. 509-637-2530

Harvest Market. Grocery store. Daily 7 a.m. to 10 p.m. 77 NE Wauna Ave. 509-493-9494

Henni's Kitchen and Bar. Eclectic menu, local ingredients, from burgers to curries. Good happy hour fare (4:30 to 6 p.m.) Daily 4:30 p.m. to close. 120 E Jewett Blvd. 509-493-1555

North Shore Cafe. Good coffee and breakfast/lunch fare. Nice big table with the Columbia River Gorge map under glass to pore over and plan. Daily 6 a.m. to 3 p.m. 166 E Jewett Blvd. 509-426-5341

Pioneer Pizza. Same owners as Henni's. Monday to Saturday 4 to 11 p.m.; Sunday 12 to 9 p.m. 216 E Jewett Blvd. 509-493-0028

Eat and Drink in Bingen

Beneventi's Pizza, Sandwiches & Pasta. Since 2004, good for a post-hike meal. Daily 10:30 or 11 a.m. to 8 or 9 p.m. 201 W Steuben St. 509-493-2177

Ayutlense, a Family Restaurant. Daily 11 a.m. to 9:30 or 10p.m. 120 E. Steuben St. 509-493-1017

Mugo Coffee. Stop before a hike for bagels, hand pies and made-to-order sandwiches. Consult the online menu then call or text your order. Monday to Saturday 6:30 or 7 a.m. to 3:30 or 4 p.m. 120 W Steuben St. Text 206-486-6080 or call 509-281-3100

Taqueria el Rinconcito Express. House-made tamales and other treats. Monday to Friday 8:30 a.m. to 5 p.m. 114 W Steuben St. 509-493-8227

W & S Liquor Store. Local spirits, wines and beers. 102 E Steuben St. 509-637-2882

Shop in Bingen and White Salmon

Antiques & Oddities. Two floors and many vendors in this large mall. Daily 10 a.m. to 5 p.m. 211 W Steuben St., Bingen. 509-493-4242

The Book Peddler. Used books for kids and adults. Tuesday to Saturday 10:30 a.m. to 5:30 p.m. 154 E Jewett Blvd., White Salmon. 509-493-4644

Klickitat Pottery. Locally made stoneware. Monday to Friday 10 a.m. to 4 p.m. 264 E Jewett Blvd., White Salmon. 509-493-4456

Discover and Learn in Bingen

Gorge Heritage Museum. May to September. Friday to Sunday 12 to 5 p.m. 202 E Humboldt St. 509-493-3228

Mount Adams Chamber of Commerce. Monday to Friday 9 a.m. to 5 p.m.; Saturday 10 a.m. to 4 p.m. Milepost 65, SR 14 (just west of the Hood River Bridge). 360-493-3630

Taste the Wine in and around White Salmon

AniChe Cellars. Only female wine-making team in the gorge. Vineyard, picnic area and tasting room. President's Day Weekend (February) to December: Wednesday to Sunday 12 to 6 p.m. 71 Little Buck Creek Road, Underwood. 360-624-6531

Ascendente Winery. Wine bar. Friday 3 to 8 p.m.; Saturday and Sunday 12 to 6 p.m. 85 NE Estes Ave. in downtown White Salmon. 509-281-3005

Gorge Crest Vineyards. By appointment only. 341 Kollock-Knapp Road, Underwood. 509-493-2026

White Salmon Vineyard Tasting Room and Cafe. April 1 to October 31: Friday to Sunday 12 to 6 p.m. 63281 SR 14 (at SR 14 and Cook-Underwood Road), Underwood. 541-490-7664

Stay in and around White Salmon

Husum Highlands B & B. Four rooms in large home on 20 acres with big views. 70 Postgren Road, Husum. 509-493-4503 [$$$]

Inn of the White Salmon. This family-run inn with elegant decor and thoughtful amenities is walkable to restaurants. Built in 1937 as the Hood View Hotel and Apartments, it once housed schoolteachers and newlyweds saving for a first home. 20 rooms; one co-ed hostel room with bunks for couples or singles; sheets and towels provided. Shuttle services offered from Portland, and for rafting or personalized outings. They'll also shuttle you and your bike to a tour of wineries. 172 W Jewett Blvd. 509-493-2335 [$ to $$$]

Steelhead Ranch Alpacas Bed and Brew. Stay in one of two units at a working alpaca farm on the White Salmon River, north of BZ Corner, where many whitewater raft trips begin. 1376 Highway 141. 425-408-2914 [$$$]

Stay in Bingen

Columbia River Gorge Hostel. Depression-era school mostly untouched since it closed in the 1970s. Minimal services, but clean and friendly. Private rooms with linens, or bunk room with a charge for linens and towels. Bring a basketball to play in the gym. Humboldt and Cedar streets. Office hours and check-in: 6 to 9 p.m. 509-493-3363 [$]

Camp near White Salmon

Bridge RV Park and Campground. RV and tent sites. On SR 14 just east of the Hood River Bridge. 509-493-1111 [$]

Lodging Cost Key			
$	$$	$$$	$$$$
<$50	$51 to $99	$100 to $200	>$200

TOUR
6

LYLE, MARYHILL AND GOLDENDALE OBSERVATORY STATE PARK

WASHINGTON

When you've just got to get away to somewhere different, a road trip to this triangle of towns in the eastern gorge fits the bill. Its rocky buttes, high plains and cliffs are more kin to the Wild West than the coastal Northwest. And the sunshine; it's abundant.

Lyle is 75 miles from Portland, and it's hard to believe that such amazingly different landscapes are less than 100 miles from Portland's green lushness. From Lyle, it's 35 miles to Goldendale, as unlike Portland as a city can be, geographically-speaking.

For the best sky-gazing at the Goldendale Observatory, take this tour during a two- or three-day stretch when the moon is new and Goldendale's forecast is for clear skies. Watching the full moon rise is pretty great too and August's Perseid meteor shower would be a spectacular time to visit.

In terms of the land, March, April and May offer wildflower displays everywhere. By June, fields are turning golden, creating a beautiful contrast with irrigated lawns, orchards and vineyards along the river. By mid-June farm stands begin their run of cherries, plums and peaches. Late spring and summer winds can be fierce and hot, a good time to take a guided raft or kayak trip on the Klickitat River (raftable through June). In September, watch salmon jump and tribal fishers dip netting from the cliffs along the Klickitat. Clear fall days offer cooler temperatures and brilliant skies.

You may want to bring your bikes and locks. Even in summer, bring warm clothes for nighttime viewing at the Goldendale Observatory (it's outdoors), where a Discover Pass is required. For weather forecasts and upcoming events or shows see goldendaleobservatory.com.

Adventure 1
Exploring the Klickitat River along the Klickitat Trail

Leave Portland so you arrive in Lyle by late morning. Have brunch or lunch at the **Country Cafe**, or wait until after you hike or bike a 4-mile round-trip stretch along the Klickitat River on the nearby Klickitat Trail, a rail line turned walking-and-biking path. The trail is fine gravel, okay for bikes with hybrid tires.

Start at the Lyle Trailhead. Rails to trails conversions can get monotonous, so veer riverward (left) at every road, fork or turn. About 1 mile in, the gravel trail becomes a gravel road. Take it downhill to an undeveloped riverfront park owned by the county and U.S. Forest Service. River access is via a steep trail. Back on the main trail heading upriver, look for a fisherman trail. Take it to a wide, flat path and spectacular cliffs above the river's gorge. It's an idyllic spot for watching swallows in spring, or for lying down and listening to nature. This is an historic fishing ground for Native Americans who still fish here with traditional dip nets. At about 2 miles in from the Lyle Trailhead is Fisher Bridge. Like all new pedestrian bridges, railings are too high for good viewing of the spectacular scene below. Find better views from the car bridge just upstream.

Intrigued and want more? You can keep going: the trail runs 31 miles, about half of it along the Klickitat and the rest through remote Swale Canyon. If not, return to the start.

Adventure 2
Scenic touring to Goldendale

Drive to Goldendale one of two ways:

Via Highway 142

Get on Highway 142 at its intersection with SR 14 in Lyle, and follow it along the Klickitat River through the community of Klickitat and on to Goldendale, a total of 34.5 miles.

Three miles beyond Klickitat, stop at the Wahkiacus Trailhead to the Klickitat Trail. Here you can take a 2.6-mile, one-way walk to Klickitat Mineral Springs. Like the Iron Mike spring in Tour 4, it's a soda spring, with naturally carbonated water. The springs were the source of several businesses: a spa in the 1890s, a soft drink bottling plant in the early 1900s and, from 1932 to 1957, the Gas Ice Corporation, which manufactured dry ice from natural carbon dioxide wells at the springs. The Depression-era *Guide to Washington* reported, "Three tons of the product, used for refrigeration in long distance shipping, are shipped daily." One building remains; its chimney is the seasonal home to migrating Vaux's swifts. Take a sip from the water bubbling up from wellheads near the old ice plant. See oregonhikers.org for route details.

Back on Highway 142, pass Blockhouse Butte. Fort Blockhouse was built here after the murder of an Indian agent at the beginning of the Yakima Indian War of 1855–56. U.S. Cavalry were stationed here until 1860. By then, Native Americans who had not succumbed to disease had been forcibly moved to reservations. Continue on Highway 142, which turns into Broadway Street as it enters Goldendale. See page 110 for things to do in downtown Goldendale.

Via the Centerville Highway

This route starts in Lyle and runs 32 miles to Goldendale. In Lyle, get on the Centerville Highway, which starts at the **Country Cafe** (SR 14 and Sixth Street). The highway soon leaves the Klickitat River canyon and climbs to High Prairie, traversing arid landscapes that offer Mount Adams views. Further east, the landscape changes dramatically as trees retreat into draws between hills. At 15.9 miles a historical marker explains the Military Road that once ran north-south through this area, along with the Dalles to Ellensburg stagecoach line. Decaying wooden barns and homes stipple fields in dryland farms. In tiny Centerville, stop at a schoolyard swing set so tall you can touch the sky with your toes. The highway ends at U.S. 97; turn left and then

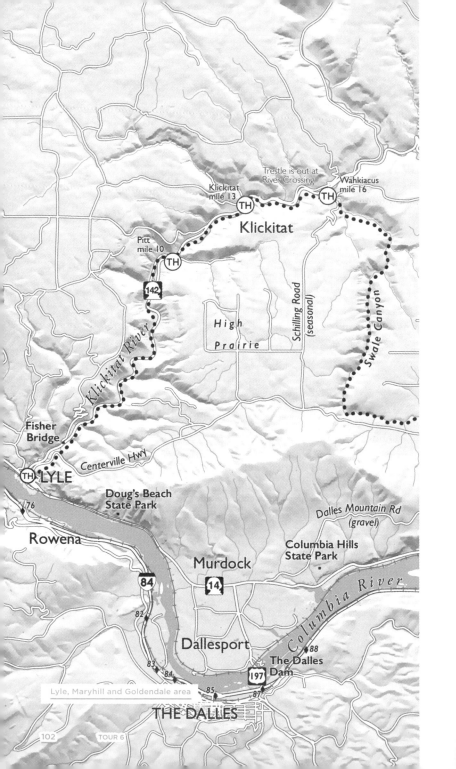

Trestle is out at
River Crossing

Klickitat
mile 13

TH

Wahkiacus
mile 16

TH

Klickitat

Pitt
mile 10

TH

142

Swale Canyon

Schilling Road
(seasonal)

High
Prairie

Klickitat River

Fisher
Bridge

Centerville Hwy

TH LYLE

Doug's Beach
State Park

Dalles Mountain Rd
(gravel)

76

Rowena

Columbia Hills
State Park

Murdock

84

14

Columbia River

82

Dallesport

88

83

84

The Dalles
Dam

197

85

87

Lyle, Maryhill and Goldendale area

THE DALLES

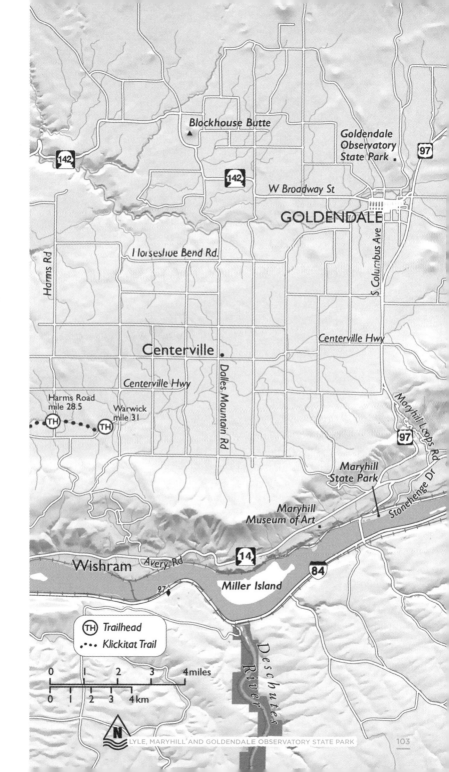

Blockhouse Butte

Goldendale
Observatory
State Park

[97]

[142]

[142]

W Broadway St

GOLDENDALE

Horseshoe Bend Rd.

Harms Rd

S Columbus Ave

Centerville

Centerville Hwy

Centerville Hwy

Dalles Mountain Rd

Maryhill Loops Rd

Harms Road
mile 28.5

Warwick
mile 31

(TH)

(TH)

[97]

Maryhill
State Park

Stonehenge Dr

Maryhill
Museum of Art

Wishram

Avery Rd

[14]

[84]

Miller Island

97

Deschutes River

(TH) Trailhead

•••• Klickitat Trail

0   1   2   3   4 miles

0   1   2   3   4 km

N

Front-yard grazing along the Centerville Highway

take the first Goldendale exit, Columbus Avenue, which leads north into the center of town, past a good dinner stop, the **Glass Onion**. See page 110 for things to do in downtown Goldendale.

DAY 1

Adventure 3
Star-gazing

After a bit of shopping and/or dinner, drive by the Art Deco-style Klickitat County Courthouse, 205 S Columbus Ave. It was finished in 1942, about the last gasp of that style's popularity. New windows in 2010 and decorative lanterns in 1998 echo the original style.

After dark, head to the **Goldendale Observatory State Park**, 5 acres atop a wooded hillside, for a guided look through one of the nation's largest publicly accessible telescopes. Rangers help you find galaxies, nebulae, shooting stars and planets. It's an internationally certified Dark Sky Park—selected for the quality of the night sky viewing and quantity of starry nights.

After star-gazing, sleep in Goldendale.

DAY 2

Adventure 1
Exploring the dreams of Sam Hill

Spend much of this day at one-of-a-kind places created a century ago by the remarkable Sam Hill. Start the day with breakfast and coffee at **Bake My Day** in Goldendale, then hit the road.

If you're driving only

From Goldendale, head south on U.S. 97. If you're not doing the bike option that follows, stop along 97 at the roadside overlook to see Hill's century-old Maryhill Loops Road. (See Sam Hill sidebar for history of the loops.) This restored segment of the loops road hosts the annual Maryhill Festival of Speed in June, when longboarders and street lugers run 2.2 miles of twisty, smooth asphalt.

Continue downhill on U.S. 97 and go east on SR 14 a short bit, then turn right on Stonehenge Drive and right again into Stonehenge, a partial replica of the original. Hill had it built as a memorial to Klickitat County soldiers killed in the Great War (WWI). See the biking route that follows for more on Stonehenge.

From Stonehenge, continue downhill to the little town and orchards of Maryhill. Farm stands open in late May, starting with asparagus, then cherries, plums, peaches and running through to walnuts in the fall. See the bike route for a side trip to a winery and details on a few more sites to see before you head to the Maryhill Museum of Art.

If you're driving to the start of the bike tour

From Goldendale, drive south on U.S. 97, cross SR 14, turn left into Maryhill State Park and park your car for a pleasant 15-mile round-trip bike ride on good roads. Discover Pass required. Bike east on the flat Maryhill Highway (a misnomer—it's a quiet road south of the railroad tracks) through irrigated orchards plush with chlorophyll and fruit. Highlights are the Gunkel Orchards Fruit Stand. See their Facebook page or call 509-773-4698 for available produce.

At Maryhill Highway and Stonehenge

Sam Hill and his landmarks

Sam Hill (1857–1931) left Minneapolis and came to Seattle in 1899 as a utility executive. His father-in-law was the famous James J. Hill of the Great Northern Railway, widely known as the Empire Builder for the many rail lines he built. They were not related until Sam married James's daughter. In 1907, Sam Hill bought 5,300 acres in Klickitat County where "the rain and sunshine meet" as he put it, including the townsite of Columbus, which he renamed Maryhill Ranch after his wife and daughter. They never saw it, having left Seattle after just six months, never to return. He developed the land with dams and irrigation, with the unrealized intention of creating a Quaker community and living here. Earlier, in 1899, he had co-founded the Washington State Good Roads Association in an era when 93 percent of the nation's roads were ungraded, unpaved and unsigned. He believed good roads would have a societal impact:

. . . .

"I believe in man on the land. We cannot afford to have our producers leave the land and come to the city and become parasites. We want our girls to stay on the farm and become the mothers of a virile race of men and not just go to the city and become manicurists, stenographers and variety actresses. We want our boys to stay on the farm and not succumb to the lure of the Great White Way or become chauffeurs and clerks . . . . We cannot keep the ambitious boy or girl on the farm unless we make life attractive and comfortable."

. . . .

Drive sits an ancient gas station and an 1888 church. A more picturesque intersection is hard to imagine. Continue east through the orchards to **Waving Tree Winery**.

From the winery, return to the church intersection and turn right on Stonehenge Drive then left into the parking lot for Sam Hill's Stonehenge. Built about 5,000 years after the original, this one is made of concrete, not stone. Hill achieved the rough, faux stone look by lining the concrete forms with crumpled tin. The site could use a little love, with its raggedy-edge parking area you'll need to crop out of your photos.

From Stonehenge, continue uphill on Stonehenge Drive to SR 14. Turn right, and ride the shoulder 0.3 mile, then turn left on Maryhill Loops Road (see the sidebar). Bike to the gate, then continue biking on the twisting, gorgeous road through open range. The cattle will find you a curious sight, and the gentle grade makes the uphill pleasant. Ride until the pavement is no longer maintained. You can hike further if you want. Retrace the route and enjoy big Columbia River views as you fly down to the start. Return to your car via Stonehenge Drive.

Adventure 2
Visiting an improbable museum

Spend the afternoon at an oasis: Sam Hill's **Maryhill Museum of Art**. On a hot windy day, the mansion's cool controlled interior is heaven and the exhibits are a wonder. The would-be home became a museum at the suggestion of Hill's friends, the modern dance pioneer Loïe Fuller (see YouTube for an amazing 1896 film of another dancer performing Fuller's famous "Dance Serpentine"); Queen Marie of Romania, a national heroine in WWI, diplomat, author and artist; and Alma de Bretteville Spreckels, a colorful San Franciscan who married into the Spreckels sugar fortune and became an art collector and philanthropist. All used their influence to procure items for the museum or contributed wondrous gifts, including Rodin sculptures, a bracelet made from Grandmama Victoria's hair (that's Queen Victoria), carved and gilded Romanian castle furniture that would look at home in *Dwell* magazine, Klickitat Indian basketry, chess sets, and a room devoted to Hill's road-building. Don't miss the cafe with patio overlooking the gorge. Lawns are lush and almost impossibly green against the desert landscape.

Maryhill Museum, with iron sculpture "Brushing" inspired by eastern gorge winds

Adventure 3
Wine-tasting at vineyards

DAY
2

From Maryhill Museum, head west on SR 14. About a mile beyond the museum, stop at **Maryhill Winery**. Throw some bocce balls, and enjoy live music on its terrace on summer weekend afternoons. West of the winery, don't miss a roadside pullout with an interpretive sign overlooking the small community of Wishram. It sits on the banks of the Columbia at the now silent Celilo Falls. Until 1957, the roar of the falls reverberated off the cliffs here. That year, the falls and fishing villages inhabited for millennia were drowned as water rose behind the new dam at The Dalles. See Tour 8 for more on Celilo Falls.

Continuing west on SR 14 is Avery Road and **Jacob Williams Winery**. Downhill from the winery is remote little Avery Recreation Area, one of the sites the Army Corps of Engineers operates along the river. Back on SR 14 come to **Cascade Cliffs Vineyard and Winery**.

Pass through Columbia Hills State Park, featured in Tour 7.

Adventure 4
A safari drive-through and beach stop

Just west of Columbia Hills State Park is one of the gorge's most unexpected sights: zebra, camel, yak and other exotic wildlife at **Schreiner Farms**. No tours are offered but it's okay to drive up the road, as far as the giraffe barn. Come during daylight hours only, and look from your car. This is private land, so drive slowly. From SR 14, turn north between MP 82 and 83, about a mile west of Dalles Mountain Road.

Next, cool off in the river, hang out on a nice beach or watch expert windsurfers at Doug's Beach State Park. You'll know you're there when you see either a mystifyingly huge, empty parking area (in winter or calm days) or an endless lineup of cars (on summer west wind days). Speedflyers and paragliders land here from the cliffs above. A couple of sweet, sandy coves between basalt outcrops make for fine swimming. At MP 79 on SR 14. Discover Pass required.

Calm winter day at Doug's Beach, when only the beavers have come out to play

Adventure 5
Sleeping in an old railroad hotel

Eat in Lyle or drive up to Klickitat to **Huntington's Steakhouse**.

Stay overnight at the **Lyle Hotel**, a historic railroad hotel. If you've got another day, raft or kayak on the Klickitat. If not, come back another time.

Adventure 1
Rafting the Klickitat

The 15-mile stretch of river run by rafts is designated one of the nation's Wild and Scenic Rivers, with Class II to IV rapids, depending on river levels. Season is April to June. Some outfitters are based in Portland, but **Blue Sky**, **Wet Planet** and **Zoller's** run this river and are local to the gorge. (See Appendix B.)

Looking down from Fisher Bridge at the Klickitat River

Eat and Drink in Lyle (unless otherwise noted)

Corner Pocket Bar and Grill. Home-cooked fries and burgers on homemade buns. Pool tables and local beer. Weekends 2 to 9 p.m.; Tuesday 4 to 9 p.m.; Wednesday to Friday 11:30 a.m. to 9 p.m. 600 State St. 509-365-0072

Country Cafe. Dinner specials change nightly: barbecue pork, meatloaf, fish tacos. Sunday 8 a.m. to 2 p.m.; Monday 7 a.m. to 2 p.m.; Tuesday to Saturday to 7 p.m. 605 State St. 509-365-6861

Huntington's Steakhouse. Rave reviews. Daily except Wednesday 5 p.m. to 12 a.m. 95 Main St., Klickitat. 509-369-4371

Lyle Hotel. Fresh, inventive menu. Excellent wine margarita and steak quesadillas. The owner is a former chef for the U.S. Tour de France team. Local beer and wine. Daily except Tuesday 4 to 9 p.m. plus Sunday brunch. 100 Seventh St. 509-365-5953

Eat and Drink in Goldendale

Bake My Day. Freshmade donuts, scones, pastries, plus breakfast fare, espresso and sandwiches. Tuesday to Friday 8 a.m. to 3 p.m.; Saturday to 2 p.m. 119 E Main St. 509-773-0403

Glass Onion Restaurant. Superb eclectic cocktails and mezze platters. Wednesday to Saturday 11:30 a.m. to 9 p.m. 604 S Columbus Ave. 509-773-4928

Golden Chinook Coffee. New in 2015, owned by two U.S. Army veterans. Monday to Friday 7 a.m. to 4 p.m.; Saturday 8 a.m. to 2 p.m. 118 Main St. 509-773-3337

Hot Rods Bar and Grill. 108 W Main St. 509-773-7005

Loïe's: The Museum Cafe. In the Maryhill Museum; see below. Wine, sandwiches, coffee overlooking the gorge. March 15 to November 15: daily 10:30 a.m. to 4:30 p.m. 509-773-3733

Sodbusters Restaurant. Country cooking. Sunday to Thursday 6 a.m. to 8 p.m.; Friday and Saturday to 9 p.m. 1040 E Broadway. 509-773-6160

Shop in Goldendale and Area

Monkeyshines Studio and Gallery. Local art and craft plus vintage clothes and housewares. Wednesday to Saturday 10 a.m. to 4 p.m. 514 S Columbus Ave. 509-250-3835

Museum Store, Maryhill Museum. Gifts, books, jewelry. March 15 to November 15: daily including holidays 10 a.m. to 5 p.m. 35 Maryhill Museum Drive, Goldendale (just off SR 14). 509-773-3733

Traditional Heirlooms. Antique consignments in downtown Goldendale. Monday to Saturday 10 a.m. to 4 p.m. 117 N Columbus Ave. 509-314-0536

Discover and Learn in and around Lyle and Goldendale

Goldendale Observatory State Park. Look through a huge telescope at the night sky in arid Goldendale where light pollution is low and air clarity is high. A ranger helps you discover what's up there. Summer: daily 1 to 11:30 p.m. October 1 to March 1: Friday to Sunday 1 to 9 p.m. 1602 Observatory Drive. 509-773-3141. For current afternoon and evening presentations see goldendaleobservatory.com.

Greater Goldendale Chamber of Commerce. Weekdays 9 a.m. to 4 p.m. 903 E Broadway. 509-773-3400

Lyle Twin Bridges Historical Museum. June through September: Saturday 12 to 5 p.m. or by appointment. 403 Klickitat St. 509-365-0060 or 509-365-3903

Maryhill Museum of Art. The common thread among its eclectic collections is Sam Hill's curiosity and connections. March 15 to November 15 daily including holidays 10 a.m. to 5 p.m. 35 Maryhill Museum Drive, Goldendale. 509-773-3733

Presby Museum. Ornate 1902 home with 22 rooms. May 1 to October 15: daily 10 a.m. to 4 p.m. 127 W Broadway, Goldendale. 509-773-4303

Schreiner Farms. Exotic animals to see from your car on a half-mile drive. Daily, daylight hours only. Between MP 82 and 83 on SR 14, Dallesport. 509-448-4580

Taste the Wine in and around Goldendale

Cascade Cliffs Vineyard and Winery. Tours, tasting room and other events. Year-round: daily 10 a.m. to 6 p.m. 8666 Highway 14 (at MP 88.6), Wishram. 509-767-1100

Jacob Williams Winery. Approx. April to October: daily 10 a.m. to 6 p.m. Call for other months. 3 Avery Road, Wishram 541-645-0462

Maryhill Winery. See the website for its many concerts. Year-round: daily 10 a.m. to 6 p.m. 9774 Highway 14, Goldendale. 877-627-9445

Waving Tree Winery. Tasting room hours June to September: daily 10 a.m. to 5 p.m.; April, May and October weekends: 10 a.m. to 5 p.m. 2 Maryhill Highway, Goldendale. 509-250-1412

Stay in Lyle and Goldendale

Lyle Hotel. A railroad hotel of eight rooms from 1905. Yes, the trains are near, so bring earplugs. 100 Seventh St. 509-365-5953 [$$]

Morning Song Acres. Rent the entire house on 40 acres in the High Prairie area between Lyle and Goldendale. 6 Oda Knight Road, Lyle. Listing on vacasa.com. 509-365-3600 [$$$ to $$$$]

Ponderosa Motel. Comfortable bed; some rooms with kitchens. Free pass to Goldendale Pool. 775 E Broadway, Goldendale. 509-773-5842 [$$ to $$$]

Quality Inn and Suites. Outdoor pool. 808 E Simcoe Drive, Goldendale. 509-773-5881 [$$$]

Camp along the River

Columbia Hills State Park. A variety of campsites. Be ready for wind. April 1 to November 1; reservations available May 15 to September 16: washington.goingtocamp.com or 888-226-7688 [$]

Maryhill State Park. Tent or RV camp in this riverfront park near the junction of SR 14 and U.S. 97. It can be very windy and noisy, with trucks air-braking downhill on U.S. 97. Year-round. Reserve at washington.goingtocamp.com or 888-226-7688 [$]

Peach Beach Camp Park. Riverfront, owned by Gunkel Orchards family, next to Maryhill State Park. Year-round. Tent and hookup sites. Reservations March to October, otherwise first come, first served. 509-250-3049 [$]

Lodging Cost Key			
$	$$	$$$	$$$$
<$50	$51 to $99	$100 to $200	>$200

Klickitat County Courthouse, an Art Deco gem in the high desert

TOUR
7

LYLE AND COLUMBIA HILLS STATE PARK

WASHINGTON

This eastern gorge getaway, with its bright light and early arrival of spring, is a cure for a rain-weary spirit. Columbia Hills State Park could easily be a national park, its scenery is that spectacular. As early as February wildflowers begin their seasonal roll-out of color, which lasts through about mid-May. Vineyards leaf out by mid-spring too. In summer, the dark green of oaks punctuate golden grasses atop black basalt cliffs. In fall vineyards are golden and cool temps return. A caveat: summer can be windy and hot, and from November to early April riverfront areas of Columbia Hills State Park are closed. That means to see Horsethief Lake and the petroglyphs, as well as the magnificent wildflowers on the upland hikes, do this tour in April or early May.

Reserve your spot in the popular guided petroglyph tours at Columbia Hills State Park; tours happen Friday and Saturday, April through October; call 509-439-9032. Discover Pass is required.

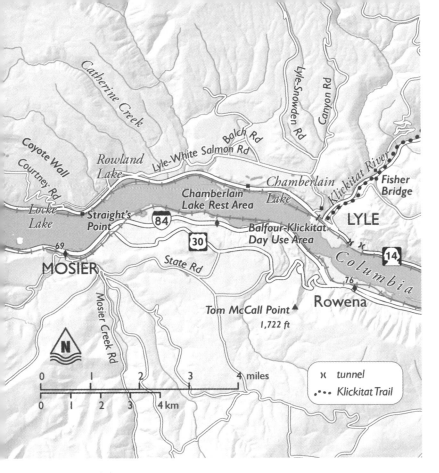

Lyle area

Bring bikes if you'd rather bike instead of drive Day 1's scenic route, and a blanket if you want to picnic overlooking the gorge. Bring snacks and drinks or picnic fare for Day 2, which is spent in Columbia Hills State Park, far from any groceries or restaurants. Stop for groceries at **Rosauers** in Hood River or **A & J Select Market** in Stevenson. If you want to visit **Klickitat Canyon Winery**, call for an appointment: 509-365-2543.

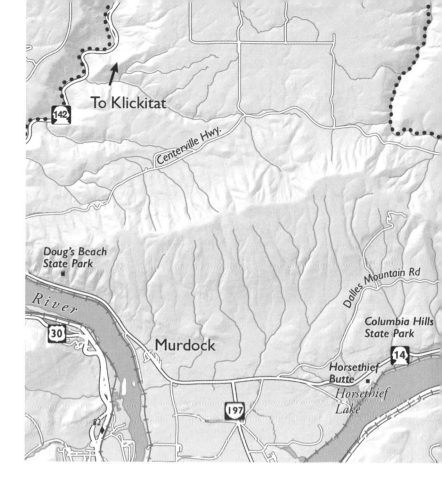

To Klickitat

Centerville Hwy.

Doug's Beach
State Park

River

Murdock

Dalles Mountain Rd

Columbia Hills
State Park

Horsethief
Butte

Horsethief
Lake

Adventure 1
Hiking at Lyle Cherry Orchard

DAY
1

Drive the 75 miles from Portland to Lyle and start with a beautiful hike. From Lyle, drive east on SR 14 a short way. Park in an unmarked gravel parking area just east of twin tunnels on SR 14 and begin hiking. The climb to Lyle Cherry Orchard is steep but views reward almost right away. The 515 acres the trail traverses are owned by Friends of the Columbia Gorge Land Trust. The land was a gift to the trust by Friends founder Nancy Russell. Highlights are views of layers of basalt flows, cut into vertical cliffs by the Columbia River. If you had been standing here when the Missoula Floods raged through the gorge, you'd be under hundreds of feet of water. At this point in the gorge, floodwaters rose to the 1,000-foot level, scouring the landscape bare of vegetation and soil.

Recovery of soils lost to floods takes a long time: 13,000 years after the water drained away, only a thin soil layer has built up. Along the trail are gnarled woodlands of Oregon white oak, also known as Garry oak, the same trees that grow to mighty titans in Oregon's Willamette Valley. A few remnants of an agricultural dream—a cherry orchard— are visible at the east end of the hike. With rainfall at 14 inches per year in this end of the gorge, blast-furnace summers and thin soils, the dream did not last.

The hike is 5 miles, out and back, with 1,500 feet of elevation gain. Eventually, Lyle and Friends of the Columbia Gorge plan to connect this trail with the streets of Lyle for a "Towns to Trails" experience. See gorgefriends.org for more on the land's history and the hiking route.

Adventure 2
Driving or biking to wine, views and a picnic

Come back to Lyle after your hike and eat at the **Country Cafe**, and then head out to enjoy this mellow, half-day outing as day turns to evening. On a century-old road bypassed by a new highway, this is the best of the gorge in a small package. Bike it if you can, but driving is great too. You can stop at wineries, wander oak-shaded Balch Cemetery, and stroll wildflower-strewn cliffs with stunning gorge views at Catherine Creek. A 1-mile segment of the old highway is not drivable: it's being reclaimed by boulders and landslides. It's bikeable, but a road bike may have to be walked over short stretches. Catherine Creek's universal access trails are paved and accessible to sight-seeing bikers. Round-trip mileage is 15 with no side trips to wineries or to Courtney Road viewpoints.

Start and end in Lyle, at the Lyle Trailhead to the Klickitat Trail, at SR 14 and WA 142. Go west on SR 14 for 0.1 mile, crossing the Klickitat River. From the broad shoulder, watch kiteboarders on windy days. A path here leads to a sandbar at the Klickitat's mouth, where they take off. The bar is where riverboats used to nose in and load cattle headed to market.

From SR 14 just past the Klickitat, turn right on Lyle–White Salmon Road (aka old Highway 8, the predecessor to SR 14). Stop in less than 0.1 mile at Balfour-Klickitat Day Use Area. Short trails and overlooks above the Klickitat River offer the best bald eagle watching in the gorge—especially in January but I've seen them other months too. In spring and summer joyful gangs of turkey vultures ride air currents bouncing off the cliffs. Once the home site of town founder James Lyle, the place had deteriorated into a dump and gravel pit. After cleanup and renovation it's again beautiful. A paved interpretive trail passes a line of Osage orange trees, immense black locust trees and a stand of ailanthus—all introduced when this was a home site, and all thriving at the rocky, sunny spot.

On Lyle–White Salmon Road climb away from the river. Canyon Road intersects at about 1.2 miles in; you can take it to **Klickitat Canyon Winery** and **Domaine Pouillon**. Both are on Lyle-Snowden Road, a left off Canyon. Staying on Lyle–White Salmon Road, at 1.5 miles is **COR Cellars**.

At 2.3 miles, turn right on Balch Road. It takes you by Western pond turtles in Balch Lake, and then by Balch Cemetery and **Synoline Winery** before returning you to Lyle–White Salmon Road.

Homer Frederic Balch (1861–91) is buried in Balch Cemetery and so is Genevra Whitcomb, the woman he loved. She loved him too, but he rejected a life with her in favor of the ministry. He officiated at her funeral when she died at 19 of pneumonia. As part of his fascination with the gorge's indigenous cultures, Balch learned Chinook jargon and recorded stories of tribal elders. His novel *Bridge of the Gods* is culturally dated but you'll never look at places like Sauvie Island the same way after you read it. Soon after the book was published, Homer died at age 30 of tuberculosis.

Next stop is the Catherine Creek Trailhead, on Lyle–White Salmon Road. On the south side of the road, take the paved Catherine Creek Universal Access Trail. (See Tour 5 for another Catherine Creek hike from this trailhead.) After the gorge became a National Scenic Area in 1986, this was one of the U.S. Forest Service's first purchases. Bike or walk the trail to some of the gorge's easiest-access and most beautiful landscapes and views. If you bike them, ride slowly and with extreme courtesy—walkers or rollers would not expect speeding bikers here. It makes a lovely spot for a picnic. Wildflowers begin in February and last until June or so when the land turns golden and rains stop. Enjoy the birdsong: this is part of the Great Washington State Birding Trail. Across the river are green, irrigated orchards and vineyards east of Mosier.

After Catherine Creek, Rowland Lake comes into view and so does the road that replaced the one you're on: SR 14, built above the water on a pile of fill.

If you're driving you'll have to park your car where Lyle–White Salmon/Old Highway 8 meets up with SR 14 and walk this next part. If you're biking, keep going. The segment that's not drivable is a decaying stretch of the old highway at the base of cliffs. In one spot, a waterfall has chewed away all but a narrow path, and boulders from above are left in place. You can bike most of it, or all of it if you've got stout tires.

At the point on the old road where you can first see tiny Locke Lake, you're at Straight's Point, where Coyote Wall's massive basalt cliffs dive into the Columbia and the wall, an anticline (a folded, convex section of rock), begins to transition to a syncline (a folded, concave section) occupied by the Columbia River. Just to add confusion, Coyote Wall is commonly, but wrongly, called the Syncline. See page 158 for more on the geology.

This decaying stretch of road ends at the Coyote Wall Trailhead (and restrooms) on Courtney Road. (Hikes from here are in Tour 5.) Turn back or, if you don't mind hills, ride uphill on Courtney Road to a couple of superb lookouts about 0.6 and 1 mile up the road. To the west are views of the Hood River Valley and Mount Hood.

Return the way you came. Don't try biking on SR 14; it'll ruin your scenic buzz as you fight to stay alive on its shoulderless segments. If you drive, take SR 14 east and stop at MP 73 at one of the world's most scenic rest stops, Chamberlain Lake.

Adventure 3
Eating along the Klickitat

After your afternoon of sight-seeing and wine-tasting, drive 13 miles up Route 142 along the Klickitat River for dinner at **Huntington's Steakhouse** in Klickitat or have a burger or fish and chips while you shoot pool at the **Corner Pocket Bar and Grill**. Sleep at the **Lyle Hotel**.

Adventure 1
Exploring Columbia Hills State Park

Eat a hearty breakfast at **Country Cafe** in Lyle, then drive 10 miles east on SR 14 to hike, kayak, swim, and tour ancient rock art at Columbia Hills State Park. If it were anywhere else, this 3,338-acre site would be a national park. Here it's just another incredibly scenic and historic place along the river. A Wishram village here called *Nix lui dix* was continuously inhabited for 3,000 years until the 1850s. Rock art on the cliffs is abundant. In this river stretch below Celilo Falls, rock ledges squeezed the river into a slot so narrow it seemed to have been turned on its side. The result: a concentration of salmon as they swam upriver to spawn. Captain William Clark said this area was "the great mart of all this country," with Native Americans from the Rockies to

Petroglyph of Tsagaglalal (She Who Watches), a chief who lived among the rocks so she could watch over her people

the Pacific Ocean meeting to trade. A small cemetery—not open to the public—on the road into the park holds remains sacred to Native Americans. They were moved before The Dalles Dam inundated gravesites along the river. Options here:

Kayaking on Horsethief Lake

Rent a kayak, available in the park in summer, and explore cliffs along Horsethief Lake. Some rock art is viewable only from the water. Or wade into the lake—the sandy bottom is lovely—and swim in its sheltered waters, unaffected by river current. Horsethief Lake, like many in the gorge, was created when a dam (The Dalles Dam in this case) flooded the lower stretch of a tributary stream. Before that, it was known as Caldwash (or Colowesh) Bottom. During fishing season, hundreds of fish-drying racks would be set up in the sandy bowl sheltered by rock ledges. The intense heat and steady winds made for a natural food dryer.

Touring the petroglyphs

Take the tour that you registered for earlier; a guide will take you to cliffs with intact petroglyphs. You can also take a self-guided tour of petroglyphs removed from cliffs before inundation by The Dalles Dam in the late 1950s.

Climbing around on Horsethief Butte

Hike the canyons and clifftops of Horsethief Butte. Listen for the twirdly sound of the cliff wren in summer. Watch rock climbers, and watch out for rattlers and poison oak as you scramble around.

Hiking at Crawford Oaks or Dalles Mountain Ranch

In spring, don't miss the wildflower trails at Crawford Oaks, and the old farm equipment and buildings at Dalles Mountain Ranch, a cattle ranch until the early 1990s. If you want to see what you're in for, Google "Dalles Mountain Ranch" images. The balsamroot, rusting equipment and big skies here will make you happy. Nine miles of looping trails meander through flower-studded pastures. Meadowlarks, nesting in the grasses, provide a glad soundtrack as you wander trails, where beauty and solitude provide a walking meditation.

Both of these park areas are upland, north of SR 14. A Crawford Oaks trailhead is on SR 14 at MP 87.2. To get to another, which offers a nice 3.5-mile loop with views, take Dalles Mountain Road (at MP 84); drive uphill 3.2 miles, take the right fork and find a parking area you can hike from. To get to The Dalles Mountain Ranch Trailhead from SR 14, turn north on Dalles Mountain Road (at MP 84). Drive uphill 3.2 miles and take the left fork; go another 1.3 to a gate; park here and wander around the old ranch buildings. See gorgefriends. org for details on both Crawford Oaks and Dalles Mountain Ranch. Discover Pass required.

After your park adventures, picnic on the green lawn by Horsethief Lake under the welcome shade of pines, tall Lombardy poplars and London plane trees. The park was created by the Army Corps of Engineers, which was required to provide recreational sites in connection with construction of The Dalles Dam. It was then the name "Horsethief" came into usage—inspired by the landscape's similarity to scenery in Hollywood westerns.

From the park, drive back to the Portland-Vancouver area or stay another night in Lyle or nearby Hood River.

Eat and Drink in Lyle (unless otherwise noted)

Corner Pocket Bar and Grill. Home-cooked fries and burgers on homemade buns. Pool tables and local beer. Weekends 2 to 9 p.m.; Tuesday 4 to 9 p.m.; Wednesday to Friday 11:30 a.m. to 9 p.m. 600 State St. 509-365-0072

Country Cafe. Dinner specials change nightly: barbecue pork, meatloaf, fish tacos. Monday 7 a.m. to 2 p.m.; Tuesday to Saturday 7 a.m. to 7 p.m.; Sunday 8 a.m. to 2 p.m. 605 State St. 509-365-6861

Huntington's Steakhouse. Raves for the steaks here. Daily except Wednesday 5 p.m. to 12 a.m. 95 Main St., Klickitat. 509-369-4371

Lyle Hotel. Fresh, inventive menu. Excellent wine margarita and steak quesadillas. The owner is a former chef for the U.S. Tour de France team. Local beer and wine. Sunday brunch; daily except Tuesday 4 to 9 p.m. 100 Seventh St. 509-365-5953

Discover and Learn in Lyle

Lyle Twin Bridges Historical Museum. June through September: Saturday 12 to 5 p.m. 403 Klickitat St. 509-365-0060

Taste the Wine in and around Lyle

Note: Lyle–White Salmon Road and Old Highway 8 are the same road.

COR Cellars. All year: Thursday to Sunday 11 a.m. to 6 p.m. 151 Old Highway 8. 509-365-2744

Domaine Pouillon. Valentine's weekend to Thanksgiving weekend: Thursday to Sunday 11 a.m. to 6 p.m. Otherwise: weekends 11 a.m. to 6 p.m. 170 Lyle Snowden Road. 509-365-2795

Klickitat Canyon Winery. Wines with no additives; some organic. Tasting room is in Stevenson (See page 63). 6 Lyle Snowden Road. By appointment: 509-365-2543

Syncline Winery. All year: Thursday to Sunday 11 a.m. to 6 p.m. 111 Balch Road. 509-365-4361

Stay in and around Lyle

Lyle Hotel. This eight-room railroad hotel dates from 1905. 100 Seventh St. 509-365-5953 [$$]

Morning Song Acres. Rent the entire house on 40 acres in the High Prairie area between Lyle and Goldendale. 6 Oda Knight Road, Lyle. Listing on vacasa.com. 509-365-3600

[$$$ to $$$$]

Camp along the River

Columbia Hills State Park. A variety of campsites, east of Lyle. Be ready for wind. April 1 to November 1. Reservations taken May 15 to September 16: washington.goingtocamp.com or 888-226-7688 [$]

Lodging Cost Key			
$	$$	$$$	$$$$
<$50	$51 to $99	$100 to $200	>$200

Looking across Horsethief Lake at Horsethief Butte

THE DALLES AND DESCHUTES RIVER STATE RECREATION AREA

OREGON

The dry side of Oregon is on full, glorious display here in the easternmost part of the gorge. Mount Hood lies on the western horizon and you're fully over the crest of the Cascades. A wondrous feature of Oregon and Washington is how quickly you can travel from one type of landscape to another that is completely different. In this case, it's 85 miles from the Portland region's lush tree-covered hills to the blocky, sculptural landscapes of The Dalles.

February to May, when lands west of the Cascades often lie under a blanket of grey skies, this end of the gorge offers heaps of sunny days with wildflowers blooming on every rocky outcrop and plateau. In irrigated farmlands that border The Dalles, cherry blossoms unfold and vineyards leaf out.

Along with nearby Mosier (Tour 9), The Dalles is a beautiful destination for spring bike rides, wildflower hikes and discovering local history. While the heat can be unrelenting in summer, hot days are perfect for The Dalles' new public pool or Riverfront Park beach. Later, crisp fall air and vineyards and hills turned golden by the long summer drought make for great biking or touring.

You may want to bring bikes and bike locks, swim suits and in early summer a cooler to carry cherries home. Reserve your jet boat tour (Day 2) in advance.

Adventure 1
Hill-walking in The Dalles
This walk also makes for a fun bike ride.

You'll want a full day for exploring, so leave home the night before and stay in The Dalles or get up early for the 84-mile drive on I-84. This approximately 5-mile urban walk (or bike ride) to the top of a bluff will give you the lay of the land, fantastic views and stories of this historic place. The route ends downtown, for lunch. Rent bikes from **Dalles City Cyclery**. (Call 541-769-0771 first to confirm availability.) Or in summer rent bikes from the **Kayak Shack** in Riverfront Park.

If you're used to biking in Portland, cruising around The Dalles is like being a kid again—friendly waves and quiet streets with big scenic rewards for the hill climb up to the bluff. Pass through neighborhoods where houses have been built around the area's many basalt outcrops— the sort of naturalistic yard ornamentation Portlanders pay to have hauled in and installed.

Begin on the west edge of downtown, at a 1930s Art Moderne building at West Second and Pentland streets. This is the Chamber of Commerce/Visitor Center. You can leave your car here; pick up an interpretive map if you want more info on the two national historic districts along the route.

Behind the visitor center, at 410 W Second Place, is the first Wasco County Courthouse, built in 1859 when Wasco was the largest county ever formed in the U.S., ranging from the Rocky Mountains to the Cascades and from California to the Columbia River. Explore the old streets west of Pentland then make your way to where Third Street curves and becomes Third Place. Here is Mill Creek, named for a flour mill built in 1866. A pedestrian bridge crosses the creek to the 50-meter, outdoor Dalles Public Pool and Splash Park, renovated in 2015. It's open mid-June to Labor Day; come back later for an early morning or evening swim. Call 541-296-9533 for hours and fees.

When you're done investigating the pool, return to Third Place and continue west to the Mill Creek Bridge. Built in 1920, it was one of the last elements of the Historic Columbia River Highway. Conde McCullough, famous in Oregon for his elegant highway bridges, was the designer. (Two other McCullough bridges are in Tour 9.)

From the bridge, retrace your steps on Third Place, passing a 1927 Arts and Crafts home with a rolled roof at 412 W Fourth St. Travelers on the old Columbia River Highway would have admired it as they rolled around the curve into town, where the highway continued as Second Street. Cross Fourth Street and turn right on Third Street.

At Third and Lincoln is the 1897 **Old St. Peter's Landmark**, a former Catholic church with a tin ceiling, stained glass, and Carrera marble—the same marble Michelangelo used for his *Pietà*. In 1970, plans were to recycle the building into a pile of bricks when the church built a replacement. Purchased for $25,000 by preservation-minded citizens, the old sanctuary is worth a stop. The 176-foot steeple was a navigational landmark for steamboat captains and a benchmark for Wasco County surveyors. The rectory (where the priests lived) and church gymnasium are adjacent to the south.

From St. Peter's stay east on Third Street and turn right on Union. Pass three gorgeous old churches and City Park, a shady spot with restrooms. Here is a stone marker placed by Ezra Meeker. As a 21-year-old, he was an Oregon Trail pioneer of 1852. He later accumulated enough wealth so that in retirement he could indulge his passion: traveling cross-country to urge states to commemorate the Oregon Trail route. He died in 1928 at age 97.

From Union, turn left (east) on 10th. Pass an enormous catalpa, with a gnarly, twisty trunk; it's across from a Depression-era stone wall at The Dalles Wahtonka High School. Don't miss the three beautiful bronze scenes above each door of the Art Moderne–style school,

What's a dalle?

A dalle is a slab or paving stone used to line gutters. The Columbia River from The Dalles upstream to Celilo, Oregon, and Wishram, Washington, was once a series of rapids called the Long Narrows, Short Narrows and Celilo Falls. In the narrows, it was said, the river turned sideways: the wide Columbia narrowed to just a few hundred yards across.

The 2-mile long "Le Grande Dalles," or Long Narrows, was named by French-Canadian fur trappers to describe the way the water rushed through gutterlike slots between basalt ledges. But the rocks here had earlier names. Humans have fished the rushing waters of the channels and traded along this stretch of the Columbia for 10,000 years. The various slots and ledges were distinct fishing sites and given names such as *tayxaytpama* or *qiyakawas*, describing whether the site was best for gaffing, spearing or netting fish.

Dalles City, downstream of the Long Narrows, was an endpoint of the 1,800-mile Oregon Trail. Here, pioneers rested before their final push to the Willamette Valley, either by traversing Mount Hood's slopes via the Barlow Trail or by launching into the Columbia River.

In 1957 most of the dalles of the Columbia were submerged behind The Dalles Dam.

In 1966, bowing to local usage, officials changed the name of Dalles City to The Dalles, with a capital T. Dalles rhymes with pals.

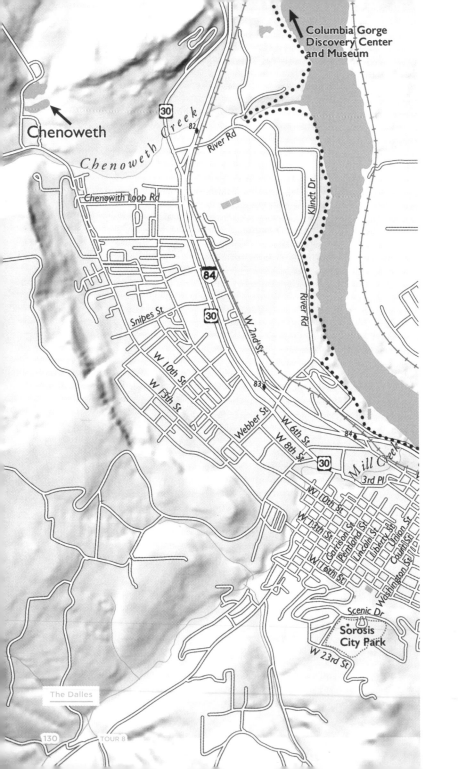

Columbia Gorge
Discovery Center
and Museum

Chenoweth

Chenoweth Creek

30

82

River Rd

Chenowith Loop Rd

Klindt Dr

84

30

Snipes St

W 2nd St

River Rd

W 10th St

83

W 13th St

Webber St

W 6th St

W 8th St

30

Mill Creek

3rd Pl

84

W 10th St

W 13th St

Garrison St

Pentland St

Lincoln St

Liberty St

Union St

Court St

W 16th St

Washington St

Scenic Dr

Sorosis
City Park

W 23rd St

The Dalles

130   TOUR 8

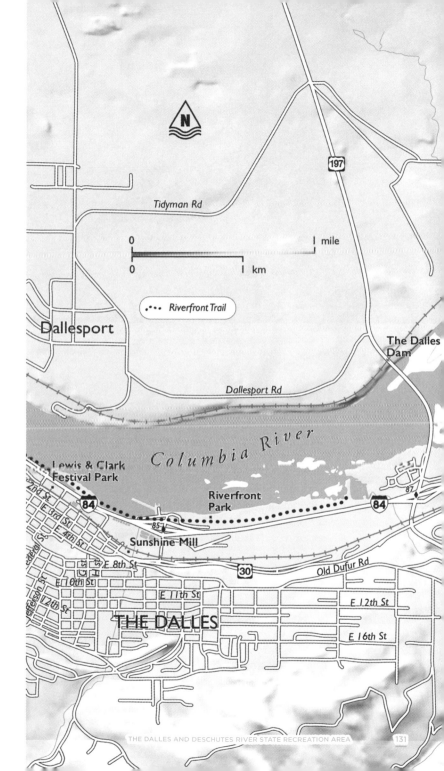

N

Tidyman Rd

0 .... 1 mile
0 .... 1 km

•••• Riverfront Trail

Dallesport

197

The Dalles Dam

Dallesport Rd

Columbia River

Lewis & Clark Festival Park

2nd St
E 3rd St
E 4th St

84

Riverfront Park

87

84

85

Sunshine Mill

E 8th St

30

Old Dufur Rd

E 11th St

E 12th St

THE DALLES

E 16th St

A short walk or ride from the river through historic neighborhoods, to big views in The Dalles

built in 1940. Cross Washington Street, passing a few of The Dalles' grandest homes. From 1933 to 1966, the 1927 Tudor Revival at 303 E 10th was home to the Seuferts, whose fish and fruit cannery is now Seufert Park, site of **The Dalles Dam Visitor Center**. A renovated stone church, **Riverenza Cafe** at 10th and Federal, is a great place for coffee.

Turn right (south) on Federal, right on 11th and left on Washington to the east facade of the school gymnasium with its artful, cast iron ticket window and bas-relief sculptures of blocky, WPA-style athletes—all men, and all looking like weary middle aged laborers rather than teens. This site was part of The Dalles Mission (also called the Wascopam Mission), founded by Methodists in 1836 to convert Indians to Christianity. They placed it near Amaton Spring, an Indian encampment. See the mural of the spring on the school's east side. The mission was sold to a Presbyterian, Marcus Whitman, in 1847 but abandoned that year after the Whitman Massacre in nearby Walla Walla. Beginning in 1841, Oregon Trail pioneers rested here before the final leg of their journey to the Willamette Valley. Try to imagine seeing this area as someone who just endured six months of walking in a dusty cloud behind livestock and wagons. After the mission years, the site became the U.S. Army's Fort Dalles. From 1850 to 1867 the

Army was charged with protecting white settlers in the area from conflicts with Native Americans.

With that info in your pocket, keep straight (uphill) one block on Washington and turn right on 12th to pass Pulpit Rock, a basalt outcrop atop which missionaries preached. Rather than move this historic rock to a grassy park, someone made the choice to leave it, in a wonderfully quirky bit of preservation, in the middle of a paved intersection. Stair-like rock footholds and two iron bolts, perhaps to hold a wooden platform for preachers, project from the west side.

Pulpit Rock

From 12th, go left on Union and right on 13th. At 13th and Lincoln is Rorick House, the oldest home in town, built in 1850 for an officer at **Fort Dalles**. Continue on 13th, then go left on Pentland and right on 15th to visit **Fort Dalles** at 15th and Garrison. The surgeon's quarters, in the Gothic Revival style, was built in 1857.

At 16th and Garrison either take the steep path east up a basalt bluff to a continuation of 16th or avoid its steepness via this route: from Garrison go east on the alley between 15th and 16th to Pentland.

Turn right on Pentland and left to get back on 16th.

From 16th, turn right on Lincoln and leave the orderly grid of streets to climb one of The Dalles many bluffs. Lincoln ends at Scenic Drive. Go uphill on Scenic, a switch-backing road built in the 1920s to take advantage of views from the bluff. The high point is 15-acre Sorosis City Park. The Indians called The Dalles region *win-quatt*, a place encircled by rock cliffs. The park sits atop one of those cliffs.

Views to the north are wonderful: Mount Adams rises to the northwest, and Dallesport, Washington, is the flat bench of land between the river's bends. The Dalles Dam is east, the cruise ship dock straight ahead, with industrial lands on the rocky shore to its west, including the giant Google data center; it came to town in 2006.

At the south end of the park, city streets end and orchards begin. West 23rd Street runs alongside a cherry orchard. Take the trail along the park's west boundary to its south boundary for beautiful rural views across Mill Creek's irrigated upper valley and up to Mount Hood. Before you hit the water towers, cut back north through the park toward a climbing structure, restrooms and other facilities. Exit the park and come to a city overlook, veteran's memorial and rose garden. Leave the cliff by heading right and downhill on Scenic Drive. Pass Columbia Gorge Community College. In 1933 the site was the Eastern Oregon Tuberculosis Hospital. Before antibiotics, TB sanatoriums and hospitals were often perched on higher ground in the belief that good food, rest and fresh air at higher altitudes would effect a cure.

Past the college's entrance road, watch on the right for Pioneer Cemetery, established in 1859 in a grove of Oregon white oaks kept small by the semiarid climate and the thin soil they cling to. These are the same species that in the deep, rain-drenched soils of the Willamette Valley become mighty trees with hugely spreading crowns. When Scenic Drive was developed, the graves of pioneers were left undisturbed, while graves in the Jewish and Chinese cemeteries were removed.

Turn left off Scenic Drive onto Terrace/Jefferson. Then go right on 10th, then left on G, which jogs right at Ninth but remains G. Then go right on Eighth and left on H, which turns into Fourth. It curves downward off the bluff, a route made elegant by a hand-carved stone wall, perhaps created by some of the Italian stonemasons who came to the gorge in the 1870s to work on the locks at Cascade Locks.

Fourth drops you into downtown. Go right on Third to the ancient Columbia Brewing building and **Sunshine Mill Winery** where wine is made in an old flour mill. Shop at nearby **Cannon Packer**, set in an old train depot.

From the winery, go west on Second Avenue into downtown. Have lunch in an 1883 courthouse at **Clock Tower Ales** or in the French style at **Petite Provence**. Walk around the building at 710 E Second St. In the 1860s, so much gold was coming out of Central Oregon that the federal government built this stone structure to mint money. By the time the building was complete, however, the placer beds (gold in streams) were tapped out so the mint never produced money.

If you left your car at the visitor center, return to fetch it by continuing west on Second. If you're on your bike, keep biking on to the next adventure.

Columbia Brewing, built in 1867 of local stone

Adventure 2
Learning about Ice Age floods and exploring a historic waterfront

Bike or drive to the **Columbia Gorge Discovery Center and Museum**. If you're on your bike and are up for a flat 12-mile round trip, start riding at Lewis and Clark Festival Park (at the foot of Union Street) and head west on the Riverfront Trail to the museum. Tour the museum and bike back. See trail highlights below, which are listed west to east.

This excellent museum is a great place to go in winter or a too-hot summer day. Don't miss the "Cargo of Lewis and Clark" exhibit. You thought you had it rough when airlines began charging for luggage and you had to hoist your gear into the carry-on bin. The amount of supplies these men hauled up and down the continent's rivers and on the many portages is shocking. Also see exhibits on the Ice Age floods that carved the gorge's walls, and on Native American culture, the missionary era and the arrival of white settlers.

Have a snack at the museum then, if you drove here, hike or bike part or all of the 6-mile (one-way) paved trail that runs east along the river. From the museum, a short stub of a trail goes west to almost opposite Crate's Point, the east end of the Columbia River Gorge. A pond near the museum was blasted by a cement company that used to occupy this site.

After exploring the trail west of the Discovery Center, head east from the trailhead at the east end of the parking lot; ride or walk past fields and single-track paths to rocky cliffs that line the river like a gutter. Some of these paths are worth investigating: they lead to secluded coves. The most scenic parts of the 6-mile trail are on the west end.

Continuing east on the path, come to the mouth of Chenoweth Creek. This is where Oregon Trail pioneers launched themselves into the Columbia. With the opening of the Barlow Trail over Mount Hood in 1846, many pioneers took the overland route rather than risk losing everything they owned to the river.

Keep on the trail, which winds inland to cross Chenoweth Creek on a bridge then passes the huge Google data center. Before Google arrived in 2006, this area was home to Martin Marietta Aluminum, which used the cheap power generated by the dam. It closed in 1984.

Further east the trail passes Rock Fort Camp, where Lewis and Clark camped on the river. Lewis recorded in April 18, 1806, that their camp was visited by a chief and 12 tribal members.

If you stay on the trail you'll come to Lewis and Clark Festival

Most of the basalt-lined river channels French-Canadian explorers called the *dalles* are now under water. This one along the Waterfront Trail is not. Note the ponderosa pines. Many pines that once grew along the river here were felled by Oregon Trail pioneers for rafts that could hold up to six wagons for the journey down the Columbia. Livestock were not allowed on the rafts: they were driven along the shore.

Park. Giant cruise ships dock here for the day during eight-day river cruises. Some of them provide passengers with bikes, so if you see scores of people on identical bikes, you know where they came from.

Adventure 3
Wine-tasting and evening options

If you didn't check it out earlier, taste local wines at the **Sunshine Mill**. Or in summer, end the day in the water at The Dalles Public Pool and Splash Park or at the broad sandy beach at Riverfront Park. Drive to the latter from I-84, exit 85. Or walk to it from Union Street in downtown: head north then turn right on the Riverfront Trail which leads to the park.

Stay downtown at **The Dalles Inn**, and walk to dinner at the **Baldwin Saloon**. Afterward, mosey the few blocks over to the riverfront and follow the Riverfront Trail east to look at boats at the Port of The Dalles Marina.

Adventure 1
Visiting Celilo Falls

Today, head to adventures east of town. Breakfast at **Momma Jane's Pancake House** then get on I-84 and drive east. Leave the freeway at exit 97 and visit Celilo Park. Managed by the Army Corps of Engineers, the park is meant to replace now-underwater Native American fishing sites used for 10,000-plus years. It overlooks where Celilo Falls poured

Riverfront Park beach on a hot summer evening

off ledges, creating a concentration of fish and a natural trading post. It's also the upper end of the 8-mile Dalles-Celilo Canal and Locks, completed in 1915 to allow steamboats passage around Five Mile Rapids (the Long Narrows), Ten Mile Rapids (the Short Narrows) and the falls.

In 2017, Celilo Park becomes home to an installation of the Confluence Project—six art installations that connect people to the river's stories along a 438-mile stretch of the Columbia River. (The other one in the gorge is in Tour 12, at the Sandy River Delta). The artist, Maya Lin, designed the Vietnam Veterans Memorial in Washington, D.C. The Celilo Park installation, a cantilevered arc, is inspired by the fishing scaffolds tribal fishermen use to project themselves out over the water. The project also involves restoration work at the park and information about this place, sacred to Native Americans. The park looks out over a calm river; if the dams ever crumble away, humans will again hear the roar of the falls that lie just offshore. Across the river is Wishram, Washington.

At the east end of the park is an in-lieu fishing site, one of 31 sites for Native Americans in the river upstream of Bonneville Dam. These sites are meant to replace traditional fishing sites and villages drowned by the dams beginning in the 1930s. Though treaties in the 1850s promised local tribes the rights to their traditional fishing and gathering sites in exchange for ceding most of their gorge lands to the United States, over the decades, settlers, businesses and the government infringed on those rights. In the late 1980s, the federal government and the four treaty tribes—Nez Perce, Yakama, Umatilla and Warm Springs—began to identify and develop 31 in-lieu sites to replace fishing access and traditional village sites. Docks, boat ramps, fish-cleaning stations and camping facilities were added. In 2012, the last site was developed in Dallesport, Washington. These sites are legally considered Indian country. Non-natives are allowed only to purchase salmon from Native Americans. Near the park and south of I-84 is the rebuilt village of Celilo, the most recent in a line of 10,000 years of encampments along the south bank of Celilo Falls.

Adventure 2
Playing at the Deschutes River

DAY
2

From Celilo Park, don't get back on I-84 but drive east on OR 206, a fast, old two-lane highway. Cross the Deschutes River and turn into the Deschutes River State Recreation Area. The Deschutes is Oregon's second largest river basin, draining the east flank of the Cascade

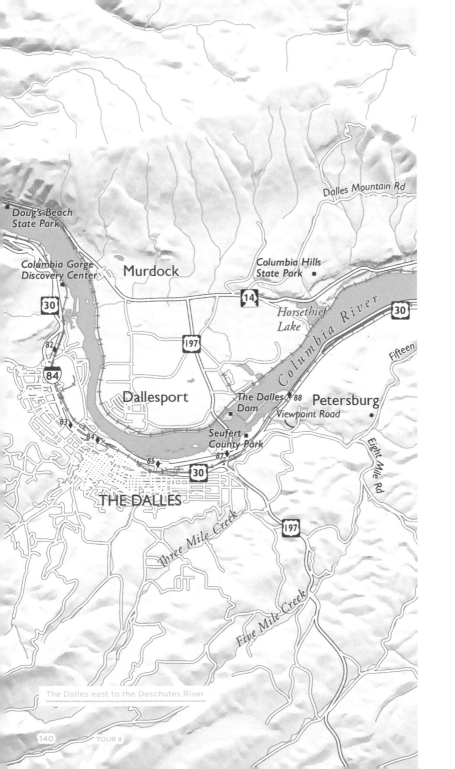

Doug's Beach
State Park

Columbia Gorge
Discovery Center

Murdock

Columbia Hills
State Park ■

30

14

82

197

Horsethief
Lake

Columbia River

30

Fifteen

84

Dallesport

The Dalles
Dam

88

Petersburg

Viewpoint Road

83

84

Seufert
County Park

87

Eight Mile Rd

85

30

197

THE DALLES

Three Mile Creek

Five Mile Creek

The Dalles east to the Deschutes River

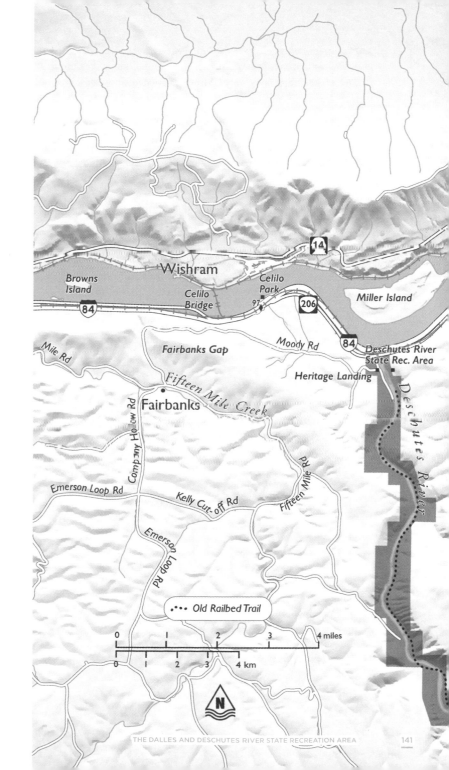

Browns Island

Wishram

Celilo Bridge

Celilo Park

97

14

206

Miller Island

84

Mile Rd

Fairbanks Gap

Moody Rd

84

Deschutes River State Rec. Area

Fifteen Mile Creek

Fairbanks

Heritage Landing

Company Hollow Rd

Emerson Loop Rd

Kelly Cut-off Rd

Fifteen Mile Rd

Emerson Loop Rd

Deschutes River

•••• Old Railbed Trail

| 0 | | 1 | | 2 | | 3 | | 4 miles |

| 0 | 1 | 2 | 3 | 4 km |

N

Mountains and much of Central and Eastern Oregon. Lewis and Clark estimated that it carried about one fourth the volume of the Columbia. That was before ranchers and farmers tapped into the Deschutes and its tributaries for irrigation. Options here:

Biking a rail to trail conversion

Bike the 16-mile (one way) Old Railbed Trail. Bring plenty of water. Great in spring or fall but not on hot days. Railroad and farm relics make this super interesting. You can also bike on the west bank of the river, along the short Rock Pile Trail. See "Deschutes River Hike" at oregonhikers.org for more details.

Hiking

For a 4-mile hike on the east bank, walk south 2 miles next to the Deschutes on the Blackberry Trail, returning via the Riverview Trail. Because of the intense summer heat, do this hike fall to spring.

Jet boat tour

If you booked ahead, drive to Heritage Landing and take your seat on a **Deschutes River Jet Boat Tour** (see "Cruising" in Appendix B) for a trip up one of the nation's Wild and Scenic Rivers

DAY
2

Adventure 3
Following the Oregon Trail back into The Dalles

After exploring the Deschutes via foot, boat or bike, retrace the route Oregon Trail pioneers walked from here to The Dalles. Most wagon trains left Missouri by mid-April, so they would've arrived in this arid semi-desert in late summer when the land was at its driest. Today on summer days, campers, cars, people and their colorful toys cluster in the rare and much-utilized shade along the Deschutes—the same place where pioneers' wagon trains stopped. The tree-lined river must have looked like a green slice of heaven to the parched walkers and animals after weeks of climbing and descending mountains and arid hills. In the shade they rested and reorganized. Goods were left behind—deemed too heavy for the perilous last segment across Mount Hood or down the wild Columbia. Wagons were planed thinner to make them lighter, and some were abandoned.

They crossed the Deschutes at its mouth, then situated downstream of the current mouth. Before The Dalles Dam raised river levels, the mouth was a wide delta with islands, rocks, channels and fast-moving water that claimed lives. In the earliest years, Native

Americans ferried women and children across in canoes. Later, pioneer entrepreneurs did the same. Oxen waded out to islands and across, and wagons were floated across.

After the river crossing, the wagons followed a route that is today's Moody Road. Find it on the west bank of the Deschutes. From OR 206, turn south on Moody. It's good gravel, although dusty, and fine even for low-slung cars. The steep, hot climb in the first 1.5 miles must have been disheartening to the tired emigrants. Keep your windows shut and watch for trucks. After the road levels, stop to enjoy stupendous views of the Columbia. You can see Wishram, and downstream of it, the Oregon Trunk Rail Bridge (aka Celilo Bridge), built in 1912 just downstream of Celilo Falls. At low water, before the dam raised the river level, all its piers were out of the water. In high water, they were in the midst of the cataracts. The Dalles-Celilo Canal, now under water, ran under the arch closest to the Oregon shore.

The thundering of Celilo Falls accompanied the pioneers on this leg of the trip. At Fairbanks Gap (about 5.5 miles from the Deschutes) they cut inland and you can too, staying on Moody Road. Open range means a few cattle may be sharing the road with you. At Fairbanks, at about mile 7, pioneers followed Fifteen Mile Creek into Dalles City. Follow their footsteps by turning right at Fairbanks on Fifteen Mile Road. Nice old barns punctuate a landscape made green from the waters of the creek. An old church is a photo stop at Petersburg, about 12.5 miles.

At about 13 miles Eight Mile Road comes in on the left; here, keep right through a beautiful valley with orchards fenced off to thwart deer. Fifteen Mile Creek is on the right. At 14.4 miles Columbia View comes in on the left. Don't take it; stay straight and roll into town via Fifteen Mile Road/State Road. At 15.4 miles, Viewpoint Road comes in on the right. It's a dead end; take it for a short out-and-back to a fine overlook of The Dalles Dam.

Back on Fifteen Mile Road/State Road, drive west to U.S. 30. Continue west on this, the original highway through town. The pioneers walked to the mission or Army fort seen earlier on this tour's hill walk, but you've already done that, so your next stop is dinner.

Adventure 4
Sleeping like it's 1959

Eat and sleep at **Hi-Way House** and **Celilo Inn**, two renovated places from the era when highways were two-lane entrepreneurial zones, lined with small businesses that thrived on visitor traffic.

Adventure 1
Taking the scenic route back to Portland

Pick up any activities you missed from the itinerary and take the scenic drive to Mosier on the Historic Columbia River Highway, stopping maybe for a hike at Rowena Crest Overlook (*see* page 152). From Mosier, take I-84 west.

Eat and Drink in The Dalles

Baldwin Saloon. Old-time style and food in an 1876 building next to the railroad tracks, where the town's action used to be. A few nearby ancient structures are worth investigating. Monday to Friday 11 a.m. to 9 p.m.; Saturday to 10 p.m. 205 Court St. 541-296-5666

Casa El Mirador. Margaritas too big to lift and other things that taste good after a hot day outside. Sunday to Thursday 11 a.m. to 10 p.m.; Friday and Saturday to 11 p.m. 1424 W Second St. 541-298-7388

Clock Tower Ales. Local beers and ciders, full bar and pub fare in a historic courthouse. Daily 7 a.m. to closing. 311 Union St. 541-705-3590

Cousins' Restaurant. Home-style cooking with microbrews. Part of Cousins' Country Inn. Daily 6 a.m. to 10 p.m. (to 9 p.m. in fall and winter). 2114 W Sixth St. 541-298-5161 or 800-848-9378

Hi-Way House. Local supper club vibe, from the days this was the old highway route. Wednesday to Sunday 4 p.m. to close. 2434 E Second St. 541-296-4994

Momma Jane's Pancake House. Recommended for carbo-loading. Just west of downtown. Daily 6 a.m. to 2 p.m. 900 W Sixth St. 541-296-6611

Petite Provence. An outpost of a Portland chain. Excellent coffee, veggie scramble, chocolate croissant. Daily 7 a.m. to 3 p.m. 408 E Second St. 541-508-0057

Rivertap Restaurant. Downtown pub fare. Daily 11 a.m. to 10 p.m.; Friday and Saturday to 12 a.m. 703 E Second St. 541-296-7870.

Riverenza Cafe. In a gorgeous stone former church. Monday to Saturday 10 a.m. to 4 p.m. 401 E 10th St. 541-980-5001

Sunshine Mill Winery. Cheese and meats accompany tasting of wines made on site in a picturesque old flour mill. Daily 12 to 6 p.m. 901 E Second St. 541-298-8900, ext. 1

Shop in The Dalles

Breezeway Antiques and Gifts. Daily 11 a.m. to 6 p.m.; Sunday to 5 p.m. 313 E Second St. 541-296-5079

Cannon Packer Gift Shop. Upscale kitchenware and more near the Sunshine Mill Winery. Monday to Friday 11 a.m. to 5 p.m.; Saturday to 4 p.m. 1006 E Second St. 541-296-3038

Columbia Gorge Discovery Center Museum Store. Daily 9 a.m. to 5 p.m. 5000 Discovery Drive. 541-296-8600

Klindt's Booksellers and Stationers. Oldest bookstore in the Pacific Northwest, since 1870. Toys and gifts too. Monday to Saturday 8 a.m. to 6 p.m.; Sunday 11 a.m. to 4 p.m. 315 E Second St. 541-296-3355

Red Wagon Antiques. Monday to Friday 10 a.m. to 5:30 p.m.; Saturday to 4:30 p.m.; Sunday to 2 p.m. 515 E Second St. 541-296-0010

Discover and Learn in The Dalles

Columbia Gorge Discovery Center and Museum. Daily 9 a.m. to 5 p.m. 5000 Discovery Drive. 541-296-8600

Fort Dalles Museum and Anderson Homestead. Spring break (late March) to October: daily 10 a.m. to 5 p.m.; January to March: weekends 10 a.m. to 5 p.m. 500 W 15th St. 541-296-4547

Old St. Peter's Landmark. Closed January. Tuesday to Friday 11 a.m. to 3 p.m.; Saturday and Sunday 1 to 3 p.m. 405 Lincoln St. 541-296-5686

Rorick House. Built in 1850 by an Army officer. Sporadic hours. 300 W 13th St. 541-296-1867

The Dalles Area Chamber of Commerce and Visitor Center. Monday to Friday 9 a.m. to 5 p.m. 404 W Second St. 541-296 2231

The Dalles Dam Visitor Center. Closed Oct. 1 to April 30. Memorial Day to Labor Day: daily 9 a.m. to 5 p.m. Call for shoulder season hours. 3545 Bret Clodfelter Way. 541-506-7819

Rent Bikes in The Dalles

Dalles City Cyclery. Call to confirm availability. 121 E Second St. 541-769-0771

Kayak Shack. City-run, seasonal bike and boat rentals at Riverfront Park. Friday to Sunday 10 a.m. to 6 p.m. I-84, exit 85. 541-296-9533

Stay in The Dalles

Celilo Inn. Remodeled 47-room motel on bluff overlooking dam. Not walkable into downtown, but huge views, an outdoor pool and deck. 3550 E Second St. 541-769-0001 [$$$]

Cousins' Country Inn. In a big box store district west of downtown. Friendly: everyone's a cousin here. Restaurant on site. 2114 W Sixth St. 541-298-5161 or 800-848-9378 [$$ to $$$]

Fairfield Inn and Suites. Part of the Marriott chain, in big box district west of downtown. 2014 W Seventh St. 541-769-0753 [$$$]

Oregon Motor Motel. 1930s-style motel on the old highway route, downtown. 200 W Second St. 541-296-9111 [$$]

R & R Guest House. Rooms, suites and a private apartment in pretty neighborhood near downtown and Sorosis Park. Saltwater heated pool and hot tub. 508 W 12th St. 541-371-2260 [$$$ to $$$$]

The Dalles Inn. Older but clean, quiet and friendly. A great downtown location for walks, restaurants, brewpubs and tasting rooms. 112 W Second St. 541-296-9107 [$$]

The Dalles Ranch. On 75 acres in the high country above The Dalles. Sleeps 21. Rent the whole place for a book club retreat or family reunion. 6289 Upper Five Mile Road. 541-298-9942 [$$$$]

Camp along the Deschutes River

Deschutes River State Recreation Area. Year-round RV and tent sites in shade along the river. 89601 Biggs-Rufus Hwy, Wasco. First come, first served November 1 to mid-April. Other months for reservations: reserveamerica.com or Oregon State Parks reservations: 800-452-5687 [$]

Lodging Cost Key			
$	$$	$$$	$$$$
<$50	$51 to $99	$100 to $200	>$200

TOUR
9

MOSIER, THE HISTORIC COLUMBIA RIVER HIGHWAY AND ROWENA CREST

OREGON

Like many gorge towns, Mosier offers a completely different vibe from Portland, giving you the feel of a real escape, but close to home. This tour is 36 hours of hikes, scenic routes to bike or drive, cherry picking and wine-tasting. It's just 68 miles, or 68 minutes, from Portland via I-84.

Mosier is a quirky town, home to about 430 people, with lots of lodging listings on peer-to-peer websites. You could stay in nearby Hood River, but you'd miss out on capturing the spirit of Slow Mo. Save Hood River for another getaway.

Spring comes early here: late February through May is wildflower season atop Mosier Plateau and Rowena Crest.

June and July are cherry harvest months, and hot summer days are made for waterfall and river play at Mosier's Pocket Park or Mayer State Park. Fall is great for wine touring. Any clear day in winter is a fine time to bike from Mosier to Hood River on the car-free Historic Columbia River Highway State Trail.

You may want to bring a cooler for cherries or produce, swimwear, bikes and locks, and dinner food if you're staying in a private rental or coming on a night when the restaurants in town are closed. If it's not summer, lunch options are slim in Mosier; best to bring your own. **Rosauers Supermarket** in Hood River is a good place to provision up.

DAY 1

Adventure 1
Hiking to Mosier Falls and the Mosier Plateau

Start early to get in a full day. Take I-84 exit 69 and follow the Historic Columbia River Highway/U.S. 30 into Mosier. Park near the Mosier Totem Pole, across from **Mosier Market and Deli**, in the graveled area between the highway and railroad tracks.

Your first adventure is a 3.5-mile Towns to Trails walk past a hidden waterfall and on to Mosier Plateau, where you'll have spectacular views of Coyote Wall across the river. Towns to Trails, a program of Friends of the Columbia Gorge, has the long-term goal of creating a network of trails accessible from gorge towns, and eventually connecting to each other.

From the totem pole you can see the 1920 warehouse of the Mosier Fruit Growers' Association, established in 1907. Cherries are a big orchard crop here. Walk east on the quiet highway about 1,000 feet and cross the Mosier Creek Bridge. It's a Conde McCullough bridge, one of three in this tour. His bridges enhance some of Oregon's most beautiful sites. Oregon City near Willamette Falls has a good one.

Just past the bridge, turn right onto the Pocket Park trail. Beyond the pioneer cemetery is an overlook into Mosier Creek's canyon and falls. Continue to the top of the 80-foot Mosier Creek Falls. Some guys rafted over it, successfully. Come back later today, perhaps, for a swim in the pool between the two falls—the pocket in Pocket Park. For now, keep hiking toward Mosier Plateau, and ascend to it via switchbacks and stairs. On top you'll encounter the foundation of a garage and remnants of a few homes. This was private land until 2005 when Friends of the Columbia Gorge founder Nancy Russell purchased acreage with two mobile homes on it. The homes were removed and sold for low-income housing. She donated the land to Friends of the Columbia Gorge Land Trust, which later bought

Mosier Totem Pole

adjacent land for the large public space you're now enjoying. See gorgefriends.org and oregonhikers.org to learn more about this site. Return the way you came.

Hiking in January as clouds lift to reveal views atop the Mosier Plateau

DAY
1

Adventure 2
Scenic touring to The Dalles

After the hike, if **The Dwelling Station** is open, shop for interesting home goods, and get a bite at **Manny's Lonchera** food truck. Then head east from Mosier for a 33-mile round-trip loop on the Historic Columbia River Highway/U.S. 30 to The Dalles. Highlights are wineries, cliff-top hikes and U-pick farms. You'll return via equally rewarding Seven Mile Hill. If you bike the route, expect 2,000 feet total elevation gain; traffic is light, speeds relatively low, and the many view stops reward you extravagantly for the hills.

From downtown Mosier, go east on the historic highway. Pass **Idiot's Grace** farm stand. It's across the road from the **Garnier Vineyards'** tasting room, which also sells produce. In season, stop to pick at **Annie's Apricots**.

Pass the large white Mayerdale house, which is not open to the public. Mark A. Mayer established Mayerdale Orchard and Ranch in 1910 and built this Colonial Revival–style home in 1913. He donated land that is today's Mayer State Park, seen later in the route.

About 3 miles in, watch for Memaloose Overlook. Below is Memaloose Island, or *Memaloose Ilahee*, Chinook jargon for "land of the dead." Native Americans placed their dead on islands to protect them from disturbance by predators. A granite obelisk marks the grave of the only white man buried on the island: Victor Trevitt, one of the founders of The Dalles. Before water rising behind Bonneville Dam reduced the original 4-acre island to about 0.5 acre, Indian remains were removed for burial on higher ground, but Trevitt's remains were not. Across the river is Catherine Creek, one of the gorge's premier wildflower hikes.

Next up: Rowena Dell. The road downhill into the dell, Canyon Way, is private, so look into the canyon only from above. Views are best from the Rowena Crest Trail, which is coming up. The canyon was created by the Missoula Floods, which worked a crack in the earth into the wide, deep cleft seen today. It was once called Hog Canyon. Early settlers fenced off the lower end and let loose their hogs, which are omnivores, in hopes of eliminating rattlesnakes.

Dry Canyon Creek is a side canyon of Rowena Dell. You'll pass over it on what seems like a nondescript bridge. It's not. Get out and walk either direction—watching for snakes and poison oak—to see its elegant arch, another classic Conde McCullough bridge.

Stop to enjoy the expansive views at Rowena Crest Overlook, the eastern gorge counterpart to Crown Point. Across the river is the mouth of the Klickitat River with its huge load of silt, and below to the east is a bird's-eye view of the Rowena Loops you'll be swooping down when you leave this plateau. On the Oregon shore is a fine swimming pond, dune-covered shoreline and windsurfing beach at Mayer State Park, the next stop on the route.

From the Overlook, hike to Tom McCall Point—2 miles with 1,000 feet of elevation gain. No dogs are allowed at this Nature Conservancy property. The trail is open May through October. Or hike the easier, 1-mile Rowena Crest Trail along the top of the plateau. It has just 250 feet of elevation gain. When the Missoula Floods raged over this tableland, they created kolk ponds here and at Mayer State Park. Kolk ponds are formed as floodwaters rip out chunks of the underlying rock. In the resulting depression, other rocks and debris churn in an underwater tornado, scouring out a round shape that can become a pond after floodwaters retreat. After the soils of this plateau were carried off by the floodwaters, the rock was left bare. Soils have not yet recovered, 13,000 year later. For trail details of either hike, see gorgefriends.org.

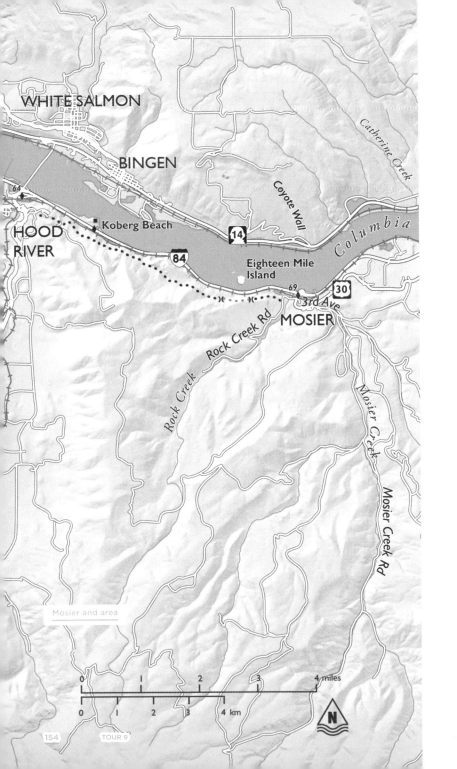

WHITE SALMON

BINGEN

Catherine Creek

Coyote Wall

Columbia

64

HOOD
RIVER

Koberg Beach

14

84

Eighteen Mile
Island

69

30

3rd Ave

MOSIER

Rock Creek Rd

Rock Creek

Mosier Creek

Mosier Creek Rd

Mosier and area

0   1   2   3   4 miles

0   1   2   3   4 km

N

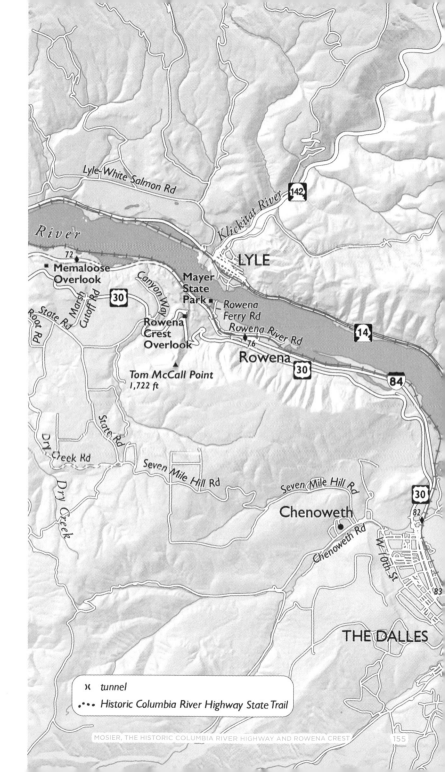

Dry Canyon Creek bridge, a gem unnoticed by many travelers

Brilliant white dunes transition to sandy beach at Mayer State Park

Leave the plateau and descend east and toward the river via the Rowena Loops, constructed in 1919. Like the loops that lift travelers up to Crown Point at the gorge's west end, this graceful stretch of roadway lays upon the land like a ribbon carefully arranged to complement the cliffs. East of the last loop is Rowena Ferry Road, named for the ferry that once crossed the Columbia between Rowena and Lyle. The road dead-ends today at I-84 but you can find its lower half in Mayer State Park.

Go to Mayer State Park: Once down from the loops, turn left in Rowena at the freeway exit. Instead of going right to head east on I-84, go left to pass under it. This puts you on Rowena River Road. Follow it 0.8 mile east to a day use area for windsurfers. After you've checked that out, go west on the same road; once past the freeway intersection, you're on the old Rowena Ferry Road. Continue west on it; after passing the boat ramp, park along the road and walk to a rare, warm-water (relatively speaking) pond with sandy beaches. It's the kolk pond described earlier. A trail west of the lake leads to some lovely sand dunes and a small beach on the Columbia. During hot summer days, west winds can be a bit much at this beach. On the old ferry road, you can explore your way to east-facing areas, though the beaches aren't as nice. After swimming or exploring, head back to the Historic Columbia River Highway and follow it east toward The Dalles.

The next few paragraphs of directions depend on if you're biking or driving: If driving, stay on the historic highway, which becomes Sixth Street in The Dalles. Cross over the third McCullough bridge, over Mill Creek, then curve left on Third Place, then right on Third Street, a one-way through downtown. Restaurants are abundant on Second and Third. See Tour 8 for a more detailed map of The Dalles, plus restaurant info.

If you're biking, the stretch along Sixth Street (the historic highway's name here), with big box stores and massive parking lots, kills the joy after all that beauty. Instead of riding all the way into downtown The Dalles, go only as far as **Cousins' Restaurant**—2114 W Sixth St. Have lunch there. It's about 1 mile into the commercial district. Afterward, bike west on Sixth, then head uphill into the countryside via Chenowith Loop Road. (See map, Tour 8.) At its end, turn right on 10th, which becomes Chenoweth Road (and the "i" in Chenowith turns to an "e"). Stay on it to Seven Mile Hill Road in the Chenoweth community. Go right, and follow the directions below, starting at the second paragraph.

Return leg: The Dalles to Mosier via Seven Mile Hill

If you drove all the way into The Dalles downtown, drive south on Union Street and right on West 10th Street. Cross Cherry Heights Road and stay on 10th (which turns into Chenoweth Road).

At the community of Chenoweth, turn right on Seven Mile Hill Road. Enjoy views of Mount Hood and Mount Adams near the summit of Seven Mile Hill.

At the State Road junction, turn right on State Road and begin dropping down the hill into the Mosier Creek Valley. As you get close to Mosier, stop at **Analemma Wines**, **Root Orchards**, **Survival Garden Country Store** or **Key Lock Orchard**.

Adventure 3
Slow-moseying in Mosier

End the day in the swimming hole at Mosier Creek Falls, dinner at **Union Tap House** or **Rack and Cloth**, and bed at whatever lodging you've lined up ahead of time.

Adventure 1
Biking or walking the Historic Columbia River Highway State Trail

After breakfast, bike or hike this wonderful 4.5-mile section of the historic highway between Mosier and Hood River. On it, views are stupendous, no cars are allowed and you pass through the Mosier twin tunnels (about 1 mile from the start). The grade is gentle with some climbing, and at times it passes inland, away from river views into quiet shady spaces.

To get to the trailhead, from the Mosier Totem Pole, go west on the old highway, then right on Rock Creek Road. Pass under the I-84 ramp, cross over Rock Creek and in less than 1 mile turn right into the Mark O. Hatfield East Trailhead. If you're driving to the trailhead, go further on Rock Creek Road to the lot on the left. An Oregon State Parks pass is required.

Once on the trail, pass through scablands scoured bare by the Missoula Floods. Stop for the excellent views of Coyote Wall's cliffs across the river. The immense vertical wall was caused by faulting; the wall's curve toward the river was caused by horizontal compression of the rock layers. Like a rug on a slippery floor when the ends are pushed together, the horizontal pressure caused the rock to fold, resulting in a system of convex ridges and concave valleys. Coyote Wall is an anticline, the ridge part of the system; the riverbed is a syncline, the valley part. Coyote Wall is commonly and incorrectly called the Syncline.

Pull off the trail to a viewpoint of Eighteen Mile Island, the rare privately owned island in the Columbia. The owners of the only home on the island boat to it from Hood River.

Next come the twin tunnels. Built in 1921, the consecutive tunnels run 390 feet total. An observation gallery between them is now covered by a rock catchment structure built in the 1990s to deflect rocks falling from the cliffs above. Masonry portals were lost in the 1930s when the tunnels were widened to accommodate larger trucks. By the 1940s, with increasing vehicle size, the tunnels were made one-way, with traffic lights. When I-84 replaced the Columbia River Highway in the 1950s, the tunnels were filled with rock and the roadway you're now on was left for nature to reclaim.

In 2000, as part of the historic highway's reemergence as a state trail, the tunnels and road reopened to bikers and walkers. Unfortunately, however, an enticing cliff walk between the tunnels is now fenced off. Stop at the windows in the east tunnel, also fenced now in these litigious times, but still offering a fantastic view. Just west of the tunnels is a concrete rock catchment structure that protects you from rocks raveling off the cliffs above. It dates from the renovation, and its monstrous size is either an example of engineering overdesign or a testament to the instability above it.

As you ride westward, across the river are log piles at Bingen, on the Washington shore. Across from that, on the Oregon side, is a rocky outcrop into the Columbia River, Koberg Beach. Swim or walk the beach there on the way back to Portland.

At the trail's west end is the **Mark O. Hatfield West Trailhead** with a nice visitor center and restrooms. It was built at the site of a former rock quarry. Buy a T-shirt to commemorate your ride. Return via the same route. Or if you don't mind climbing a hill on your return, keep going 1.2 miles downhill on the Hood River loops—a classic bit of the old Columbia River Highway, much like the Rowena loops and the figure eight loops at Crown Point. At the bottom, cross over the Hood River and now you're on State Street at the edge of downtown Hood River. Turn right at Front and left on Oak for lots of eating/shopping/drinking options. (See Tour 10 for restaurants and a map.) After your lunch or coffee break, climb back up the loops and enjoy the cruise back into Mosier.

On the way back to the Portland area, stop to swim at or explore Koberg
Beach, a nice sandy beach sheltered from the noise and sight of I-84.
This land was owned by John and Emma Koberg who once farmed the
floodplain that's now underwater. From 1915 to 1950, a resort with a
dance hall operated here. The east end is an in-lieu fishing site—off
limits unless you're a tribal fisher. Find the trail to the beach at the
west end of the parking area. Access Koberg Beach only from I-84
westbound, an unnumbered rest stop exit a few miles west of exit 69.

Eat and Drink in Mosier

Manny's Lonchera. Eat on picnic tables under the trees and visit with other travelers at this food cart. Summer only: Tuesday to Friday 9 a.m. to 6 p.m.; Saturday 10 a.m. to 4 p.m.; Sunday 12 to 4 p.m. 1104 First Ave. 541-980-6080

Mosier Market and Deli. Daily 8 a.m. to 8 p.m.; June 1 to August 31: to 9 p.m. 1010 First St. 541-478-3763

Rack and Cloth. Cider, wine, beer plus seasonal, local meals. Weekends 12 to 10 p.m.; Thursday and Friday 4 to 10 p.m. 1104 First Ave. 541-965-1457

Shop in Mosier

The Dwelling Station. Home goods and repurposed items. Friday to Sunday 11 a.m. to 6 p.m. 1202 First St. 503-880-1233

Mosier Farmers' Market. June to September: Sunday 4 to 7 p.m. Downtown. 541-999-5439

Discover and Learn near Mosier

Mark O. Hatfield West Visitor Center. Operated by Oregon State Parks. At the west end of the Hood River-to-Mosier segment of the Historic Columbia River Highway State Trail. Daily 10 a.m. to 2 p.m. 541-387-4010 or 800-551-6949

Taste the Wine in Mosier

Analemma Wines. April to November: weekends 10 a.m. to 5 p.m. 1120 State Road. 541-478-2873

Garnier Vineyards. 330 acres of wine grapes, cherries, peaches and pears. Tasting room/farm stand is at the west end of the Mayerdale estate. April through early October: weekends 12 to 5 p.m. 8467 Highway 30 W. 541-478-2200

Pick Fruit in Mosier

Annie's Apricots. Easy-to-pick trees; minimal spraying. Early July. 8264 Highway 30. 541-478-3502

Idiot's Grace. Certified-organic farm. 8450 Hwy 30 W. 541-490-5249

Key Lock Orchard. During cherry harvest: 10 a.m. to 7 p.m. 270 State Road.

Root Orchards. In 1878 Amos Root established this farm, the area's first commercial orchard. During cherry harvest, June to early July: 8 a.m. to 6 p.m. 1111 Root Road. 541-478-3425

Survival Garden Country Store. Fresh milk and eggs. No U-pick. 1150 State Road. 541-980-2085

Stay in Mosier

Three Sleeps Vineyard B and B. Two rooms with private entrances and patios overlooking a vineyard. Two-night minimum July to September and holiday weekends. Call the Wednesday before the weekend for one-night stays. 1600 Carroll Road. 541-478-0143 or 541-490-5404 [$$$]

Camp near Mosier

Memaloose State Park. Good viewing of the nighttime sky. RV and tent sites. No river access; views of Memaloose Island. Get there via an unnumbered exit, "Memaloose Rest Area and Campground," east of Mosier, I-84 westbound only. March 13 to October 31. Oregon State Parks reservations: 800-452-5687 [$]

Lodging Cost Key			
$	$$	$$$	$$$$
<$50	$51 to $99	$100 to $200	>$200

Cherry picking in June, Mosier

HOOD RIVER

OREGON

When you want a fun getaway in a town that's like a more athletic younger cousin to Portland, spend a weekend in Hood River. The town sits in the spectacular Hood River Valley, with Mount Hood's snowy flanks embracing the beauty that flows from its peak. Adventures here are all about outdoor sports, orchards, wine, beer, cider, local foods and shopping. This two-and-a-half day getaway in and around the gorge's busiest town covers these bases by bike, train, board, foot and air.

All this and it's a 60-mile, 60-minute drive from Portland, easy to get to at the end of a workweek. In summer west winds blow reliably and windsurfing and kiteboarding action is high. Spring is when cherry and apple orchards bloom white and pink, fall brings wine and other harvest festivals, and year-round, the shopping, eating and drinking are superb.

You may want to make reservations for the **Mount Hood Railroad** excursion train or reserve the services of a guide/instructor for mountain biking, horseback riding, windsurfing, or air-touring. (See Appendix B.) You may want to bring your bike, a lock and swimsuit. If you want to bike—road or mountain—reserve in advance at **Discover Bicycles** or **Mountain View Cycles**, especially on summer weekends.

Find free parking at Hood River County Chamber of Commerce on East Port Marina Drive, at Waterfront Park, or on residential streets west of Seventh Street and south of Sherman Avenue.

Adventure 1
Taking a town walkabout

Leave Portland with several hours of daylight left. After the quick, hour-long drive out on I-84, check into your hotel or inn, then stretch your legs and figure out the lay of the land with this approximately 3-mile, one-hour walkabout. It starts where the first settlers, Nathaniel and Mary Coe, built their home in 1854, and ends with dinner.

Park at Tsuruta Park, State and 13th streets. Adams Creek makes an appearance here in a stone-lined gutter, then disappears into a pipe, the sad fate of urban streams everywhere. Walk east on State. At 1022 State is a home built on the site where the Coes first settled in 1854.

From State, go right on 12th. Climb the hill then turn left on Sherman Avenue, occupied by the sort of impressive homes people build when given a steep bluff to perch on. Cross 11th, and look left at the red-roofed Dutch Colonial at 1006. It was built in 1927 atop the foundation of a house built by Henry Coe in 1875. Henry was Nathaniel and Mary's son; his home was surrounded by berry crops. A big copper beech in the yard is a nonnative beauty that probably dates from the 1920s.

Still on Sherman, cross 10th and notice the land dropping, this time toward the valley of the Hood River. From Sherman, turn left on Ninth, then right on State and pass lots of nice old homes, many from the Craftsman era of the early 1900s. Number 621 is a Colonial-style home from 1902. At Sixth, in the northeast corner, is the 1886 home of Ezra L. and Georgiana Smith. They arrived here with few possessions in 1876 and did quite well their first 10 years, based on the look of this house. The **Stoltz Winery Tasting Room** occupies it now. Go around to the view side of the house to a grand staircase that once delivered the Smiths from their perch up here down to the commercial district, where Mr. Smith owned a building (seen later on the route).

Descend the staircase to the rock cairn in Georgiana Smith Park. The building above the cairn is a Carnegie library, built with funds from Andrew Carnegie's foundation, which offered communities worldwide a chance to apply for grants to build public libraries. Between 1904 and 1921, 31 Carnegie libraries were built in Oregon.

From the cairn, head downhill to Oak Street and go east. The siren call of shopping stalled me out for an hour or so here and if you need some new activewear, there's no better place to buy it. While downtown, perhaps have dinner at one of the many options on page 185.

At the southeast corner of Third and Oak is the building Ezra Smith walked to from his home. He organized the town's first bank in 1904 and it occupied this building until 1910 when a newer structure that says "trustworthy local bank" in every way was built kitty-corner from this one.

From Oak, turn right (south) on Third and walk to State, where a bike hub offers a pump, restrooms and place to lock up. Go left (east) on State to Second and State. Here, Overlook Memorial Park remembers Hood River soldiers who died in wars from World War I to Vietnam. One name inscribed in the basalt column is Frank Hachiya, born in 1920 in Odell where his father, one of many Japanese immigrants in the Hood River Valley, worked in the Rodamar family's orchards. After Japan attacked Pearl Harbor in 1941 and the nation went to war, Frank enlisted as a translator for the U.S. Army's Military Intelligence Service. His father was sent to an internment camp in Idaho, along with all West Coast Japanese-American citizens, victims of the xenophobia that engulfed the nation during the war. Frank was shot to death in 1945 on his way to interview a Japanese prisoner of war on Leyte Island.

From the memorial at Second and State, begin climbing Hood River's famous Second Street steps. Detour into the Stratton Garden, a stair-side rose garden. If you do, the total steps in this epic staircase is 409, the second longest in Oregon. (The first, in Happy Valley, has 441 steps). Without the detour it's 413 steps. This route does not make you climb all 409, although I recommend you do them all. This is super fit Hood River and when in Rome . . . . One flight between landings has 150 steps. Not interested? Okay, so then after the 59 steps up to the rose garden, climb 27 more to Sherman Avenue. Cross it and climb the 150-step flight. It leads to Hazel Avenue, your exit from the stairs.

From the stairs, turn left on Hazel, an intriguing street with an off-the-grid feel. No sidewalks here, but great views of the sandbar at the mouth of the Hood River. At a fork, stay high (right). Cross East Pointe Court with its big glassy homes, and watch on the left for a small wooden sanctuary with an old bell in a cupola. A sign says, "We welcome you to see the little house of prayer."

At the corner of East Third and Hazel, come to a sign for the Indian Creek Trail. The actual trailhead is slightly to the right, uphill on Third. Begin walking on the trail. Soon, oak woodlands open up at a bench that offers excellent views of the Hood River, downstream of where Indian Creek flows into it. This trail was once a service

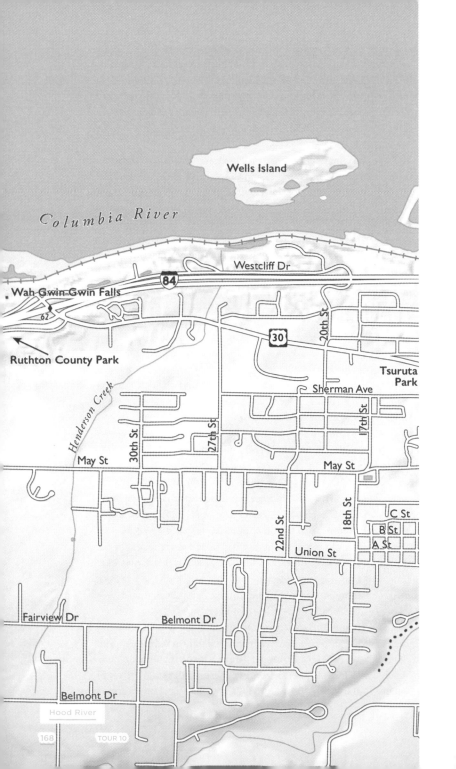

Wells Island

Columbia River

Westcliff Dr

84

Wah-Gwin-Gwin Falls

62

30

20th St

Ruthton County Park

Tsuruta
Park

Henderson Creek

Sherman Ave

17th St

27th St

30th St

May St

May St

22nd St

18th St

C St

B St

A St

Union St

Fairview Dr

Belmont Dr

Belmont Dr

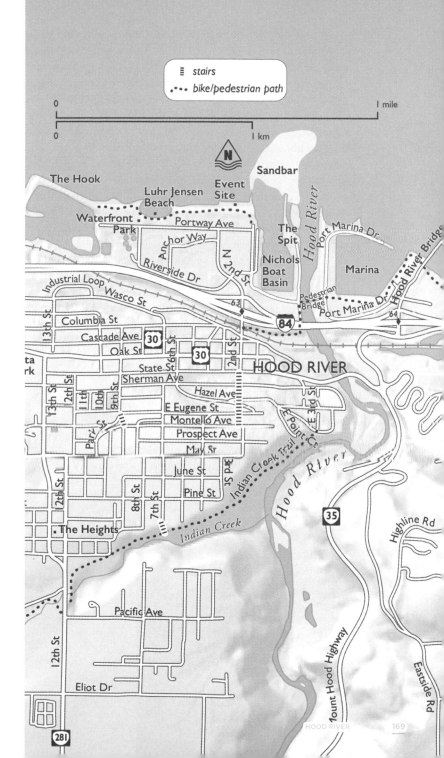

stairs

bike/pedestrian path

0   1 mile

0   1 km

N

Sandbar

The Hook

Luhr Jensen
Beach

Event
Site

Hood River

Waterfront
Park

Portway Ave

The
Spit

Port Marina Dr

Anchor Way

Riverside Dr

N 2nd St

Nichols
Boat
Basin

Marina

Port Marina Dr

Hood River Bridge

Industrial Loop

Wasco St

63

Pedestrian
Bridge

84

64

13th St

Columbia St

6th St

Cascade Ave

30

Oak St

2nd St

30

HOOD RIVER

ta
rk

State St

Sherman Ave

Hazel Ave

13th St

12th St

11th

10th

9th St

E Eugene St

E 3rd St

Montello Ave

E Point Dr

Prospect Ave

Park St

May St

Indian Creek Trail

Hood River

June St

8th St

7th St

Pine St

4th St

35

The Heights

Indian Creek

Highline Rd

12th St

Pacific Ave

Mount Hood Highway

Eastside Rd

Eliot Dr

281

road for a water pipe, which you'll soon see. Just west of Fifth Street (which you cannot see—it's on the bluff above the trail), a wooden pipe begins. As was true all over the planet, in the Pacific Northwest many old water systems relied on wooden pipes. This relic supplied water to the Diamond Fruit cannery (now the home of Full Sail Ale). It's made of milled lumber cut into staves and bound with iron cording. (Early wooden pipes in Portland were made of old-growth Douglas fir trees with their cores drilled out, joined by metal sleeves.) In some places the Indian Creek pipe is wonderfully intact; in others, it's being reclaimed by the earth. Take your photos now.

Shortly after the pipe begins running along the trail, come to a set of wooden steps up the bluff. Climb them to the dead end of Seventh Street, where interesting homes and big trees give you something to admire and Mount Adams grows larger as you walk north.

At the northwest corner of Seventh and May Street, don't miss the incredible London plane tree, with its enormous blobby, peely trunk. This tree species, a cross between an American sycamore and an Oriental plane tree, is popular in big cities because it can withstand air pollution and root compaction. It first gained popularity during the Industrial Revolution of the nineteenth century, when London's air was a dark stew of pollutants.

From Seventh, turn left on Montello. Just before Eighth, look over the roofs of houses to Underwood Mountain across the river. At an open space across from 729 you can look directly up the valley of the White Salmon River to Mount Adams. At 813 Montello is a grand Queen Anne Victorian from 1901. At 911 is the beautiful Simpson Copple House, built by a fruit grower in 1906.

From 911 Montello, come back a bit east to Waucoma Park, with

Wooden water pipe,
Indian Creek Trail

its sculpture memorial of a young baseball player. Take the 65 steps down to Eugene and Park streets. Go left on Eugene, passing more handsome old homes and Coe Primary School. At 11th and Eugene is a strikingly attractive Episcopal church. Built in 1925 on land donated by the Coe family, its architect was Percy Bentley, who moved here from the Midwest after steeping in the architectural ambience of Frank Lloyd Wright and Louis Sullivan. It's not Prairie style, but has spare Gothic lines that echo the form-follows-function bible of Wright and other modernist architects.

Continue west on Eugene; carefully cross 12th where Eugene jogs, then stay west on Eugene again, past homes with huge old trees. At 1207 is a five-trunk tulip poplar, a tree native to the Smoky Mountains of Tennessee and North Carolina; across from it is a tiny old cottage with an enormous native Oregon white oak. Turn right at 13th to return to the start.

Or, for dinner options in the Heights, walk left (south) on 13th five blocks or so. Or head downtown or to the waterfront. See page 187.

Adventure 1
Choosing your next adventure

DAY
2

This first half of the day is about outdoor adventures: mountain biking, horseback riding, water sports, or an aerial tour. Have breakfast at **Hood River Taqueria, Ten Speed Coffee, Knead** or **Ground Coffee**, then get out there.

Appendix B has details and contact info for outfitters and guides listed here.

Mountain biking

Mountain biking's not all about stunts and steep, rocky trails. Mitchell Buck, owner of Hood River's **Dirty Fingers Bicycle Repair**, says you can find a "low-consequence environment" with lots of chances for skills building at the Family Man area in Post Canyon, a large mountain bike trail system on the west end of town. Park at the trailhead at Riordan Hill Drive and loop around a flat, treed area with smooth terrain. Find how to get there or to more challenging rides at Dirty Fingers, where you can buy the Hood River Oregon Trail Map.

Or hire a guide. Greg Galliano of **Hood River Mountain Bike Adventures** has been guiding bikers since 2005. He'll drive you to and guide you on the best trails, tailored to your skills. Rent or bring your own. He'll also take you on a wine tour by bike.

If you want to find your own way, rent road or mountain bikes downtown at **Discover Bicycles** or **Mountain View Cycles**.

Hood River street view

Horseback riding

See **Double Mountain Horse Ranch's** website for ride options or call to create a custom ride.

River sport lesson or rental

Hood River has protected waters for beginners. You won't be out there in the main channel with the barges. Lessons are generally offered mid-May to mid-September. Too windy? Rent a kayak or standup paddleboard in the Nichols Boat Basin, which is protected from the west winds. See Appendix B for guides, lessons, excursions and rentals for kayaks, Jet Skis, sailboats, standup paddling and windsurfing/kiteboarding.

Aerial tour

Classic Wings Aero Services offers 30-, 60- and 90-minute air tours of Mount Hood, the Hood River Valley and the Columbia River. If you've never taken a sightseeing flight, the scenery here makes this a good place to start. You can also design your own tour.

Train ride

Take a half-day excursion aboard the **Mount Hood Railroad** train from Hood River to Parkdale. The 22-mile route climbs through Hood River Valley orchards, June to late October.

For swimmers only

Plan a weekend around the annual **Roy Webster Cross-Channel Swim** in September. (See Appendix A.) Jump off a sternwheeler in the early morning with 500 grinning, shivering, orange-capped folks and swim the mile-wide Columbia between Bingen, Washington and Hood River. Swimming amidst the gorge's incredible scenery, you'll feel like a frisky kid. The river temperature is usually in the high sixties that time of year—warmer than the morning air. Preregistration recommended. Afterward regain the calories at Hood River's **Egg River Cafe**.

Adventure 2
Scenic driving in the Hood River Valley

DAY 2

After your active morning, have lunch on the water, downtown or in the Heights, then set out for a classic scenic driving tour. This route is a combination of picturesque old barns and farm houses, orchards, views of mounts Hood and Adams, and stops for hiking, wine-tasting, fruit-buying, shopping, alpaca-petting, and museum-going. It also follows part of the Hood River Fruit Loop, which promotes local businesses. (See the 30-plus sites on the loop at hoodriverfruitloop.com.) Find details on businesses visited on this scenic drive at Shop, page 189.

Apples had been the first orchard crop in the valley until a deep freeze in 1010. After that, growers turned to pears, which remain the major commercial crop, although sweet cherries and vineyards are increasing.

Start the route at Second and State in downtown. Go east on State, cross the Hood River and U.S. 35, following the sign that says "State Park," and begin climbing the historic highway's Hood River Loops. In a 300-foot climb from the river, road builders created a series of curvy switchbacks that never exceed a 5 percent grade—much like the curves at Rowena Crest and Crown Point.

Turn off the highway onto Highline Road, then keep south on Eastside Road. Pass through pear orchards and stop at Panorama Point. It looks out at Mount Hood and the green, irrigated Hood River Valley that incises its northern flanks. Back on Eastside Road, red barns poke their tops up out of green orchards. Pass Old Dalles Drive, a road from the 1870s; it crosses privately owned Hood River Mountain. A gate blocks further access about midway to Mosier.

Come to the community of Pine Grove, at Wells Drive and Pine Grove School. Turn right here on Van Horn Drive for a short out-and-back investigation of many interesting sites along Van Horn. One is Juanita's Tortilla Factory (not open to the public), started by Antonio and Juana Dominguez. The Dominguez family moved here in 1953 and were one of the first three Mexican families to move to the Hood River Valley. In 1977 Juana and family members started making and selling tortillas commercially.

Stop on Van Horn Drive at **The Fruit Company**, which packs and ships fruit and gourmet food gift baskets in an old Diamond Fruit packing warehouse. It's a family operation, run by descendants of Roy and Olive Webster, who moved here in 1942 and began growing and shipping fruit. Roy also swam across the Columbia that year, an annual event now named for him. (See Appendix A.) Take a quick tour of the company's antique orchard equipment (Monday to Friday 11 a.m. to 3 p.m.). On Fridays, buy at discounted prices any fruit, cheese, nuts and other items that don't meet the company's standards for its gift baskets.

Also on Van Horn Drive and open March to November is **Mount Hood Winery**. And east of the rail tracks on Van Horn Drive is the serene and lovely Pine Grove Butte Cemetery. Investigate all these stops, then come back to Eastside Road and Wells Drive. I recommend driving west on Wells—it's a loop—if you like photographing picturesque wooden barns in scenic settings.

Back at the intersection of Eastside and Wells, go south on Eastside. Stop for a photo at the 1907 Carpenter Gothic–style Pine Grove Methodist Church. Turn right at Fir Mountain Road, and drive west to OR 35, turn left and immediately right to **Fox Tail Cider** and **Smiley's Red Barn**, at the southwest corner of this intersection. After this stop, drive a bit further south on OR 35 and turn left into **Wy'East Vineyards**. From there carefully cross OR 35 to Neal Creek Mill Road; pass Cardinal Glass Industries, a Minnesota company that makes residential insulated glass (hence this plant's name: Cardinal IG for "insulated glass"). Follow the road to **Glassometry Studios** at 3015 Lower Mill Drive.

From Neal Creek Mill Road, turn right on Davis/OR 282. This is the heart of Odell, the fruit-packing hub for the valley. Huge processing facilities are on the right. Since 1919, Duckwall Fruit has packed pears that today are eaten all over the planet, including Fiji, United Arab Emirates and India. From Davis, turn left on Graves Road to **Cody Orchards Farm Stand**, with one of the valley's oldest packing sheds.

From the Cody Orchards stand, come back out to Davis, go left and then left on Straight Hill Road to **Hood River Lavender Farms** at 3801. In summer, its gardens of purple flowers with a snow-capped mountain behind them are a great place to spark the flame in young photographers.

From Straight Hill Road, turn right on Central Vale Road. Pass Columbia Gorge Organics, which grows and processes orchard crops into juices sold at specialty retailers. From September to December they're packing pears and apples. No drop-in visits, but call 541-354-1066 if you'd like a tour during those months. Then go right on Wyeast Road, and left on Sylvester Drive to **Cascade Alpacas of Oregon and Foothills Yarn and Fiber**. Pet one of the two-toed wonders, buy an alpaca hat and ask questions of the friendly, knowledgeable staff.

From the alpacas, turn left on Canyon Road, which follows Odell Creek, then left on Lippman, left on Summit and left on Dee Highway (OR 281). Stop at **The Old Trunk** in a 1900s general store, for antiquing, sweets and fruit.

Punchbowl Falls is the next stop. Drive 4 miles south on Dee Highway then turn right on Punchbowl Road. Right after crossing the

Underwood
Mountain
2,755 ft ▲

Underwood

Drano
Lake

Columbia River

62

84

56

84 30

HOOD RIVER

Viento
State Park

Tucker Rd

281

Acree Dr

Tucker County Park ▪

Wyeast Rd

Summit Dr

Lippman Rd

282

Hood River

281

Odell

Dee Hwy

Davis Dr

Canyon Rd

The Hood River Valley

Sylvester Dr

Straight Hill Rd

Punchbowl
Falls

Punchbowl Rd

Central Vale Rd

Odell Creek

W. Fork

E. Fork

Middle Mountain
2,644 ft
▲

Dee

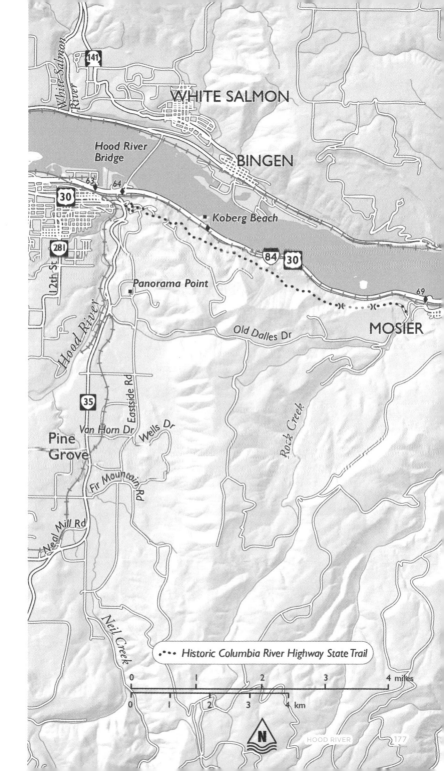

WHITE SALMON

Hood River
Bridge

BINGEN

141

White Salmon River

30

63

64

281

12th St

Koberg Beach

84 30

Panorama Point

Hood River

69

Old Dalles Dr

MOSIER

35

Eastside Rd

Van Horn Dr

Wells Dr

Pine
Grove

Fir Mountain Rd

Neal Mill Rd

Rock Creek

Neil Creek

•••• Historic Columbia River Highway State Trail

0   1   2   3   4 miles

0   1   2   3   4 km

N

East Fork Hood River, veer right, staying on Punchbowl Road. At Green Road, stay straight on Punchbowl Road. Park in a gravel area on the right just before the road crosses the canyon of the West Fork Hood River. Begin hiking north on a logging road. This land, once owned by timber companies, now belongs to Western Rivers Conservancy. It was long a de facto local park and in summer 2015 funds were found to make it official. Selective logging in April 2015 removed diseased trees and thinned the forest. Avoid side trails that lead to the cliff edge, where a stumble could result in a fatal fall. Instead, look for trails that show you the waterfall without taking you near the edge.

Rafters drop their rafts in below the falls to raft the Class III to IV water of the lower Hood River, which has run free since the Powerdale Dam downstream was removed in 2010. At the falls an old wooden ladder hangs off the far cliff; it once serviced the ugly concrete box in the river: a fish ladder installed in 1959. Keep going north on the logging road; it narrows to a steep but manageable footpath that descends to the confluence of the West Fork and East Fork. A gravel bar makes a great place to enjoy this incredible setting. Volcanic debris off the mountain sometimes turns the East Fork a latte color. In November 2006, a huge debris flow washed through here, dropping heavier boulders and cobbles along the way, and creating the large sandbar at the mouth of the Hood River (seen later in the tour). Return the way you walked in.

Before you get into your car, walk onto the bridge just beyond where you parked for a view of the canyon. Return to the Dee Highway/ OR 281 and turn left (north). Stop at **Riversong Sanctuary** at 3226 Dee Highway, an organic farm. Learn how they turn herbs into medicinal products. Buy soaps and oils or relax by their pond. Then if you fancy more river-walking, stop at **Tucker County Park** for a hiking trail along the Hood River. Find the trail at the upstream end of the group picnic area.

From Dee Highway, turn right at Tucker Road and stop for an hour or more at **WAAAM—the Western Antique Aeroplane and Automobile Museum**. The exuberant use of steel and style in the land yachts, restored planes and motorcycles is astounding. You'll return to your aerodynamic little nugget of a car and heave a sigh of nostalgia for the days when America produced such beautiful, mobile objects of art. The best part: on second Saturdays from 10 a.m. to 2 p.m., old planes taxi out of the museum to the runway behind it and fly over Hood River. Cars are also aired out and visitors can sometimes come along for a ride (in the cars, not the planes).

Columnar basalt cliffs along the West Fork Hood River

After the museum, go right on Tucker. On the left at 1400 Tucker Road, is Tallman Ladders, founded by the aptly named Bob Tallman Sr. after World War II. Knowing aluminum's lightweight properties from his work on war planes, he made a few aluminum ladders for use in his own orchard. Soon other orchardists were asking for them, to replace the heavy wooden ladders then in use. The company is still family run.

Follow Tucker's bends until it loses its rural character. At this point, you're in Hood River Heights, a commercial district that sprung up to serve growers. Stop in the Heights for dinner (see page 186 for options) or follow Tucker as it turns into 12th and drops you down the hill.

Adventure 3
Watching the sun set from the sandbar

DAY
2

After dinner, a walk out to the sandbar is a nice way to end the evening. See the map for how to get there.

Let the day and the winds heat up while you have breakfast and shop along Oak Street and Cascade Avenue. Then head out for a bike ride with lots of scenic stops for beach-walking, eating, drinking local beer, watching windsurfers and kiteboarders and photographing wily goats. The distance, about 8 miles, isn't much but with the many stops you can make a half-day of this or more. The map on page 168 has the detail you need for this adventure.

The Hood River waterfront is a perfect place to explore by bike: it's flat and you can whiz through less scenic parts to get to the good stuff. Much of the route is on paths or streets with little traffic. Even if you're heading into a stiff west wind, the terrain and frequent stops make it eminently doable. In the early 1980s windsurfers (aka sailboarders) discovered Hood River, and since then the City and Port have focused on revivifying the waterfront for tourism, recreation and industry. Today it's a still-evolving and really interesting blend of all these economic engines. The second part of the ride takes you out to cliffs above the river, and involves some hill climbing on quiet streets on the way out; it's pretty much all downhill on the way back.

Start on Port Marina Drive at the **Hood River County Chamber of Commerce**, source of info and maps. At the east side of the building, take the asphalt path east along the marina, pass under the Hood River Bridge and ride to where the path ends at a beach just beyond the Best Western. Before Bonneville Dam raised river levels here you could ride out to the next point in the river, Koberg Beach. Now an exit off I-84 westbound is the only option to get to Koberg Beach.

From the Best Western, turn around and ride back to the Chamber office, then go west. If you ride north alongside the green lawns of Marina Park, you'll get great views of boats in the marina and will end up at the Columbia Gorge Sailpark and Swim Beach.

But for now, the goal is to get to the sandbar: from the Chamber, bike west and cross the pedestrian bridge over the Hood River. In 1804, Lewis and Clark reported that people living here at the mouth of the Hood River called it *Waucoma*, "the place of the cottonwoods." Today's river mouth with its straight channel and bare ground would be unrecognizable to those nineteenth-century people. Historically, the river mouth was an alluvial fan—a Y-shaped mix of islands, channels, sloughs and cottonwood forest. When Bonneville Dam raised river levels, much of that was inundated. Starting in the 1950s, the marina was dredged, and fill placed to create a jetty. More fill in the 1960s created land for industry, port facilities and space for I-84.

At the end of the pedestrian bridge, you can go north to the Spit, and get right out to the sandbar without wading, but it's prettier if you follow these directions: after coming off the bridge, stay straight (west), riding along the base of the Nichols Boat Basin.

Beginning in 1939, Nichols Boat Works built tugboats and towing vessels here. The sternwheeler *Columbia Gorge*, home port at Cascade Locks, was built here in 1983. The boat works operated until 1988. In the early 2000s, up to 200 cruise ships moored in the basin each year. That changed in 2006, when debris flows came down the Hood River from Mount Hood and rebuilt much of the delta lost to the dam. The flows created a freeform, 26-acre sandbar at the artificially straight mouth of the Hood River, and nearly closed the entrance to the boat basin. The boat basin facilities were razed in 2008. In 2015 construction began for a hotel, park and commercial buildings.

From the base of the Nichols Boat Basin, turn right to ride up its west bank. You'll end up at the Event Site, with a big lawn for watching kiteboarders launch from here and the sandbar. Lock your bike to the rack near the restroom and wander out to the sandbar. It extends far into the Columbia and is being left to Mother Nature to engineer, except where it reaches into the shipping channel. You'll have to wade across the now-shallow mouth of the boat basin to get to the sandbar. (One summer night as winds died, the narrow passage clogged with kiteboarders leaving the sandbar, bringing to mind wildebeests leaving a Serengeti watering hole.)

After investigating the sandbar, come back to the Event Site and continue west on the paved Waterfront Trail. Pass Northwave Sails, maker of sails for windsurfers since 1982, and a windsurfing launch at Luhr Jensen Beach. Luhr Jensen was born in 1888 and lived in Dee, up the Hood River Valley. He worked at lumber mills and farmed. When the Depression slashed his income to a trickle, he began making fishing tackle. His meticulous lures (another felicitous name-pairing of product and creator) led to a multimillion dollar company, Luhr-Jensen and Sons. It was sold in 2006 to Rapala, a Finnish lure maker. Until then, its headquarters was here on the waterfront. A little further on is Hood River Waterfront Park, with its playground and climbing wall.

From the park, ride over a thin bit of landfill on loose gravel to the Hook, where beginners learn to windsurf. The blue-roofed complex across the river is the Spring Creek National Fish Hatchery—a premier windsurfing site for experts. Underwood Mountain, a shield volcano, rises to 2,755 feet above it. Wells Island is just west of the Hook. It

One of the wary Ruthton Park goats

wasn't an island until Bonneville Dam raised river levels. The Port of Hood River planned in the 1980s to turn it into an interpretive and conference center. Instead, it was conserved and is now managed by the Forest Service. It has an active heron rookery on its west end, and bald eagles use it to perch and peer.

Head back off the Hook and if hunger calls have a meal or beer on Portway Avenue at **pFriem Family Brewers** or pizza at **Solstice Wood Fire Cafe and Bar**. Then meander back eastward via streets that are home to fruit processing of two different kinds: Hood River Juice Company/Ryan's Juice makes apple cider (not hard cider) in the large structure south of Anchor Way. **Hood River Distillers** on Riverside Drive got started in 1934 as a way to glean more profits from the town's orchard crops. With Prohibition recently ended, it began making brandies from apples and pears. Taste its gin, whiskey and other spirits downtown on Oak Street.

Leave the waterfront by riding south on Second Street's sidewalk. Cross over I-84 and turn right on Cascade Avenue. At Third and Cascade, stop at the **Columbia Art Gallery** at the Columbia Center for the Arts for locally made art and jewelry.

From Cascade, turn north (right) on Third and left on Columbia. Ahead is the Union Building, the oldest warehouse associated with the valley's fruit-growing economy; one section dates from 1905. Veer left to stay on Columbia. Pass **Full Sail Brewing**, one of Oregon's oldest craft brewers. It's in the former Diamond Fruit cannery and cold storage plant. Free tours daily, 1, 2, 3 and 4 p.m., ages 12 and older. Its pub is just west on Columbia. Just across from Full Sail is **Double Mountain Brewery and Tap Room**, at 8 Fourth St. "Double Mountain" is a Hood River–specific term—referring to mounts Hood and Adams, bookends to the area's beauty.

From Columbia, turn right on Seventh, which rolls downhill and becomes Wasco. Offices for the **Columbia River Gorge National Scenic Area** are in the big white Waucoma Center (enter on the east end of the building). Here buy detailed maps of the gorge.

From Wasco, go right on 20th. On the corners here are the Rotary Skate Park and the Morrison Disc Golf Park. Follow 20th downhill as it crosses under I-84, then turn left on Westcliff Drive, which sees hardly any traffic. Turn into **Columbia Gorge Hotel** and walk the trails along the cliff to 200-foot Wah Gwin Gwin Falls. The hotel was built in 1921 and later spent a few decades as a retirement home for the Neighbors of Woodcraft fraternal organization. It is back to business these days. You can eat here or get something to drink in the gift shop.

From the hotel continue west on Westcliff and don't miss Ruthton County Park. If you're stealthy you can snap off a few photos of the resident goats before they see you and split down the cliffs. From near their escape route under the west fence check out one of the best gorge views: looking west with Ruthton Cove and Ruthton Point in the foreground. The point is private land, in the same family for generations, and before that was home to Native Americans who called it *Polalla Illahee*, or Sand Land. After settlement, it was named Riverside Farms. The sandy beaches and 200 acres of the farmland are gone now, lost to the rising river level behind Bonneville Dam. The family, now in its sixth generation farming the land, grows, presses, ferments, ages and bottles apple and pear cider, selling it locally as Rivercider.

This county park is on the route of the Columbia River Highway, dedicated in 1916 and largely superseded by I-84. The park will eventually be a trailhead for a future section of the Historic Columbia River Highway State Trail, a restoration/recreation of the old highway. The new trail segment westward approximates the route of the original highway by running along the north shoulder of I-84 to an existing stretch of historic highway at Ruthton Point.

Retrace your route to return. Have lunch at one of the brewpubs on Columbia Street seen earlier. Afterward, from Cascade and Second,

turn north on Second and get up on its northbound sidewalk. Before
the I-84 eastbound on-ramp, turn right on the pedestrian path to
the right; it leads under I-84, then crosses the Hood River on the
pedestrian bridge you crossed earlier. Once across, you're near the
History Museum of Hood River on Port Marina Drive. Check it out
if it's open and then go east a short ways to the start.

Adventure 2
Investigating Viento State Park

On the way back to Portland via I-84, stop at Viento State Park, exit
56. To get to the park's wide (in summer) rocky beach, park at the day
use area on the north side of I-84, by the swing set. Walk through lawn
to stairs to a road; cross railroad tracks and continue to a parking area
for windsurfers. A path to the river leads to amazing views: a landslide
on the slopes of 2,948-foot Dog Mountain and, east of it, 3,014-foot
Cook Hill (a less-visited version of popular Dog).

After checking out the beach you can ride a 1-mile segment of
the Historic Columbia River Highway State Trail west to Starvation
Creek Falls. Beginning in September 2016 you can ride another 1.25
miles west from Starvation Creek, to Lindsey Creek, passing Hole in
the Wall Falls on Warren Creek and Cabin Creek Falls. The trail at
Viento starts south of I-84, at the west end of a day use area.

Eat and Drink in Downtown Hood River

Andrew's Pizza and Skylight Theatre Pub. First-run movies. Afternoon and evening show times. 107 Oak St. Movie line: 541-386-1448. Theater: 541-386-4888

Bette's Place Restaurant. Four-decades-same-family-owned diner. Daily 5:30 a.m. to 3 p.m. 416 Oak St. 541-386-1880

Boda's Kitchen. Gourmet deli. Get a box lunch to take on your adventures. Daily 10 a.m. to 7 p.m. 404 Oak St. 541-386-9876

Brian's Pourhouse. Elegant food and drink in a converted home. Eat inside or on the deck. Sunday to Thursday 5 to 10 p.m.; Friday and Saturday to 11 p.m. 606 Oak St. 541-387-4344

Celilo Restaurant and Bar. Seasonal and local food. Daily 11:30 a.m. to 3 p.m., and 5 to 11 p.m. 16 Oak St. 541-386-5710

Dog River Coffee. Serves Stumptown. Weekdays 6 a.m. to 6 p.m.; weekends opens 7 a.m. 411 Oak St. 541-386-4502

Doppio. Espresso, pastries, panini, beer, wine. Daily 7 a.m. to 6 p.m. 310 Oak St. 541-386-3000

Double Mountain Brewery and Tap Room. Great beer and pizza in this friendly, busy place. Kids allowed until 9 p.m. Daily 11 a.m. to 10 p.m.; Friday and Saturday to 11 p.m. 8 Fourth St. 541-387-0042

El Rio Burrito Bar. Traditional and fusion burritos. Daily 10 a.m. to 9 p.m. 112 Oak St. 541-436-0099

Full Sail Brewing. Seasonal, local food to complement the beer. Come for lunch and stay for a free brewery tour. Kids okay with parent. Daily 11 a.m. to 9 p.m. 506 Columbia St. 541-386-2247

Ground Coffee. Plus breakfast sandwiches, pastries, smoothies, panini, soup, sandwiches, beer, wine. 12 Oak St. Daily 6 a.m. to 6 p.m.; Friday and Saturday to 7 p.m. 541-386-4442

Horse and Hound British Pub. Tuesday to Sunday 11 a.m. to 11 p.m. 403 Oak St. 541-386-2099

Knead. Pastries, rustic tarts, cinnamon rolls, fougasse (pretzel bread), sandwiches. Tuesday to Saturday 8 a.m. to 5:30 p.m. 102 Fifth St. 541-436-2866

Mike's Ice Cream. Sit on the lawn and enjoy your scoops. Daily 11 a.m. to 11 p.m. 504B Oak. 541-386-6260

River Daze Cafe. Baked-in-house breads and sweets; locally sourced meats and vegetables. Monday to Friday 7:30 a.m. to 3:30 p.m.; Saturday and Sunday 8:30 a.m. to 3:30 p.m. 202D Cascade Ave.

Romul's. Old world Italian. Daily 4 p.m. to close. 315 Oak St. 541-436-4444

Sixth Street Bistro. Local brews and locally grown, inventively prepared fare. Outdoor patio. Daily 11:30 a.m. to 9:30 p.m. 509 Cascade Ave. 541-386-5737

Stonehedge Gardens Wine Country Bistro. Not downtown, but in an 1898 home on 7 well-tended acres in the hills near I-84 exit 62. Outdoor seating with fire pit. Daily 5 p.m. to close. 3405 Wine Country Ave. 541-386-3940

The Subterranean. Retro supper club feels just right after a day in the sun amid the superfit. Steaks, burgers. Daily 4:30 p.m. to 9:30 or 10 p.m. 113 Third St. 541-436-4600

Three Rivers Grill. Northwest fare in a repurposed home with a big deck and view. Daily 11 a.m. to 10 p.m. 601 Oak St. 541-386-8883

Trillium Cafe and Bar. Great pub food and service. Happy hour 4 to 6 p.m. Daily 11 to 2:30 a.m. 207 Oak St. 541-308-0800

Vintage Grille (in the Hood River Hotel). Northwest food and martinis. Monday, Wednesday, Thursday 4 to 10 p.m.; Friday to Sunday 11:30 a.m. to 10 p.m. 102 Oak St. 541-288-8264

Eat and Drink in and near the Heights

Egg River Cafe. Big view, organic coffee and eggs. Daily 6 a.m. to 2 p.m. 1313 Oak St. 541-386-1127

Farm Stand in the Gorge. Organic market and deli. Monday to Friday 7 a.m. to 8 p.m.; Saturday 9 a.m. to 8 p.m.; Sunday 9 a.m. to 6 p.m. 1009 12th St. 541-386-4203

Hood River Taqueria. From Jalisco to Hood River. Outdoor seating. Weekdays 9:30 a.m. to 10 p.m.; Friday and Saturday to 11 p.m. 1210 13th St. 541-387-3300

Mesquitery Restaurant and Bar. Old-style steakhouse, complete with Caesar salad. Daily 4:30 to 9 p.m. 1219 12th St. 541-386-2002

Monagon's Pancake House. Family run. Daily 7 a.m. to 3 p.m. Dinner Wednesday to Saturday 3 to 9 p.m. 1301 Belmont St. 541-436-4035

Pine Street Bakery. Breakfast sandwiches, coffee, salads, soups. Daily 7 a.m. to 3 p.m. 1103 12th St. 541-386-1719

Rosauers Supermarket/Huckleberry's Natural Market. Two grocery stores, side by side. Daily 6 to 12 a.m. Hood River Shopping Center: 1867 12th St. 541-386-1119

Ten Speed Coffee Roastery. Good food and coffee next to Dirty Fingers bike repair shop/bar. Daily 7 a.m. to 7 p.m. 1235 State St. 541-386-3165

Thai House. Family-owned. Monday to Friday 11 a.m. to 9 p.m. (closed 2 to 5 p.m.); Saturday 12 to 9 p.m. (closed 2 to 5 p.m.) 1302 13th St. 541-436-0509

Eat and Drink along the Waterfront

Pfriem Family Brewers. Good food and beer. Weekdays 11:30 a.m. to 9 p.m.; Friday and Saturday to 10 p.m. 707 Portway Ave., Suite 101. 541-321-0490

Solstice Wood Fire Cafe and Bar. Pizza, beer, wine, cocktails. Happy hour weekdays: 2 to 5 p.m.; Wednesday to Monday 11:30 a.m. to 9 p.m.; Friday and Saturday to 10 p.m. 501 Portway Ave. 541-436-0800

Shop in Downtown Hood River

Ananas Boutique. Custom and off-the-rack women's clothes. Summer daily 10 a.m. to 5 p.m.; Sunday to 6 p.m. 206 Oak St. 541-386-1116

Apland Jewelers. Craftsmen jewelers design and make fine jewelry here. Tuesday to Friday 10 a.m. to 5:30 p.m.; Saturday to 5 p.m. 216 Oak St. 541-386-3977

Art on Oak. Artist-owned gallery: paintings, ceramics, fiber and jewelry. Daily 10 a.m. to 6 p.m. 210 Oak St. 541-436-4472

ArtiFacts: Good Books and Bad Art. Used and new books; great selection plus gifts and bumper stickers. Daily 10 a.m. to 6 p.m. 202 Cascade Ave. No phone, no email.

Columbia Art Gallery in the Columbia Center for the Arts. Lush gallery of visual art for sale in renovated American Legion hall that's also home to a theater and classes. May 31 to September 30: daily 11 a.m. to 6 p.m.; October 1 to May 1: Wednesday to Sunday 11 a.m. to 5 p.m. 215 Cascade Ave. 541-387-8877

Dream Street Boutique. Women's clothing. Monday to Friday 10 a.m. to 6 p.m.; Saturday to 5 p.m. 209 Oak St. 541-386-1530

The Enchanted Alpaca. Farm-to-store alpaca and other natural fiber clothing. Daily 10 a.m. to 6 p.m. 314 Oak St. 541-386-1240

Footwise Hood River. Quintessential Northwest styles. Monday to Saturday 10 a.m. to 6 p.m.; Sunday to 5 p.m. 413 Oak St. 541-308-0770

G Williker's Toy Shoppe. Toys to withstand time's test, plus books. Monday to Saturday 10 a.m. to 6 p.m.; Sunday to 5 p.m. 202 Oak St. 541-387-2229

Goodwill on Oak. Better quality retail thriftware, part of Goodwill Industries of the Columbia Willamette's chain of stores. Monday to Saturday 9:30 a.m. to 7 p.m.; Sunday 10 a.m. to 6 p.m. 304 Oak St. 541-308-0513

Gorge Fly Shop. Since 1992, gear plus info on where to fish, and local guides. Monday to Saturday 9:30 a.m. to 6 p.m.; Sunday 10 a.m. to 4 p.m. 201 Oak St. 541-386-6977

Gorge Dog. Gifts and gear for your BFF. Monday to Saturday 10 a.m. to 6 p.m.; Sunday to 5 p.m. 412 Oak St. 541-387-3996

Hood River Jewelers. Fine jewelry. Monday to Saturday 10 a.m. to 5 p.m. 415 Oak St. 541-386-6440

Hood River Stationers. Cards, gifts and art kits and supplies. Monday to Friday 10 a.m. to 6 p.m.; Saturday 10 a.m. to 5 p.m.; Sunday 11 a.m. to 4 p.m. 213 Oak St. 541-386-2344

Knot Another Hat. Yarn, gift kits and craft supplies. Tuesday to Sunday 11 a.m. to 5:30 p.m. 11 Third St., No. 103. 541-308-0002

Made in the Gorge Artists' Cooperative. Pottery, metal arts, body products, jewelry, paintings and more. Daily 10 a.m. to 5 p.m. 108 Oak St. 541-386-2830

Melika Activewear. Oregon-made (Pistil, Melika and Outside Baby) plus other women's active, casual and casual business-wear brands. Also: clothes for girls and babies. Monday to Saturday 10 a.m. to 6 p.m.; Sunday 11 a.m. to 5 p.m. 316 Oak St. 541-387-4400

Mystic Mud Studio. Local pottery inspired by the valley's produce. 104 Oak St. Call for hours: 541-386-6463. Studio line: 541-354-1238

Pacifica Gifts. Greeting cards, soaps and gifts. Monday to Saturday 10 a.m. to 5 p.m.; Sunday to 4 p.m. 410 Oak St. 541-490-1957

Parts + Labour. Casual, elegant women's clothes. Monday to Saturday 10 a.m. to 6 p.m.; Sunday 11 a.m. to 5 p.m. 311 Oak St. 541-387-2787

Plenty. Women's clothes and beauty products. Closed Wednesday. Monday to Saturday 11 a.m. to 6 p.m.; Sunday 12 to 5 p.m. 310 Oak St., Suite 102. 541-386-5000

Shortt Supply. Outdoor wear and running gear. Monday to Friday 10 a.m. to 6 p.m.; Saturday 10 a.m. to 5 p.m.; Sunday 11 a.m. to 4 p.m. 116 Oak St. 541-386-5474

Silverado Jewelry Gallery. Monday to Saturday 10 a.m. to 6 p.m.; Sunday 11 a.m. to 5 p.m. 310 Oak St. 541-386-7642

The Wearhouse: Carhartt Store. Tough, American-made clothes; kids' clothes too. Monday to Friday 10 a.m. to 6 p.m.; Saturday 10 a.m. to 5 p.m.; Sunday 11 a.m. to 4 p.m. 208 Oak St. 541-386-9010

Twiggs. Nature-styled jewelry, home goods and gifts. Monday to Saturday 10 a.m. to 6 p.m.; Sunday 11 a.m. to 4 p.m. 305 Oak St. 541-386-6188

Waucoma Bookstore. Indie bookstore, since 1976. Gifts and toys too. Monday to Friday 10 a.m. to 6 p.m.; Sunday 9:30 a.m. to 6 p.m. 212 Oak St. 541-386-5353

Shop along Day 2's Scenic Drive through the Hood River Valley

Cascade Alpacas of Oregon and Foothills Yarn and Fiber. June 1 to end of October: daily 11 a.m. to 5 p.m. Late October to Christmas: Friday to Sunday 11 a.m. to 4 p.m. 4207 Sylvester Drive. 541-354-3542

Cody Orchards Farm Stand. Conventional and organic produce. March or April to late October: Wednesday to Sunday 10 a.m. to 6 p.m.; Sunday 12 to 5 p.m.; Monday 10 a.m. to 5 p.m. Other months: available produce set out on honor system. 3475 Graves Road. 541-354-1085

The Fruit Company. Buy excess inventory of fruit, fruit candies, cheese, nuts and more at discounted prices. Friday 8 a.m. to 2 p.m. 2900 Van Horn Drive. 541-387-3100 or 800-387-3100

Glassometry Studios. Blown art glass: functional and sculptural, glass sinks, chandeliers and sconces, cast glass. Friday to Sunday 11 a.m. to 5 p.m. 3015 Lower Mill Drive. 541-354-3015

Hood River Lavender Farms. 75 varieties, organically grown. U-pick. May 1 to October 1: Wednesday to Saturday 10 a.m. to 5 p.m.; Sunday 11 a.m. to 5 p.m. 3801 Straight Hill Road. 541-354-9917

The Old Trunk. Antiques, ice cream, coffee, candy, produce. May to November: daily 10 a.m. to 5:30 p.m. 2958 Dee Highway. 541-354-1181

Riversong Sanctuary. Organic, herbal beauty products. Late May to early September: Wednesday to Sunday 11 a.m. to 6 p.m. 3226 Dee Highway. 541-354-9909

Smiley's Red Barn. Produce, jams, replicas of old fruit-packing labels, snacks. Mid June through October: daily 10 a.m. to 6 p.m. 2965 Ehrck Hill Road. 541-386-5989

Discover and Learn in Hood River

Columbia River Gorge National Scenic Area. Administrative office for the U.S. Forest Service–managed scenic area also sells maps and other useful items. Monday to Friday 8 a.m. to 4:30 p.m. 902 Wasco Ave., Suite 200. 541-308-1700

History Museum of Hood River. Local stories and artifacts. Monday to Saturday 11 a.m. to 4 p.m. Call for winter hours. 300 E Port Marina Drive. 541-386-6772

Hood River County Chamber of Commerce. City and county maps and tourist info. Monday to Friday 9 a.m. to 4 p.m. 720 E Port Marina Drive. 541-386-2000

WAAAM: Western Antique Aeroplane and Automobile Museum. Amazing collection of machines from the pre-plastics era. Daily 9 a.m. to 5 p.m. 1600 Air Museum Road. 541-308-1600

Taste the Wine, Spirits and Cider in and around Hood River

Camp 1805 Distillery and Tasting Room. See the still, have a cocktail and small plate, and take a bottle home with you. Monday to Thursday 3 to 9 p.m.; Friday and Saturday 1 to 10 p.m.; Sunday 1 to 9 p.m. 501 Portway Ave. 541-386-1805

Fox Tail Cider. Daily 11 a.m. to 6 p.m. 2965 Ehrck Hill Road. 541-716-0093

Hood River Distillers. Daily 12 to 6 p.m. 304B Oak St. 541-386-1588, ext. 234

Mount Hood Winery. March to November: daily 11 a.m. to 5 p.m. 2882 Van Horn Drive. 541-386-8333

Pheasant Valley Winery. Thursday to Monday 11 a.m. to 5 p.m. 3890 Acree Drive. 866-357-9463

Stoltz Winery Tasting Room. Wednesday to Saturday 12 to 6 p.m.; Sunday to 5 p.m. 514 State St. 541-716-1330

Wy'East Vineyards. Closed Thanksgiving to mid-February. Otherwise: daily 11 a.m. or 12 p.m. to 5 p.m. 3189 OR 35. 541-386-1277

Rent Bikes in Hood River

Discover Bicycles. Mountain, road and hybrid bikes; women-specific bikes, bikes for older kids plus third wheels. Monday to Saturday 10 a.m. to 6 p.m.; Sunday to 5 p.m. 210 State St. 541-386-4820

Mountain View Cycles. Road and mountain bikes, including kids' bikes and trailers. Reserve early. Sunday 9 a.m. to 5 p.m.; Monday and Thursday 10 a.m. to 6 p.m.; Friday and Saturday 9 a.m. to 6 p.m. 205 Oak St. 541-386-2453

Stay in Hood River

Best Western Plus Hood River Inn. Only hotel in town with a river beach. Outdoor, riverside pool, great view of the Columbia and Hood River Bridge. Pay a bit more for a riverside room. 1108 E Marina Way. 541-386-2200 or 800-828-7873 [$$ to $$$$]

Columbia Cliff Villas Hotel. This luxury suite hotel is a newer version of the Columbia Gorge Hotel to its west. Stay here for more modern rooms, and still enjoy the gardens and grounds of the older hotel. Pay extra for riverside rooms and avoid highway noise. 3880 Westcliff Drive. 866-912-8366 [$$$$]

Columbia Gorge Hotel. 39-room historic Italian–villa style hotel on cliffs above the river. From the grounds, Wah Gwin Gwin Falls drop 208 feet to the river. Pay $20 more for a riverside room; you'll hear the trains at the base of the cliff but the views are worth it. The garden rooms face the din of I-84. Room 339: river and waterfall view. 4000 Westcliff Drive. 541-386-5566 or 800-345-1921 [$$$]

Comfort Suites. Industrial/suburban setting off the freeway. 2625 Cascade Ave. 541-308-1000 [$$$]

Hood River B n B. Three blocks from downtown. Cheerful, basic and close to everything. 918 Oak St. 541-387-2997 [$$ to $$$]

Hood River Hotel. Vintage, railroad-era hotel near downtown restaurants and shops. 102 Oak St. 541-386-1900 [$$ to $$$]

Inn at the Gorge. Big, inviting porches in a friendly looking 1908 Colonial Revival/Craftsman home. Walk to shopping and restaurants. 1113 Eugene St. 541-386-4429 or 877-852-2385 [$$$]

Oak Street Hotel. Century-old boutique hotel, with nine rooms, walkable to downtown's shops and restaurants. 610 Oak St. 541-386-3845 [$$$]

Riverview Lodge. Budget motel, clean and quiet, a few blocks west of walkable area. Discounted lift tickets to Meadows. 1505 Oak St. 541-386-8719 [$$]

Sakura Ridge. Bed and breakfasts don't get better than this; 72 acres of orchard trees, gardens, organic vegetables and fruits, and frolicking lambs with Mount Hood as backdrop. Two-night minimum. 5601 York Hill Road. 541-386-2636 or 877-472-5872 [$$$ to $$$$]

Sunset Motel. Same comment as for Comfort Suites. 2300 Cascade Ave. 541-386-6322 [$$]

Vagabond Lodge. Third-generation, family run motel on 5.5 clifftop acres. Big lawn, rock outcrops and views. Rooms 30 to 37 are closest to the cliff and views. Ask about rafting and windsurfing discounts. Also: secluded cliff-front platform tents, with beds and electricity June to September; these have an outdoor solar shower and portable toilet. 4070 Westcliff Drive. 541-386-2992 [$$ to $$$$]

Vineyard View Bed and Breakfast. Four rooms in a vineyard close to Post Canyon trails. 4240 Post Canyon Drive. [$$$]

Camp in and around Hood River

Tucker County Park. No-reservation camping along the Hood River, far from freeways or trains. RV and tent sites, some on the river. 2440 Dee Highway. 541-386-4477 [$]

Viento State Park. Has 56 woodsy sites north of I-84, some are close to the river; others look out on I-84. South of I-84 are 18 tent sites; some back to Viento Creek, but road sounds pervade. May through October. Exit 56. Park office: 541-374-8811. Reservations: 800-452-5681 [$]

Lodging Cost Key			
$	$$	$$$	$$$$
<$50	$51 to $99	$100 to $200	>$200

Tracks in the sand along the Hood River

TOUR
11

CASCADE LOCKS AND THE HISTORIC COLUMBIA RIVER HIGHWAY STATE TRAIL

OREGON

As part of this tour in the heart of the gorge, you bike a 7-mile section of the Historic Columbia River Highway State Trail. Along the way, stop to watch salmon spawn in fall, pick a waterfall for a short hike, get incredible views from the old highway and visit sturgeon at Bonneville Dam. Spend the night next to the gorge's most picturesque bridge, and walk down the street to good beer and food. On day two, choose your adventure: mountain biking the Easy CLIMB trail, hiking to Dry Creek Falls or the falls along Eagle Creek, or taking an easy bike cruise out to Wyeth with gallery shopping afterward along WaNaPa Street.

In summer, waterfalls here are less crowded than those further west; and, when Portland bakes and the eastern gorge sears, this is a cool destination with its shady, tree-filled canyons and many chances to get wet in a waterfall.

In autumn, bigleaf maples turn golden and salmon spawn in the creeks. This is the wettest part of the gorge, so in winter and spring watch the forecast; come during clear, crisp weather for a treat: creeks and waterfalls at full bore. This is when the gorge is at its most beautiful: crowds are gone and the greenery is lush and brilliant.

You may want to bring bikes, bike locks and a cooler in fall so you can bring back fish from Native Americans selling out of their coolers at the base of the Bridge of the Gods or behind Thunder Island Brewing. Year-round, you can buy fish caught by tribal fishers from Brigham Fish Market.

Adventure 1
Biking the Historic Columbia River Highway State Trail

Leave Portland early for the 44-mile, 45-minute drive out I-84. You have a full day of exploring ahead. Even if you're not an avid biker, this spectacular ride is worth doing, especially because there are no cars to contend with. You can take it at a meandering pace, with many stops for exploring and taking in views. Bring food and water. The only food options are packaged snacks and coffee at the Bonneville Dam gift shop.

Ride the entire 7 miles from Cascade Locks to McCord Creek, or turn back at any point. Stop often. Expect 90 minutes to four hours, depending on how fast you ride and how often you stop to investigate sites. The trail gains and loses about 100 feet of elevation several times over the route, with a gentle grade never more than 8 percent. Find restrooms at Eagle Creek and Bonneville Dam.

Leave the freeway at exit 44 and park at the Cascades Lock trailhead under the Bridge of the Gods. This pretty 1926 bridge was built at the spot where the Columbia squeezes itself through into a narrow channel. The bridge, part of the Pacific Crest Trail, is named for the Native American tale of the rock bridge that spanned and dammed the river here after a great landslide roared down from Table Mountain on the Washington shore. A walk or bike across the bridge offers big thrills and views. (See Tour 3.)

The Historic Columbia River Highway State Trail heads west from the bridge, and at first parallels the freeway on-ramp, but soon enters dappled forest. Pass through a tunnel under I-84, built in 1998 using the same stonework style as the historic highway. Now on the south side of I-84 you'll see a signpost for Gorge Trail 400. The trail runs from Angel's Rest on its west end to Wyeth Campground, sometimes using the old highway.

One of many view stops along the state trail

Stop at the first of many century-old bridges, this one built in 1915 over Ruckel Creek. The 46-foot falls are easy to see but easy to miss too. Look over the short but stout bridge to the right.

The next creek is famous Eagle Creek, one of the earliest developed gorge recreation areas. In 1915, the new Columbia River Highway had become so popular for auto-touring that the U.S. Forest Service created its first-ever public campground here.

The first stop at Eagle Creek is the Cascade Hatchery. It was built in the late 1950s on the site of a roadhouse lodge and cabins that operated from 1915 to 1937. Take a self-guided tour, 7:30 a.m. to 4 p.m., of the coho salmon ponds. Each year, millions of fingerlings raised for the Umatilla, Nez Perce and Yakama tribes leave here by tanker truck to be released in other creeks. Other fingerlings are trucked to the Oxbow hatchery in Cascade Locks to be released into Herman Creek. A display on the east side of the building has good information on salmon.

In fall Eagle Creek is an excellent place to watch Chinook salmon. After living in the Pacific Ocean, the fish return to spawn and die in

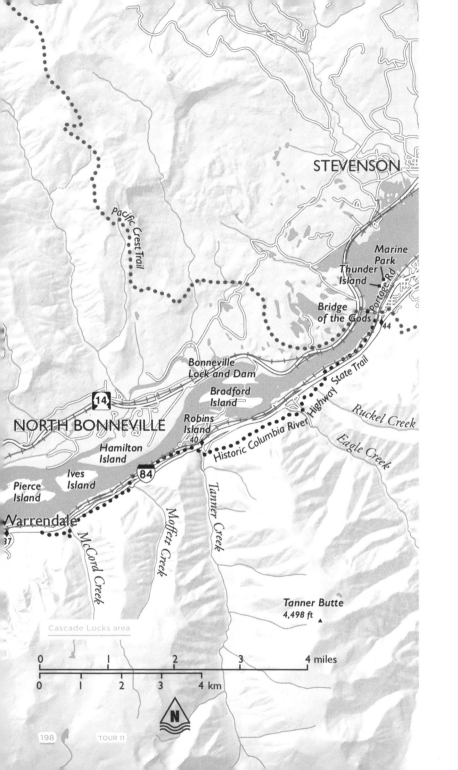

STEVENSON

Pacific Crest Trail

Marine
Park

Thunder
Island

Portage Rd

Bridge
of the Gods

44

Bonneville
Lock and Dam

Bradford
Island

Historic Columbia River Highway State Trail

Ruckel Creek

14

Robins
Island

Eagle Creek

NORTH BONNEVILLE

40

Historic Columbia River Highway State Trail

Hamilton
Island

Ives
Island

84

Tanner Creek

Pierce
Island

Warrendale

McCord Creek

Moffett Creek

37

Tanner Butte
4,498 ft

Cascade Locks area

0   1   2   3   4 miles

0   1   2   3   4 km

N

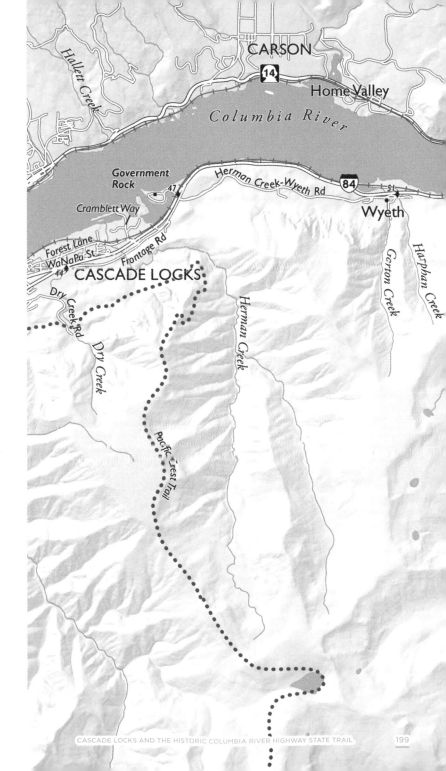

the stream they were born in. Watch them spawn from a charming fish-viewing observatory built into the old highway on the west bank, or from vantage points along the creekside road. Viewing is best where the water riffles over rocks. The female swishes her tail above the gravel to create a redd, or nest site. With the male beside her, she releases eggs and he releases milt (sperm). The fertilized eggs attach to gravel in the redd, and the female swims upstream and fans her tail to cover the eggs with more gravel. She protects the redd for a few days; the male leaves to find other females. Both soon die. Their bodies become food for eagles and scavengers.

The bridge over Eagle Creek is one of the few bridges on the historic highway made of local stone rather than concrete.

Bike upstream on the road along Eagle Creek to the often-jammed parking area at the Eagle Creek Trailhead. If you fancy a hike, lock your bike to something sturdy. (See the hike description, page 208.) To the left as you ride up to the trailhead are old campsites with stone grills scattered on the hillside, and a large old group camp building, work of the Civilian Conservation Corps (CCC) in the 1930s. The current campground is a half-mile ride uphill. It has old growth firs, but it's noisy from I-84.

Don't miss this last Eagle Creek nugget: bike downstream on the road signed "dead end." Ride under I-84, along the creek and to the

A common Eagle Creek sight on fall weekdays:
school kids learning about the salmon life cycle

gate for the Eagle Creek Overlook. It's now a group campground, so if the gate's open, stay away to give campers their privacy. If the gate's shut, proceed on: that means no one is using the group campsite. Rangers gate the road because they don't want hikers parking here for the Eagle Creek Trail. Ride the road to the top or take a foot trail that begins near the mouth of Eagle Creek. Up on the bluff the Northwest-style shelter and stonework were built by the CCC in the 1930s as an observation overlook of Bonneville Dam, then under construction. It feels surprisingly remote. East of the shelter, a trail downhill toward the river leads to an overlook with views of Native American fishing scaffolds and the slide scarps of Table Mountain, Red Bluffs and Greenleaf Peak. Land that slid off those peaks around 1700 formed the Bonneville Landslide that blocked the Columbia and created the Cascades of the Columbia. You can also see, off the Washington shore, Powerhouse 2, built in the 1970s at Bonneville Dam. You might also see the sternwheeler churn by close to shore here.

From the Overlook come back to where the Historic Columbia River Highway State Trail crosses Eagle Creek. Head west, riding against traffic on the I-84 eastbound exit ramp a short way; then follow arrows in the pavement that direct you left, off the exit ramp and back on the trail. Come to a staircase, perhaps built to connect the newer version of the road (built in the 1930s, now I-84), to the old highway and its viewpoints. Carry your bike or roll it up the staircase using the gutter. At the top of the stairs you're on the state trail again.

Now comes a very interesting segment: along the white-railinged section, look over and down to the Toothrock Tunnel. It was completed in 1932 when it was clear the Columbia River Highway—today's trail—was not big enough for increasing traffic loads. For years, traffic in the tunnel was two-way. Westbound lanes of I-84 weren't built until the 1960s. Keep going and you're riding over the tunnel itself. Don't miss pullouts for views of the slide, dam and lock (the leftmost channel in the dam infrastructure), plus the pillar that is Beacon Rock on the Washington shore. Below you, on I-84 westbound, drivers zoom past, this incredible scenery obscured by speed.

A mile or so west of Eagle Creek, turn right to go north, biking under I-84 to **Bonneville Lock and Dam**, a National Historic Landmark. Here there are cars, but slow ones. The landscaping and architecture are beautiful and it's the only place on the route to get a snack (at the gift shop). Stop at the fish-rearing ponds, and at pretty ponds where you can watch enormous sturgeon and feed rainbow trout. You can bike out to Robins Island, which is not too special, but you can't bike or

Rusting water pipe on the trail to Upper McCord Creek Falls

walk to the Visitor Center on Bradford Island. Only visitors in cars are allowed past the checkpoint. To see the mouth of Tanner Creek, ride past the fish-rearing ponds, and go left on the roadway along the Columbia. As that road curves inland watch for and take a right turn to a bridge across Tanner Creek. Stop at a parking area at its mouth. Here the Columbia narrows; all fish heading upriver pass by, making for prime fishing. The map in Tour 2, page 45, shows roads at the dam in more detail.

Come back to the historic highway trail. If you want a spectacular hike, you'll be happy with Wahclella Falls on Tanner Creek. It's 0.9 mile one way to the two-tiered falls (48 and 79 feet). The trail gains only 300 feet of elevation. You can bike as far as the small dam on Tanner Creek, then walk. In spring, sheet-like Munra Falls near the start of the trail is at its best. The trail loops at the end and comes back via the same path.

Back on the main biking trail, go west. Cross the Tanner Creek Bridge, with views of the especially pretty creek. After that the trail is not so pretty except for some excellent viewpoints. At one viewpoint you can see Hamilton Island, the large, largely treeless island in the river. Its strangely smooth hump is landfill from powerhouse construction. Downstream is Ives Island. At low water you can walk to it from Hamilton. The water spewing from a concrete pipe is part of a fish hatchery; its spray prevents birds from picking off fish as they're released.

Cross Moffett Creek on its impressive bridge, a 205-foot flat arch built in 1915. Cross under I-84 and bike to the gleaming white McCord Creek Bridge, completed in 2013. A short distance beyond is the John B. Yeon Trailhead. It's your turnaround point. Here, hike 0.8 mile to 213-foot Elowah Falls on McCord Creek or 1.1 miles to Upper McCord Creek Falls, a 64-foot twin fall formation. Upper McCord is excellent if you like looking at industrial artifacts being reclaimed by nature. The water in the creek had been harnessed to run a pulp mill on the river, and plenty of old hardware remains. Find a map at gorgefriends.org.

Return to Cascade Locks via the same route.

Adventure 2
Exploring Cascade Locks National Historic Site

DAY
1

After your ride, come back to Cascade Locks and eat locally caught salmon or clam chowder at **Brigham Fish Market**; it's the first brick-and-mortar fish shop in the gorge owned by tribal fishers. Or bike down to **Thunder Island Brewing**. If the weather is fine, sit on its deck and enjoy the gorgeous scenery: across the river are the cliffs of Greenleaf Peak and Table Mountain. In front of you are the above-water parts of the nineteenth-century Cascade Locks, the next stop.

After you eat, head to **Cascade Locks Marine Park**, on the lower level of town. (See the Tour 3 map, page 54 for more detail on the streets of Cascade Locks.) To get to the marine park, travel east on WaNaPa Street. Just past **East Wind Drive-In**, go left on Portage Road, passing under the railroad tracks to enter the park. Once inside, go straight then left to head to the locks. Park near the pedestrian bridge to Thunder Island.

The Cascade Locks had two 46-foot-long chambers, most of which are now submerged, but their above-water remnants are fascinating to explore. While you're looking at the canal and what's visible of the locks, here's a short explanation: On a river, locks are like a smooth set of water stair steps that enable boats to avoid unnavigable stretches such as rapids or waterfalls. When traveling up the Columbia, a boat would enter the lock canal through the lowest of three gates, which put it in the lower chamber. The gate would shut, and the boat would sit in the placid water as the chamber slowly flooded. When the lower chamber's water level rose to the level in the upper chamber, the middle gate opened and the boat would move smoothly into the upper chamber. The middle and upper gates would then close and the process repeat. When the water level in the upper chamber rose to the level of

The Great Cascades of the Columbia

The Columbia River has been vital to humans for over 10,000 years in part because it offers the only nearly sea-level passage through the Cascade Mountains. But in several places in the gorge, nature blocked that passage with major obstacles such as the Cascades of the Columbia. It was a series of rapids formed when part of Table Mountain collapsed into the river. After being temporarily dammed by the slide's boulders, soil, trees and gravel, the river began chewing through the slide debris, carrying much of it downstream. The rock remaining in the river was named the Great Cascades of the Columbia by early white explorers. This series of whitewater stretched from the Lower Cascades (Bradford Island, now the location of Bonneville Dam) to the Upper Cascades, at today's Cascades Locks. The name "the Great Cascades" is the origin of the name for the surrounding Cascade Mountains, a term used by botanist David Douglas in the 1820s.

Because the Cascades were an obstacle to river travel, Native Americans and early explorers and pioneers portaged around them on footpaths. A portage road in the 1850s and a portage railway in 1862 made shipping and travel on the river progressively easier. Then, in 1878, the Army Corps of Engineers, in one of its first waterworks in the Pacific Northwest, began building a canal and locks at the Cascades. Construction was challenging: it wasn't until 1896 that the first steamboat passed through. And, by the time the locks opened, the Cascades had already been circumvented via the railroad. Beginning in 1883, it gave people and goods an easier alternative to river travel. Still, the locks were a vital transportation link that prevented the railroad from developing a monopoly on freight and passenger traffic. In 1906 the locks saw their peak use: 65,556 passengers on two round-trip steamboat trips per day between Portland and The Dalles.

the river upstream of it, the uppermost gate opened and the boat proceeded out of the lock canal and into the river. Traveling downriver, the process was reversed.

You can see the locations of the lock chamber gates from near the footbridge to Thunder Island. They are the curved indentations in the wall. You can also tell where the gates were because each one lined up with a corresponding lock-tender's house, which remain in the park. The gates were removed in 1953, 15 years after the locks became submerged.

The chambers at Cascade Locks are handcrafted of basalt quarried from the site and nearby. Stonecutters were recruited from Italy for the task. At times up to 100 men cut the rock in huge stone-working sheds on land that is now the Marine Park's lawn. The staircases that today disappear into the water lead to lower walls that people would promenade along as they watched boat traffic in the lock chambers.

Walk across the footbridge, built in 1969, to Thunder Island and explore the path along its north shore. Before the dam flooded the Cascades, you would have been looking out at whitewater here. In the 1880s much of the island was topped with rock removed during excavation of the lock canal. In 1901, trees were planted to make Thunder Island more park-like. The island's east and south slopes are sheathed in hand-carved basalt blocks from the island's days as the north wall of the lock canal.

From the island, return to the park. The entire park area, situated on a flat bench of land below the town level, was a U.S. Army reservation during the lock's operating years. The supervisor was granted the eastern half of the reservation; his grand home was

The locks at Cascade Locks, repurposed for Indian fishing platforms

surrounded by flower and vegetable gardens, a pasture for the family cow, a chicken yard, pond, privacy hedges, fruit trees and several outbuildings. Only a lilac, maples and white oak remain from that era. The hawthorn hedge along the rail tracks near the cougar sculpture dates from 1901. The west end of the reservation was for the workers; on it are the three lock-tenders' homes, all built in 1906. They're good examples of the military architecture common in early twentieth century America.

The **Cascade Locks Historical Museum** is in the middle lock-tender house. Next to it is the Oregon Pony, the steam engine on the portage rail line that operated along the rapids beginning in 1862.

At the east end of the park is the **Port of Cascade Locks Visitor Center**, where the sternwheeler *Columbia Gorge* and cruise ships dock. A marina and sandy river beach are to its east. Look for Sacagawea, her baby Pomp and the big dog Seaman, plus a cougar ready to pounce; all are the work of local sculptor Heather Soderberg.

After exploring Marine Park, come back to WaNaPa Street. Check into your hotel. For a view so fine you'll have to drag yourself out for dinner, stay at the **Best Western Plus** and get a riverfront room. Walk to dinner at **Cascade Locks Ale House**.

Adventure 1
Biking, hiking or dam-touring

Eat breakfast at **Bridgeside Family Dining**, which has some of the best views in the gorge. Then take your pick of these hike and bike options:

Gallery-shopping and biking to Gorton Creek Falls

On WaNaPa Street, find local art and crafts at **Lorang Fine Art, Gifts and Antiques** and at **Soderberg Studio and Bronze Works**. If they're not open before your ride to Gorton Creek, visit them on the way back into town.

The ride is 8 miles, one way, on flat to rolling roads with little traffic. From downtown, head east on WaNaPa Street and Forest Lane. (See pages 54 and 198 for maps.) Cross over I-84, then turn left on Frontage Road. Pass Herman Creek Campground (closed) and trailhead. The elegant old park building dates from 1936; it's now a maintenance shed.

From Frontage Road, turn right on Herman Creek Road and stay on it to **Wyeth Campground**, a camp for conscientious objectors during World War II. Instead of combat, men served by building trails and planting trees. Their meticulous stonework still lines the roadways. If it's summer, lock your bike and do the Gorton Creek Falls hike and scramble—a very fun hike for kids. The creek is on the west side of the campground. Follow a trail about 0.6 mile into its canyon. Then on a narrow scramble path on the east bank, head up to the falls. Retrace your steps out of the canyon. Northwest Forest Pass required.

After the hike to the falls, travel west on Herman Creek Road. At its junction with Frontage Road, bike under I-84 toward the Columbia where you can hike around and picnic on castlelike Government Rock, a 32-acre former rock quarry with a grassy mesa on top and huge views. In 1999, Confederated Tribes of Warm Springs purchased the land from Cascade Locks and announced plans to build an off-reservation casino here. In 2013 after years of plans, studies, lobbying and contentious negotiations, the plans were dropped.

After leaving Government Rock, go west on Frontage Road. Stay on it past its intersection with Forest Lane. Pass a lovely pond and follow Frontage Road as it passes under I-84, where it becomes

An Arizonan soaking up the green at Gorton Creek Falls

WaNaPa Street. Continue west, stopping at the galleries before you return to the start.

Biking the Cascade Locks Easy CLIMB Trail

The CLIMB (Cascade Locks International Mountain Bike Trail) is a single-track trail that offers two miles of fun for beginners with beach stops, less than 200 feet of climbing and views of the Oregon cliffs. To get there, from the Bridge of the Gods, bike WaNaPa Street about 1 mile east. Go left on Forest Lane. Stay on it 1.8 miles then turn left on Cramblett Way and right at the first street. The trail begins at the dead-end.

Hiking the Pacific Crest Trail to Dry Creek Falls

This 4-mile morning hike wakes you up nicely with about 700 feet of elevation gain. If you read or watched *Wild*, you'll doubly appreciate this lovely hike. Download more detailed trail directions before you go; see gorgefriends.org. Start at the Bridge of the Gods Trailhead parking area (Northwest Forest Pass required). This trailhead for the Pacific Crest Trail (PCT) is near the tollbooth. Take the PCT, cross under I-84 then walk on a gravel road a short distance. Where Gorge Trail 400 comes in, turn left to follow the PCT.

In a mile, turn right on a road and walk it until you see the sign on the left to pick up the PCT again. In about another mile come to a gravel road (Dry Creek Road). Turn right and walk to the falls. Water from Dry Creek was used from 1896 to 1937 to operate the lock gates.

To return, stay on Dry Creek Road as it descends to town. At its end at Ruckel Street, turn left, go under I-84 and mosey northwest on city streets toward **East Wind Drive-In** for ice cream or espresso. Walk west on WaNaPa to return to the start.

Hiking Eagle Creek and its many waterfalls

Depending on how far you hike into the canyon, this out-and-back trail can be a short afternoon jaunt or an all-day hike. The trail, dynamited out of basalt cliffs in the early 1900s, has steep drop-offs that have claimed the lives of more than a few off-leash dogs. Cable railings bolted to the wall are a welcome sight in places. Metlako Falls is the first major falls, an 82-foot drop, about 1.5 miles in off a side trail. Along with other falls on the creek, it's popular with law-breaking kayakers when the water is running high. At 1.7 miles in, get out your camera for Punchbowl Falls, a 36-foot drop. A hike to it has 500 feet of elevation gain. Tunnel Falls, with a 165-foot drop is 6 miles in.

A hike to it has 1,640 feet of elevation gain. The Forest Service dynamited the cliff behind the falls, creating the tunnel for walkers. For trail details see oregonhikers.org.

Access Eagle Creek by car from I-84 exit 41, eastbound only, or by biking on the Historic Columbia River Highway State Trail. If you're westbound on I-84, you'll have to get off at exit 35 and get back on the freeway, this time heading east so you can get to Eagle Creek via exit 41. Northwest Forest Pass required.

Exploring Bonneville Lock and Dam

A few hours at Bonneville Dam should be on every Northwesterner's list; it was the second of 11 dams built on the U.S. sections of the Columbia from 1933 to 1971, and it forever changed the river ecosystem. Built to generate hydroelectric power and improve river transportation, it was dedicated by Franklin and Eleanor Roosevelt in 1937, during the same trip on which they dedicated Mount Hood's Timberline Lodge. Both the dam and the lodge were WPA projects that provided good jobs to hundreds of grateful workers who had been unemployed by the Great Depression. The grounds have the Depression era beauty found in many WPA projects around the nation.

Say hi to Herman the 6-foot white sturgeon—the species is North America's largest freshwater fish—and feed rainbow trout in the ponds, visit the Chinook and coho salmon fish hatchery, take a dam tour, or drive out to the mouth of Tanner Creek in fall to watch the fisherfolk when fall Chinook return to spawn. See Day 1's description for more details on this site. You can also tour Powerhouse 1 from the **Bonneville Lock and Dam Bradford Island Visitors Center** and in summer watch boats lock through at the **Bonneville Lock and Dam Navigation Lock Visitors Center**.

Two-day Columbia River jet boat and bike loop

The river used to be the main transportation route through the gorge. Now a river trip is rather novel and makes for a fun adventure. See "Cruising" in Appendix B for half or full day round trips from Portland or Cascade Locks, plus longer cruises.

A more unusual option is to take your bike on the jet boat *Explorer* and cruise east to Cascade Locks. Spend the night so you can explore around. The next day, bike west on the Historic Columbia River Highway to Troutdale, where you can catch TriMet back into Portland.

From June to September, board the 35-passenger boat at 8:15 a.m. in downtown Portland. Arrive in Cascade Locks around lunchtime and eat at **Locks Waterfront Grill** or **Thunder Island Brewing**, then check into your lodging. Afternoon options: hike from downtown to Dry Creek Falls or bike/hike to Gorton Creek Falls (details earlier in this tour). Explore WaNaPa Street, with its galleries and restaurants, and historic Cascade Locks Marine Park. The next day, tank up at **East Wind Drive In** or **Bridgeside Family Dining** and ride west on the Historic Columbia River Highway State Trail. See Day 1's description and Tour 12 for highlights of the route. There's one big hill—up to Crown Point—but the grade is gentle and the spectacular views on the loop road are something you can't fully enjoy in a car.

Near the end of the 27-mile ride, the historic highway takes you across the Sandy River on a century-old bridge. On the river's east bank is Troutdale's Glen Otto Park. There, board TriMet bus 80 or 81 for a 20-minute ride to Gresham Transit Center. From there ride the MAX Blue Line into Portland.

Reserve a space on the *Explorer* at portlandspirit.com. (See Appendix B.) Let them know you have a bike, as space is limited.

You can rent a bike in Portland, picking it up the night before, from Pedal Bike Tours at 133 SW Second Ave. 503-243-2453.

To hear daily and year-to-date fish passage numbers at Bonneville, call 541-374-4011. The Army Corps of Engineers tallies Chinook, sockeye, coho, steelhead, shad and lamprey, and also lets you know the river temperature. Information is updated daily by 9 a.m., April into November. If numbers are running high, look through the underwater fish-viewing windows to watch the fish climb the ladders that enable them to get around the dam. The best months to watch: June for lamprey, sockeye salmon and American shad, August for steelhead trout and September for Chinook and coho salmon. Sturgeon, unfortunately, cannot pass the dam; in between the river's dams are landlocked populations. In 2008, cameras sent underwater to inspect the dam revealed huge "sturgeon balls" at the foot of Bonneville Dam, in which thousands of fish huddle in a lazily-moving scrum. When salmon are running listen for the barking of California sea lions, which like salmon just as much as we do.

Eat and Drink in Cascade Locks

Bridgeside Family Dining. Formerly Char Burger, this restaurant serves spectacular, best-in-town views of the Bridge of the Gods. Daily 7 a.m. to 9 p.m. 745 WaNaPa St. 541-374-8477

Brigham Fish Market. Eat chowder here, or get smoked or canned salmon or smoked fish dip for later. Monday 12 to 6 p.m.; Tuesday, Thursday, Friday and Saturday 10 a.m. to 6 p.m.; Sunday 10 a.m. to 5 p.m. 681 WaNaPa St. 541-374-9340

Cascade Locks Ale House. Great service and food; huge beer and cider variety. Daily except Tuesday 11 a.m. to 9 p.m. 500 WaNaPa St. 541-374-9310

East Wind Drive-In. Ice cream is an after-hike tradition at the neon penguin. Burgers and breakfast too. Monday to Friday 7 a.m. to 8 p.m.; Saturday and Sunday 7:30 a.m. to 8 p.m. Shorter off-season hours. 395 WaNaPa. 541-374-8380

Jumpin' Jax Java Espresso and Snacks. Longbottom coffee. Monday to Friday 5:30 a.m. to 5 p.m. (closed Tuesday and 12 to 2 p.m. other weekdays); Saturday and Sunday 8 a.m. to 4 p.m. 651 WaNaPa St. 541-374-5420

Locks Waterfront Grill. Part of the Visitor Center at the Port of Cascade Locks Marine Park. May to October: daily 10:30 a.m. to 6 p.m. June and July: to 9 p.m. 541-645-0372

Native American Fish Sales. In the parking lot east of the Bridge of the Gods and at the in-lieu site behind Thunder Island Brewing. Available seasonally. See Appendix C.

Thunder Island Brewing. Beer and good sandwiches made here. Picnic tables overlook the historic locks from the river level. Monday to Wednesday 11 a.m. to 9 p.m.; Thursday to Sunday to 10 p.m. Winter hours vary. 515 Portage Road. 971-231-1599

Shop in Cascade Locks and at Bonneville Dam

Bonneville Lock and Dam Gift Shop. Near the fish-rearing and sturgeon ponds. Daily 9 a.m. to 5 p.m. 70741 NE Sturgeon Lane at Bonneville Dam. I-84, exit 40. 541-374-8447

Lorang Fine Art, Gifts and Antiques. 120 artists represented. Monday to Saturday (closed Tuesday) 10 a.m. to 5 p.m.; Sunday 12 to 5 p.m. From November to April, also closed Wednesday. 360 WaNaPa St., Cascade Locks. 541-374-8007

Soderburg Studio and Bronze Works. Heather Soderberg's father worked in a foundry and by age three she was selling her own sculptures. See her work at Cascade Locks Marine Park. Foundry tours available (call ahead). Monday to Thursday 10 a.m. to 6 p.m. 96 WaNaPa St. 503-869-6459

Discover and Learn in Cascade Locks and at Bonneville Dam

Bonneville Lock and Dam, Bradford Island Visitors Center. Guided tours of Powerhouse 1 (call for times), plus underwater viewing of fish migration, observation deck and displays. Daily 9 a.m. to 5 p.m. I-84, exit 40. 541-374-8820. nwp.usace.army.mil

Bonneville Lock and Dam, Navigation Lock Visitors Center. View boats passing through the lock. Memorial Day to Labor Day: daily 1 to 4 p.m. I-84, exit 40. 541-374-8820. nwp.usace.army.mil

Cascade Locks Historical Museum. Native Americans in the gorge, fish wheels, Cascade rapids, steamboats, locks and more local history. In a historic lock-tender home at the Cascade Locks Marine Park. May to September: Tuesday to Sunday 12 to 5 p.m. 541-374-8535

Port of Cascade Locks Visitor Center. At the east end of Cascade Locks Marine Park, adjacent to Locks Waterfront Grill. May 1 to October 31: daily 10:30 a.m. to 6 p.m. 541-374-8619

Stay in Cascade Locks

Best Western Plus: Columbia River Inn. Right on the river, next to the Bridge of the Gods. Get a riverfront room for stunning views. Walk to restaurants. 735 WaNaPa St. 541-374-8777 [$$ to $$$$]

Bridge of the Gods Motel, Cabins and RV Park. Many rooms with kitchenettes. 630 WaNaPa St. Walk to restaurants. 541-374-8628 [$$$]

Cascade Locks/Portland East KOA. In a forested setting, nine cabins without baths, four cottages with baths. Extra charge for bedding. Also tent and RV sites. March 15 to October 15. 841 NE Forest Lane. 541-374-8668 or 800-562-8698 [$$ to $$$]

Cascade Motel. 11 renovated tourist cabins of varying sizes, circa 1947. A remnant of when this quiet road was part of the old highway. 300 NW Forest Lane. 541-374-8750 [$$ to $$$]

Camp in and around Cascade Locks

Ainsworth State Park. Has 40 full-hookup RV and 6 walk-in tent sites in a 180-acre forested setting. The original picnic facilities and trails were constructed in 1935 by the CCC. Mid-March to the end of October. Reserveamerica.com or 800-452-5687 [$]

Cascade Locks/Portland East KOA. See listing in Stay in Cascade Locks. [$]

Cascade Locks Marine Park. Has 15 year-round sites for RVs and tents in park lawn. Walk to restaurants. Restrooms open March to November. Hookups May through November. Reservations: 541-374-8619 [$]

Eagle Creek Campground. Has 17 sites for tents and small (under 20 feet) RVs. No hookups. May 1 to September 30. Big trees, walk to the Eagle Creek Trail, but be prepared for freeway sounds. I-84, exit 41. Reservations: recreation.gov or 541-308-1700 [$]

Wyeth Campground. Lightly used campground of 14 sites east of Cascade Locks. No hookups or water but it has a restroom. Many trails take off from the campground. On Gorton Creek. I-84, Exit 51. Reservations: recreation.gov or 541-308-1700 [$]

Lodging Cost Key			
$	$$	$$$	$$$$
<$50	$51 to $99	$100 to $200	>$200

TOUR
12

TROUTDALE AND WATERFALLS ALONG THE HISTORIC COLUMBIA RIVER HIGHWAY

OREGON

This two-day tour—which starts only 17 miles from Portland—is a quick, easy mini-vacation. Sure, you can drive there and come home in a day, but staying overnight delivers much more of a getaway, and how often do you get to investigate the sights at a former poor farm? That's what you can do at one of Oregon's most inventive and richly landscaped resorts, **McMenamins Edgefield**, a perfect base for adventures in the greenest part of the Columbia River Gorge National Scenic Area.

The century-old Historic Columbia River Highway takes you through the gorge's Waterfall Alley, with many of the 96 falls on the Oregon side.

The concentration of falls is due to the Ice Age floods that roared down the Columbia River 13,000 to 17,000 years ago. Roiling with ice, trees, rocks, sand and soil, the floodwaters chewed away at the valley's slopes. After the floods had passed, creeks that once dropped down gentle hillsides now plunged off vertical cliffs. There are more waterfalls on Oregon's side than Washington's because the cliffs were carved more steeply in Oregon, and more at the west end of the gorge than the east, due to higher rainfall amounts.

Waterfall Alley—roughly from Latourell Falls to Oneonta Creek—is the most visited section of the 83-mile long Columbia River Gorge National Scenic Area. Summer crowds make biking or driving the old highway not so much of a getaway, as you jockey for parking and share your wilderness experience with hundreds of others. On the plus side: in summer you can play in the creeks, drench yourself under waterfall spray, or swim from beaches. Come in summer but also try this getaway in winter and spring when waterfalls are full of runoff, the forest is lush and the crowds are gone. Fall is also gorgeous, golden with big leaf maples, and peaceful. If you choose a mild-weather window, and bike or drive the old highway, you may have sections of it to yourself, making this unique place even more of a marvel. And if there's a hard freeze, the waterfalls become even more spectacular.

The tour also takes you to the federally designated Wild and Scenic Sandy River in Troutdale, where a short walk from this glacier-fed river takes you to a charming main street stuffed with restaurants, shops, galleries and museums.

You may want to bring bikes and locks, and swimsuits and towels for playing in the Sandy River or in the Columbia at Rooster Rock State Park.

Adventure 1
Scenic touring along the Historic Columbia River Highway

Start with breakfast in Troutdale at the **Troutdale General Store** or **Ristorante di Pompello**. Afterward, drive east on downtown's main street, Columbia River Highway (US 30 on the map).

Just before you cross the Sandy River, pass Glenn Otto Park. Come back at day's end to walk its beaches and trails. Cross the river on an old bridge, and turn right. The historic highway hugs the Sandy's bank for a while and passes a couple of midcentury roadhouses. See Eat and Drink for info.

Climb to Springdale, a pretty rural community with a great-looking old school, and further to another rural community, Corbett. Stop at the **Corbett Country Market** for picnic food or snacks. It's the last food option until Multnomah Falls Lodge.

Pass the sign for **Menucha Retreat and Conference Center**, once a family estate but now owned by Portland's First Presbyterian Church. Its grounds are open only to guests attending a conference or retreat.

Just beyond Menucha, turn left into the Portland Women's Forum overlook, where you get your first panoramic view of the gorge. No matter how many times you see it, the view is shockingly beautiful. Just to the east, Crown Point and its Vista House observatory are more famous but this is where to stand to take the classic photo of Vista House crowning the gorge. The cliffs of Crown Point and the Women's Forum are the head scarp (cliff-edge) of a massive landslide. Rooster Rock, the pillar below at the water's edge, slid down from these cliffs in an upright position.

Beginning in 1912, the clifftop here was home to the Chanticleer Inn. It predated the scenic highway by three years, so visitors took a train from Portland to a station at Rooster Rock. From there, they were driven up the steep hill to the inn. You can hike the old Rooster Rock Wagon Road as far downhill as the train tracks; find it behind the gate in the Women's Forum parking lot. The road's not a top destination but if you're a long-time gorge explorer, it offers fresh angles and scenes. Hike at least to the old iron gate.

The inn burned down in 1930. The Portland Women's Forum bought the land in 1956, and donated it to the state in 1962. The forum was a group who disseminated information on public issues, from local to international. Men who built the historic highway receive a lot of recognition, but it was Gertrude Glutsch Jensen, a forum member, who first lobbied the state legislature to protect Oregon's side of the gorge. When the state created the Columbia River Gorge Commission in 1953, she was named chair and remained so for 16 years. During that time thousands of acres were preserved for public enjoyment. Her work laid the foundation for the Columbia River Gorge National Scenic Area. She died one month after President Ronald Reagan signed it into law in 1986.

From the Women's Forum, consider a detour if the day is clear: drive to Sherrard Point on Larch Mountain to a spectacular viewpoint 4,000 feet above the river. (Northwest Forest Pass required.) The road is snow-free and open generally from May to November. On the historic highway east of the Women's Forum, turn right on Larch Mountain Road. Drive 14 miles to a picnic area and a trailhead for a 0.3-mile

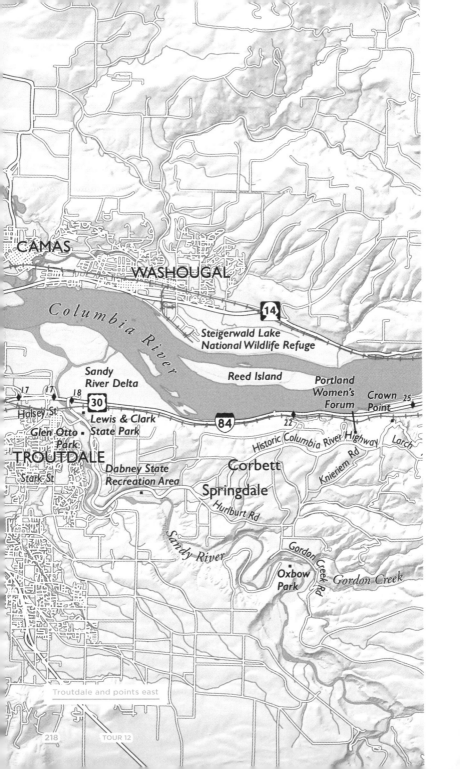

CAMAS

WASHOUGAL

Columbia River

14

Steigerwald Lake
National Wildlife Refuge

Sandy
River Delta

Reed Island

Portland
Women's
Forum

Crown
Point

17 17 18

30

25

Halsey St

84

22

Lewis & Clark
State Park

Historic Columbia River Highway

Larch

Glen Otto
Park

Knieriem Rd

TROUTDALE

Dabney State
Recreation Area

Corbett

Stark St

Springdale

Hurlburt Rd

Sandy River

Gordon Creek Rd

Oxbow
Park

Gordon Creek

Troutdale and points east

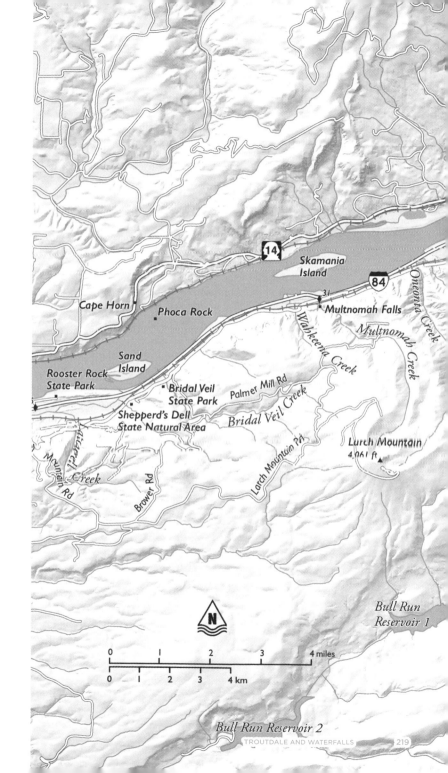

14

Skamania
Island

84

Oneonta Creek

Cape Horn

Phoca Rock

31

Multnomah Falls

Wahkeena Creek

Multnomah Creek

Sand
Island

Rooster Rock
State Park

Bridal Veil
State Park

Palmer Mill Rd

Bridal Veil Creek

Shepperd's Dell
State Natural Area

Larch Mountain Rd

Larch Mountain
4,061 ft

Latourell Creek

Mountain Rd

Brower Rd

*Bull Run
Reservoir 1*

N

0   1   2   3   4 miles

0   1   2   3   4 km

Bull Run Reservoir 2

Historic Columbia River Highway

paved (with stairs) trail to an observation platform, with a locator beacon that points out five Cascade volcanoes. It's the only place on this tour that lifts you above the gorge to a view of the mountains the gorge bisects. Retrace your route to the scenic highway.

On the scenic highway just east of Larch Mountain Road is **Vista House** at Crown Point. Spend time here with the view that invites "silent communion with the infinite," in the words of Samuel Lancaster, the highway's chief engineer. Vista House was dedicated in 1918 as a highway rest stop and observatory. Handcrafted of stone, glass and tile, the Art Nouveau–style octagon wonderfully enhances the cliff it perches on. Inside is an interpretive center, espresso stand and gift shop that sells maps, books and local crafts. Outside, hold onto your hat. When the winds blow, just standing still is heroic. Don't miss the balcony. Sights, west to east: Reed Island, the lowlands of Steigerwald Lake National Wildlife Refuge, the cliffs of Cape Horn, Phoca Rock—a 100-foot high peak in the river, Beacon Rock, a free-standing 800-foot pinnacle on the Washington shore, and Sand Island on the Oregon shore. People-watching is also noteworthy, as are the wood-and-marble restrooms. Carefully walk across the scenic highway below Vista House to look at the view from the sidewalk (across from the base of a gated-off grand staircase). From here you can edit out the crowds and roadway for a view that's even more spectacular.

Beyond Vista House, the scenic highway drops down from the cliffs in figure eight loops. Once the road levels out, the first stop is Latourell Falls. If you saw a photo of the iridescent chartreuse lichen that frames these 224-foot falls, you'd think it had been photoshopped. If you're going to do one hike today, make it the 2.4-mile Latourell Falls Loop hike to the upper falls. (Elevation gain: 520 feet.) It's less busy than other gorge waterfall hikes, and right away you lose the sounds of I-84. The path begins on the east side of the falls viewpoint, and for a good ways you have incredible views of the lower falls as you go deeper into the canyon and then pass through a forest of big cedars and firs to the upper falls. Come back down on the west side of the canyon. Here the trail travels west and you may think you missed a turn; but don't worry, it switches back toward the start eventually. Take a photo at the trailhead of the map for this hike; it's easy to follow.

For a shorter walk, hike to the base of the lower falls then downhill to other park facilities at Guy Talbot State Park. Talbot was a Portland executive in the early 1900s with the Oregon Electric Railway, Pacific Power and Light, and Portland Gas and Coke. This area was his family's summer home and instead of keeping it in the family, in 1914 and 1929 he donated the land at the falls and the canyon above. The Talbot home is gone but the barn remains on Latourell Road in the community of Latourell. Loop back up to the highway via Falls Street and Latourell Road.

The next falls is at Shepperd's Dell State Natural Area. It's 220 feet in eight tiers, some of which are visible from the highway bridge—placed by Lancaster to maximize the beauty of the falls and the road. A short path leads to a viewpoint of the falls and the highway arch joining the canyon walls.

Next up is Bridal Veil State Park and Scenic Viewpoint. A paved, accessible trail leads to semi-secluded overlooks atop the cliffs, some with picnic tables, and all with amazing views. To the west are basalt towers called the Pillars of Hercules. In the 1880s, the first rail line through the gorge ran between them. Across the river are the cliffs of Cape Horn. A 0.3-mile trail leads downhill to the base of 118-foot Lower Bridal Veil Falls. The falls are substantial even in the driest of summers because Bridal Veil is one of the biggest creeks draining Larch Mountain. It once supplied water for three flumes which fed mills at Bridal Veil. The Bridal Veil Inn (now the **Bridal Veil Lodge**) on the scenic highway here housed workers at the Bridal Veil Lumbering Company's mill.

East of Bridal Veil is Wahkeena Falls, about which

Steps to the balcony in Vista House

View from Vista House, spectacular even in winter and with more available parking

waterfallsnorthwest.com says: "Any serious photographer should plan to spend a good hour or two here at least once in their lifetime." See if you agree. An accessible path leads to a stone overlook. Or hike the 0.2-mile, steep paved path to the stone bridge at the base of the falls. Turn around here, or climb on into the narrow canyon and Fairy Falls (2 miles round trip, 800 feet of elevation gain).

The state's most-visited tourist attraction is next: **Multnomah Falls**. The parking lot and walkway to the 620-foot falls can be a melee. Investigate the 1925 stone guest lodge, with its restaurant (reservations: 503-695-2376). It's an Oregon architectural icon, designed by Portland's A.E. Doyle. Take the easy walk to the stone footbridge at the base of the 542-foot upper falls, or walk the 1-mile trail to the top of the falls. Another 0.4 mile on the trail takes you to 50-foot Wiesendanger Falls, where you can find the solitude that's lacking below. They're named for Albert Wiesendanger, a longtime Oregon forester. For a longer hike, do the 4.8-mile Multnomah Falls to Wahkeena Falls Loop. It has 1,540 feet of elevation gain. See gorgefriends.org.

East of Multnomah Falls on the old highway is Lower Oneonta Falls, hidden far back in Oneonta Gorge. Old steps from the highway to the creek hint at a long history of splashy walks up to the 100-foot falls, but since the 1990s, rockfall and a massive log jam have turned a shallow creek walk into a scramble and swim that has claimed a life. Despite the increasing crowds, it's magical. Adventuring up the creek, over the logjam and through a stretch of water that sometimes requires a swim is a lot of fun, BUT, this is not advised unless you're willing to accept the significant risks of climbing over slippery and unstable logs with water below them.

The last falls in this series is Horsetail Falls. See it with a short walk from the historic highway. The big pool at the base of the 214-foot falls is a nice cool-off spot in summer. From there, hike a steep 0.25 mile to 88-foot Ponytail Falls, and step behind it. For a 4.7-mile hike to the wonderful Triple Falls, keep going after Ponytail Falls, cross Oneonta Creek to 60-foot Oneonta Falls, and then go on to Triple Falls, also on Oneonta Creek, where the many pools above the falls make a good lunch and play destination on a hot afternoon. (Or after Oneonta Falls, skip the 1.2-mile out-and-back leg to Triple Falls to shorten the hike.) For a fuller description, see the Horsetail-Ponytail-Triple Falls Hike at gorgefriends.org.

Original highway tunnel at Oneonta Gorge, once filled
and abandoned, reopened to non-motorized traffic

Adventure 2
Hiking and swimming

Head back to Multnomah Falls Lodge for lunch, then on the way back to Troutdale take a waterfall hike you missed, or try one of these great options:

Rooster Rock State Park

If you want to swim or take a flat walk, go to Rooster Rock. The best gorge swimming I've found is here at Sand Island, made even better by the spectacular views across the river of Cape Horn's cliffs. You can wade to the island by August, or earlier in a dry year. Beaches along the island's downstream tip and north side are superb: shallow, with the vast areas of swimmable water warmed by the hot sand. This area is affected by tides and even more by water releases at Bonneville Dam, so beach levels change daily.

The sandy lowland below the high-water mark east of the vast parking lot, including Sand Island, is one of Oregon's two official clothing-optional beaches. Also from the parking lot is a 2-mile flat walking loop in an area that is not clothing optional.

This part of the gorge gets blasted by winter's east winds, recorded at 110 mph at Rooster Rock. Come on east wind days to watch windsurfers. Other winter visitors are tundra swans, who stop at the park's Mirror Lake on the south side of I-84. A walkable roadway runs along it. To get to the park, you have to be on I-84. Take exit 25. $5 day use parking fee.

Sandy River Delta

Another flat walk, 7 miles west of Rooster Rock, is at the Sandy River Delta. Once farmed, this floodplain is being restored with native plants and is seamed with trails where dogs get to shuck their leashes. The 1.25-mile Confluence Trail is the exception: on it, dogs are supposed to be leashed but on a summer weekday afternoon I encountered 14 dogs, only three of whom were leashed, for a 21 percent compliance rate.

In the delta, the Confluence Trail leads to Bird Blind, part of the Confluence Project, a series of art installations along the Columbia River by Maya Lin. Its vertical wooden slats are inscribed with the names and current status of the 134 species Lewis and Clark noted on their westward journey. It's fun to compare the spellings the men used with the species' common and scientific names.

Sandy River beaches

Other good options for playing in a river are the roadside pullouts along the Sandy River at Lewis and Clark State Park or the beaches at Glenn Otto Park.

Access the Sandy River Delta, Lewis and Clark State Park and Glenn Otto Park via I-84 exit 18 or from the Historic Columbia River Highway.

Adventure 3
Dinner in Troutdale and relaxing at McMenamins

After your day outdoors, have dinner downtown at **Troutini** or at one of the two historic roadhouses along the Sandy River, **Tad's Chicken 'n Dumplins** or **Shirley's Tippy Canoe**. Head back to your home away from home, the Multnomah County poor farm, now **McMenamins Edgefield**, where creative reuse has reached its apex. Have a nightcap from one of its many bars, wander around and enjoy the superb landscaping, or relax in the outdoor heated soaking pool.

Adventure 1
Moseying at the poor farm and beyond

Wake up at and have breakfast at Edgefield. Take your coffee and explore the gardens, paths and various buildings, then head into Troutdale for a river walkabout or bike ride. All three of the following options are capped off with a pass through downtown Troutdale with its many eating and shopping destinations.

Troutdale walkabout: bluff, town and beach

Leave your car at Glenn Otto Park and walk this eclectic 2-mile route (not including any trail meandering you might do at Glen Otto Park). From the park, turn left (west) onto the Historic Columbia River Highway. You're on a floodplain; below the bluffs, this wide river bench was under water in the May 1948 flood (known throughout the Portland area as the Vanport Flood). At Jackson Park Road is a 1912 Craftsman home turned artists' live/work space. It's owned by sculptor Rip Caswell, who also owns the pond to the south. The pond was dug in 1915. It's like other, earlier ponds dug in the 1870s along the base of this bluff by Captain John Harlow as part of a farm retreat he called Troutdale. Harlow stocked his ponds with trout, and in 2013 Caswell stocked this pond with trout, in part to honor the town's history but also for the visiting eagles, osprey, wood ducks and other wildlife. It's fine to walk over and enjoy this scenic spot.

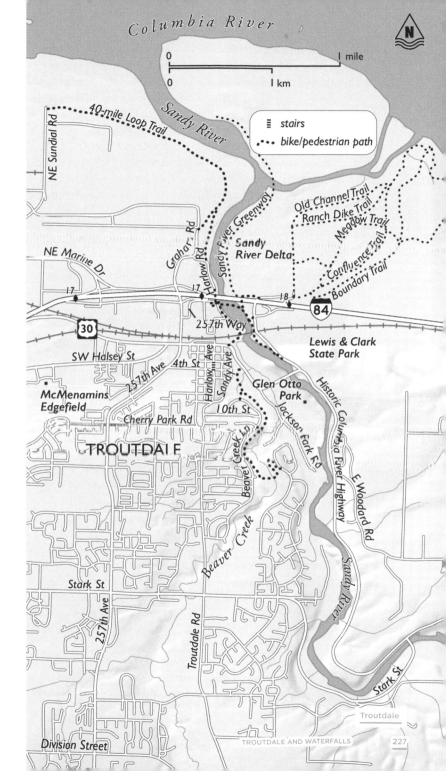

Columbia River

0   1 mile

0   1 km

Sandy River

≡ stairs

••• bike/pedestrian path

NE Sundial Rd

40-mile Loop Trail

Graham Rd

Harlow Rd

Sandy River Greenway

Old Channel Trail

Ranch Dike Trail

Meadow Trail

Sandy River Delta

Confluence Trail

Boundary Trail

NE Marine Dr

17

17

18

84

257th Way

Lewis & Clark State Park

30

SW Halsey St

257th Ave

4th St

Harlow Ave

Sandy Ave

Glen Otto Park

Historic Columbia River Highway

McMenamins Edgefield

Cherry Park Rd

10th St

Jackson Park Rd

TROUTDALE

Beaver Creek Ln

E Woodard Rd

Sandy River

Stark St

Beaver Creek

257th Ave

Troutdale Rd

Stark St

Troutdale

Division Street

TROUTDALE AND WATERFALLS

Walk further on the historic highway. Captain Harlow's home is gone but the 1900 house built by his son on the family's land is now the **Harlow House Museum**. Next to it in a barn is the **King of Roads Museum**. Behind the museums, take the Robin's Way Trail, which follows an old path improved in memory of Robin Dix, who died as a teen in 1982, and his sister Julie, who also died young. His parents owned the strawberry fields that once grew at the top of the path.

When you emerge from the path at the top of the bluff take the first right, which leads to wooden steps. Climb them and come to a path that leads to Beaver Creek Court. Turn right on it, and then right on Beaver Creek Lane. This neighborhood, Strawberry Meadows, was built in the 1990s on land that was Bob and Louise Dix's berry farm.

From Beaver Creek Lane, turn right on 10th, then right on Sandy Avenue. Follow Sandy downhill, along the top of Harlow Canyon. Turn left at Fourth and take steps downhill at Harlow and Fourth (they're at the west end of a red-and-white barrier), and end up in downtown Troutdale on the Columbia River Highway, where good food, art galleries, antique shops and stores invite a ramble. Afterward, go east on the highway, stopping at the excellent **Depot Rail Museum**. Spend a half hour with a docent learning about the town's rail story. Keep east on the historic highway. Just before the river bridge, turn into Glenn Otto Park, where you can swim, hike bottomland trails and laze on the Sandy River's beaches before you head back to Portland.

Walking or biking to Sandy River beaches

This approximately 3-mile loop can be extended to any length by walking along the dike trail on the Sandy's west bank to the 40-Mile Loop Trail. Start the loop at the parking area for Lewis and Clark State Park. Cross the road to the paved path along the Sandy River. Here, near its confluence with the Columbia, the channel is wide and braided with islands. Turn right to walk or bike downstream on the Sandy's east bank. Make use of several places where stone steps lead down to beaches, which get wider as summer progresses. On hot summer days they're colorful with people and their water toys. Keep on the trail as it forks left toward a bike-and-pedestrian path on the I-84 bridge over the Sandy. Cross over the river. You can continue downstream along the west bank, which leads to a path on a dike and more offshoot paths to the river. At any point, return the way you came.

Alternatively, if you like to combine eclectic elements on your walks, do this: once you cross over the river, take the permeable-pavement sidewalk along 257th Way, which runs west alongside

Columbia Gorge Premium Outlets. Then turn left on Graham Road/257th Avenue. Dip into the mall to your left if you see a store that looks irresistible.

From the mall, continue south on 257th, then turn left on the Columbia River Highway, where the Troutdale Arch welcomes you. Shop, eat or visit galleries or the Rail Depot Museum downtown.

From downtown Troutdale, follow the historic highway downhill and eastward; pass Glenn Otto Park. If you feel like more trail-walking, depending on river levels it has plenty to offer along the forested banks of the Sandy. Then cross the old and tiny Sandy River Bridge and turn left, walking the road a short distance (traffic is not heavy) to return to Lewis and Clark State Park.

Biking two bridges and the Sandy River gorge

This route offers spectacular views about half of its length as it hugs the banks and cliffs of the Sandy River. Bike the 7.5-mile route only if you're confident of going uphill without weaving or wobbling—parts of the Stark Street section are steep with little shoulder, sheer drop-offs and 45-mph traffic. But for strong riders, the many places to stop and savor views of the Sandy River gorge are worth it.

Start at Glenn Otto Park and ride east across the narrow highway bridge, built in 1912. Bike on the bridge sidewalk so you can stop to enjoy the middle-of-the-river view without impeding traffic.

From the bridge, turn right (south) on the Historic Columbia River Highway, biking upstream along the Sandy. Pass two classic riverfront roadhouses. Further south, the bluff to your left is full of rounded cobbles. That's the Troutdale Formation, rocks carried here by the ancestral Columbia River two to ten million years ago. Turn right onto the route's second narrow and scenic bridge, the Stark Street Bridge, built in 1914. Cross on the sidewalk so you can stop for views. The private home on the west bank was built in the 1910s as the clubhouse for the Portland Automobile Club in the early days of auto-touring.

From the Stark Street Bridge, the route hugs the cliffs of the Sandy River and climbs steeply for about 1.5 miles. This section of Stark Street gets too little love these days, which is a shame: the hand-carved rock walls, benches and canyon overlooks created in 1916 and in 1940 by WPA crews are worthy of a national park.

After the climb the road levels. Turn right off Stark onto Troutdale Road, passing one of the last in-town berry patches. In about a mile, veer right onto Sandy Avenue and follow it downhill and on into downtown Troutdale. After a snack, shopping or lunch, continue east on the highway to return to Glen Otto Park.

Scenic bike rides on the Historic Columbia River Highway

These segments offer lots of waterfalls, short hikes and big views. The parts of the highway that are car-free are called the Historic Columbia River Highway State Trail. On other parts, shoulders are slim to none but drivers are out there to enjoy the scenery too and so cars are generally respectful and following the posted speed (35 mph or less). Off-season and midday traffic can be extremely light.

Recommended segments:

- **Troutdale to Cascade Locks.** 27 miles one way. A great overnight bike tour: spend the night in Cascade Locks. Stop often to visit waterfalls, scenic overlooks and Bonneville Dam. It's a 900-foot climb from Troutdale to Portland Women's Forum, then a gentle, long downhill and rolling terrain into Cascade Locks. Return via the same route for a 54-mile round trip.

- **Portland Women's Forum to Multnomah Falls.** 10 miles one way past waterfalls and overlooks. Lovely 700-foot looping downhill then rolling flats on roadway shared with cars. Bring a lock so you can lunch at **Multnomah Falls Lodge**; call ahead to reserve a table. Then hike 1 mile to the top of the falls. On the return, you'll have a 700-foot climb, but on the ascent the stupendous views bikers have over the stone wall can't be seen from a car.

- **Guy Talbot State Park/Latourell Falls to Multnomah Falls.** 9 miles one way, rolling flats on roadway shared with cars. Six major falls, plus the Bridal Veil Scenic Overlook. Want to ride just one way? Pedal Bike Tours offers one-way trips. Its van leaves from Portland, drops you off at Latourell Falls, meets you at waterfall stops, and loads you back into the van at Horsetail Falls. See Appendix B.

Eat and Drink in Troutdale

Brass Rail Tavern. Daily 10 a.m. to 2:30 a.m. 108 E Historic Columbia River Highway. 503-666-8756

Brewligan's Bottle Shop and Taproom. Monday to Thursday 3 to 10 p.m.; Friday and Saturday 12 to 10 p.m.; Sunday 12 to 8 p.m. 275 E Columbia River Highway. 503-489-5919

Celebrate Me Home Espresso Bar. Monday to Friday 8 a.m. to 5:30 p.m.; Saturday 9 a.m. to 5:30 p.m.; Sunday 10 a.m. to 5 p.m. 319 E Columbia River Highway. 503-618-9394

McMenamins Edgefield. 10 food and drink venues on 74 acres of the former Multnomah County Poor Farm, including a tea house, wine bar, distillery tasting room, brewpub and upscale restaurant. 2126 SW Halsey St. 503-669-8610

Ristorante di Pompello. Generous portions of food, wine and service. Tuesday to Saturday, 8 a.m. to 10 p.m.; Sunday and Monday, 11 a.m. to 10 p.m. 177 E Columbia River Highway. 503-667-2480

Siam Sushi. Small and friendly. 165 E Columbia River Highway. 503-618-8862

Troutdale General Store. Breakfast and lunch fare are hiding in this warren of giftiness. See Shopping for more details. Monday to Friday, 7:30 a.m. to 9 p.m.; Saturday and Sunday 9 a.m. to 5 p.m. 289 E Columbia River Highway. 503-492-7912

Troutini. Great happy hour and small plate menu. Tuesday to Thursday 11 a.m. to 10 p.m.; Friday 11 a.m. to 11 p.m.; Saturday 10 a.m. to 11 p.m.; Sunday 10 a.m. to 9 p.m. Closed daily 3 to 4 p.m. 101 W Columbia River Highway. 503-912-1482

Ye Olde Pub. Friendly, straight-up family pub with patio. Monday to Thursday 11 a.m. to 10 p.m.; Friday 11 a.m. to 1 a.m.; Saturday 7 a.m. to 1 a.m.; Sunday 7 a.m. to 10 p.m. 202 W Historic Columbia River Highway. 503-328-9303

Riverview Restaurant. Cocktails or dinner under the firs overlooking the Sandy River. Tuesday to Sunday 4:30 to 8 p.m. or 9 p.m. 29311 SE Stark St. 503-661-3663

Eat and Drink along the Historic Columbia River Highway

Listed in the order encountered as one travels from Troutdale to Multnomah Falls

Tad's Chicken 'n Dumplins. One of the last of the old roadhouses on the historic highway. Sit on the patio over the Sandy River or in a wood-paneled bar and dining room. Look through tall trees at drift boats in winter and tubers on the river in summer. You're not in Portland anymore. Weekdays 5 to 10 p.m. Weekends: opens 4 p.m. 1325 E Historic Columbia River Highway. 503-666-5337

Shirley's Tippy Canoe. Another vintage roadhouse on the Sandy River; it dates from the 1940s. 28242 E Columbia River Highway. Daily 8 a.m. to close. 503-492-2220

Big Bear's Country Market and Deli. Dine in or take out. Ice cream shakes. Daily 8 a.m. to 3 p.m. except Thursday: 8 a.m. to 8 p.m. 31515 E Historic Columbia River Highway, Springdale. 503-695-6255

Springdale Pub and Eatery. Daily from 11 a.m. Monday to Thursday to 1 a.m.; Friday and Saturday to 2 a.m.; Sunday to 12 a.m. 32302 E Historic Columbia River Highway. 503-695-2676

Corbett Country Market. House-made smoked salmon and other meats. Provision up for a day exploring the gorge. Daily 6:30 to 8 a.m. to 8 to 10 p.m. 36801 E Historic Columbia River Highway. 503-695-2234

Multnomah Falls Lodge. Make a reservation and plan your explorations so you can enjoy a meal in the historic lodge. Daily 8 a.m. to 9 p.m. 53000 Historic Columbia River Highway. 503-695-2376

Shop in Troutdale

Bev Frank Antiques. Wednesday to Saturday 11 a.m. to 5 p.m.; Sunday 12:30 to 5 p.m. 387 E Columbia River Highway. 503-665-1640

Caswell Gallery. Bronze sculptures by Rip Caswell; paintings, glass art, pottery too. He created the Troutdale Arch and other outdoor bronze sculptures throughout town. Tuesday to Saturday 10 a.m. to 5:30 p.m.; Sunday and Monday by appointment. 253 E Columbia River Highway. 503-492-2473

Celebrate Me Home/Rustic with a Twist. Furniture, home goods and gifts. Monday to Friday 8 a.m. to 5:30 p.m.; Saturday 9 a.m. to 5:30 p.m.; Sunday 10 a.m. to 5 p.m. 319 E Columbia River Highway. 503-618-9394

Columbia Gorge Premium Outlets. 45 stores. Daily 10 a.m. to 8 p.m. Sunday to 6 p.m. 450 NW 257th Way. 503-669-8060

Columbia River Gallery. Tuesday to Saturday 10 a.m. to 5 p.m. 303 E Columbia River Highway. 503-491-8407

Damenpura. Metaphysical and consciousness-enhancing boutique and classes. 373 E Columbia River Highway. Tuesday to Saturday 1 to 5:30 p.m. 503-826-8899

Infusion Gallery. Artists with developmental disabilities. Classes too. Tuesday to Friday 10 a.m. to 5 p.m.; Saturday 12 to 5 p.m. 345 E Columbia River Highway. 503-489-6565

Fenske Galleries. Luminous, or invisible, art. Wednesday to Friday 10:30 a.m. to 5:00 p.m.; Saturday 10:30 a.m. to 5:00 p.m. 255 E Columbia River Highway. 971-232-0742

McMenamins Edgefield. An extensive gift shop, with spirits distilled on site, wine, tee shirts, books and more. See Eat and Drink in Troutdale. 2126 SW Halsey St. 503-669-8610 or 800-669-8610

Oregon Log Furniture. Locally hand-crafted furniture plus accessories. Daily 10 a.m. to 5 p.m. Weekends to 4 p.m. 111 W Columbia River Highway. 503-557-3144

Timeless Designs. Gifts and antiques. Sunday 11 a.m. to 4 p.m.; Tuesday to Saturday 10 a.m. to 6 p.m. 149 E Columbia River Highway. 503-328-6278

Troutdale Antique Mall. Two floors of vendors. Daily 11 a.m. to 5:30 p.m. except Sunday 12 to 5 p.m. 359 E Columbia River Highway. 503-674-6820

Troutdale Art Center. Various artists and media. Friday to Sunday 11 a.m. to 4 p.m. 903 E Columbia River Highway. 503-515-5673

Troutdale General Store. Part old-timey country store, lunch counter, gifts, candy, ice-cream and espresso. Great candy selection in bushel baskets. Weekdays 7:30 a.m. to 5 p.m. Weekends: from 9 a.m. 289 E Columbia River Highway. 503-492-7912

Shop along the Historic Columbia River Highway

Multnomah Falls Lodge Gift Shop. Daily 8 a.m. to 9 p.m. 53000 Historic Columbia River. 503-695-2376

Vista House. Gift shop and espresso bar. Early May to late September: daily 9 a.m. to 6 p.m. Early November to early March: Friday to Sunday 10 a.m. to 4 p.m. Shoulder seasons: daily 10 a.m. to 4 p.m. 40700 Historic Columbia River Highway. 503-695-2240

Discover and Learn in Troutdale and along the Historic Columbia River Highway

Depot Rail Museum. Excellent railroad station displays; take the docent-led tour. Summer: Tuesday to Saturday 10 a.m. to 2 p.m. Call for winter hours. 473 E Columbia River Highway, Troutdale. 503-661-2164

Harlow House Museum. Every third Saturday. Call for winter hours. 726 E Columbia River Highway, Troutdale. 503-661-2164

King of Roads Exhibit, Barn Exhibit Hall. A great introduction to the spectacular Columbia River Highway. Basalt stone archwork inside was done by artisans who do restoration work on the old highway. May 1 to September 30: Monday to Saturday 9 a.m. to 4 p.m. and Sunday 1 to 4 p.m. Shorter winter hours. 732 E Columbia River Highway, Troutdale. 503-661-2164

Multnomah Falls Visitor Center. Staffed by the U.S. Forest Service and Friends of Multnomah Falls. East of Corbett at 53000 Historic Columbia River Highway. Daily 9 a.m. to 5 p.m. 503-695-2372

Vista House Visitor Center. Operated by Friends of Vista House. Early May to late September: daily 9 a.m. to 6 p.m. Early November to early March: Friday to Sunday 10 a.m. to 4 p.m. In the shoulder seasons: daily 10 a.m. to 4 p.m. East of Corbett at 40700 Historic Columbia River Highway. 503-695-2240

West Columbia Gorge Chamber of Commerce and Visitor Center. Monday to Friday 10 a.m. to 4 p.m. 107 E Historic Columbia River Highway, Troutdale. 503-669-7473

Stay in Troutdale and along the Historic Columbia River Highway

Brickhaven Bed and Breakfast. A room and a suite within a home located between Menucha and Portland Women's Forum at the west edge of Waterfall Alley. A quirky, arty place of bricks and barn timbers. 38717 Historic Columbia River Hwy, Corbett. 503-695-5126 [$$$]

Bridal Veil Lodge Bed and Breakfast. This lodge in the heart of Waterfall Alley dates from the early auto-touring era. Across the road is Bridal Veil State Park. 46650 Historic Columbia River Highway. 503-695-6152

Comfort Inn Columbia Gorge Gateway. Though near I-84 in Troutdale, it's on prime bike routes: leave your car in the lot and ride short loops around Troutdale and the Sandy River or long excursions into the gorge. 1000 NW Graham Road. 503-493-2900 [$$$]

McMenamins Edgefield. At Multnomah County's former poor farm in Troutdale are 100 artfully restored rooms, some with private baths. If you're a fan of trees and plants, the lush landscaping here will make your day. Rooms for single travelers plus 12-person hostel rooms; separate male and female rooms with towels/bedding provided. 74 acres of vineyards, a brewery, distillery, gardens, a golf course and soaking pool. About 0.75 mile west of downtown Troutdale. 2126 SW Halsey St. 800-669-8610 or 503-669-8610 [$$$$]

Menucha Retreat and Conference Center. For personal retreat room. In 1914, this cliff top in the gorge became the country estate of Julius and Grace Meier, who named it Menucha (Hebrew for "waters of refreshment"). He was Oregon's governor from 1931 to 1935. Julius died in 1937. After World War II, the family sold Menucha to First Presbyterian Church of Portland, which converted the home into a retreat and conference center for nonprofit or faith-based groups, family reunions or individuals. Menucha's mission: to enrich lives through hospitality, learning, reflection and renewal. Grounds are open only to participants—do not cruise through to look around. One space is available, depending on capacity, for personal retreats for one to four people. 38711 Historic Columbia River Highway (0.25 mile west of Portland Women's Forum). 503-695-2243 [$$]

Lodging Cost Key			
$	$$	$$$	$$$$
<$50	$51 to $99	$100 to $200	>$200

FESTIVALS AND EVENTS BY MONTH

Find music, fine arts, crafts, sports, harvest, food and drink events here. Months can vary slightly, year to year and info is subject to change; check the websites. Not every gorge event is listed. Check the visitor center in the area you're visiting for other upcoming events:

Oregon, west to east

West Columbia Gorge Chamber of Commerce. westcolumbiagorgechamber.com

City of Cascade Locks Tourism. cascadelocks.net

Hood River County Chamber of Commerce. hoodriver.org

The Dalles Area Chamber of Commerce. thedalleschamber.com

Washington, west to east

Camas-Washougal Chamber of Commerce. cwchamber.com

Skamania County Chamber of Commerce. skamania.org

Mount Adams Chamber of Commerce. mtadamschamber.com

Greater Goldendale Area Chamber of Commerce. goldendalechamber.org

Year-round

Troutdale First Friday Art Walk. Historic Columbia River Highway, downtown Troutdale. Many galleries, antique stores, shops and restaurants. 5 to 9 p.m. On Facebook.

January

None

February

Valentine's Wine and Chocolate Weekend. Individual gorge wineries. Discounts, wine and chocolate pairings, special releases. columbiagorgewine.com

March

None

April

Birds of Prey Hybrid Half Marathon and 5K. On trails along the river on Strawberry Island (Hamilton Island), North Bonneville. columbiagorgerunningclub.com

Blossom Craft Show. Hood River County Fairgrounds. 125 vendors of art, craft and plants. Quilt display and sale too. hoodriver.org

Community Garage Sale. Skamania County Fairgrounds Exhibit Hall, Stevenson. skamaniacounty.org

Hard Pressed Cider Fest. 3315 Stadelman Drive, Hood River. Local cideries, with food and music. All ages. hoodriver.org

Hood River Valley Blossom Time. Businesses and organizations in Hood River. Three weeks of events to celebrate the valley's foods and wine. hoodriver.org

Iron Man Strong Ale Festival. Skamania County Fairgrounds, Stevenson. Local microbrews with 8 percent or higher alcohol content, plus food and music. ironmanstrongalefestival.com

Northwest Cherry Festival. Downtown The Dalles. "Cherry of a Ride" bike ride, street fair, food, music and a run. thedalleschamber.com

Open Studios. Various sites. Gorge artists open their studios to visitors. Self-guided map at gorgeartists.org/guide

Passport Month. $25 wine passport gives access to special events at gorge wineries such as food pairings, discounts and reserve tastings, plus nearby lodging and dinner specials. columbiagorgewine.com

May

Color Dash 5K, The Dalles. Get splashed with color dust as you run for a local charity. thedalleschamber.com

Gorge Cup Races. Event Site, Hood River. Generally every second Saturday May to August. gorgecup.com

Grape to Table Weekend. Various wineries. Special releases, food pairings and music. Memorial Day weekend. columbiagorgewine.com

Spring Festival. Rheingarten Park, White Salmon. Forty years of celebrating small town life and spring. whitesalmonspringfestival.com

Stevenson to Carson Ridge Run. 10 miles, nearly 2,000 feet elevation. Ends at a brewpub. columbiagorgerunningclub.com

Teardrops, T@Bs and Tiny Trailers. Skamania County Fairgrounds, Stevenson. Four-day campout of cuteness on wheels. teardroptrailers.org

June

Best of the Gorge Art Show. Columbia Center for the Arts, Hood River. Two-month-long juried show of fine arts. columbiaarts.org

Columbia Gorge Windsurfing Association Beach Bash. (Formerly Gorge WindFest) Event Site, Hood River. Demos, music, beach party, contests, kid play area. gorgewindsurfing.org

Gorge Blues and Brews Festival. Skamania County Fairgrounds, Stevenson. Blues on the water, plus local beer, wine and hard cider. Camp onsite or walk to your lodging gorgebluesandbrews.com

Gorge Cup Races. Event Site, Hood River. Generally every second Saturday May to August. gorgecup.com

Gorge Ride. The Dalles to Hood River. Supported bike ride along the Historic Columbia River Highway. hcrh.org

Maryhill Festival of Speed. Maryhill Loops Road, Goldendale. 250 of the world's top downhill skateboarders and street lugers race the historic loops. Food, music, vendors. maryhillfestivalofspeed.com

Sternwheeler Days. Marine Park, Cascade Locks. Annual celebration of the sternwheeler's return. cascadelocks.net

White Salmon Backyard Half. Challenging half-marathon course with big views and stray cows, potentially. columbiagorgerunningclub.com

July

Antique Car Tour. Starts at Western Antique Aeroplane and Automobile Museum, Hood River. Ride in an antique vehicle or walk the Historic Columbia River's Mosier Twin Tunnels. hcrh.org

Art and Wine Fusion. Downtown White Salmon. Street festival of local art, wine and cider plus music. artwinefusion.com

Best of the Gorge Art Show. Columbia Center for the Arts, Hood River. Two-month-long juried show of fine arts. columbiaarts.org

Bridge of the Gods Kiteboarding Festival. East Point Kite Beach, Stevenson. Pros and serious amateurs battle with tricks and speed. botgkitefest.com

Columbia Gorge Bluegrass Festival. Skamania County Fairgrounds, Stevenson. American roots music in beautiful Rock Cove. columbiagorgebluegrass.net

Cracked Pots: Art from Recycled Materials. McMenamins Edgefield, Troutdale. Indoor, outdoor and wearable art from 100 artists. crackedpots.org

Fort Dalles Days and Pro Rodeo. Ten days of museum open houses, music, street fair, chili cook-off and parade. fortdallesdays.com, fortdallesrodeo.com, thedallesmainstreet.org

Gorge Cup Races. Event Site, Hood River. Generally every second Saturday May to August. gorgecup.com

Gorge Days. North Bonneville. Annual street rod and classic car show, citywide garage sale, music and food. gorgedays.net

Gorge Downwind Paddling Festival. Weeklong surfski, kayak and outrigger events, including clinics and downwind races. gorgepaddlingfestival.com

Hood River County Fair. Rural Odell, 7 miles south of downtown Hood River. hoodriverfair.org

Maryhill Winery Summer Concert Series. SR 14 east of Lyle. Seating for 4,000 on a lawn amphitheater overlooking the Columbia River. maryhillwinery.com

Wildside Relay. Bob's Beach, Stevenson. Part of the Gorge Downwind Paddling Festival. Racers in narrow outrigger kayaks paddle upriver to Bingen. Watch at Stevenson's waterfront, Home Valley Park, Spring Creek National Fish Hatchery or Bingen's Sailboard Park. nwoutrigger.com

August

Blow Out. 17-mile downwind race, on the river from Stevenson to Hood River. Kiteboarders and windsurfers. botgkitefest.com

Bridge of the Gods Half Marathon and 10K Run. Cascade Locks and Historic Columbia River Highway. Run or walk across the gorge's most intriguing bridge. bridgeofthegodsrun.com

Columbia Gorge Paddle Challenge. Waterfront Park, Hood River. Standup paddling: professional and recreational races, music. gorgepaddlechallenge.com

Cruise The Gorge. The Dalles. Vintage and classic cars on display. Friday night Cruise-In, downtown and Saturday Show in the Shade at Sorosis Park. midcolumbiacarclub.org

Gorge Cup Races. Event Site, Hood River. Generally every second Saturday May to August. gorgecup.com

King of the Hook. The Hook, Hood River. Good spectating—Hood River's version of the World Naked Bike Ride, but with wetsuits, costumes and vintage boards. gorgewindsurfing.org

Klickitat County Fair and Rodeo. Goldendale. A classic Western fair. klickitatcountyfair.com

Maryhill Winery Summer Concert Series. SR 14 east of Lyle. Seating for 4,000 on a lawn amphitheater overlooking the Columbia River. maryhillwinery.com

Pacific Crest Trail Days. Cascade Locks Marine Park. Hike, walk the Bridge of the Gods, buy outdoor gear, camp on Thunder Island. pctdays.com

Rally in the Gorge. Hood River County Fairgrounds. Motorized sport bike and touring rides, vendors, clinics and classes. soundrider.com

Skamania County Fair and Timber Carnival. Stevenson. Livestock, equitation, chainsaw and pie-baking contests, music, carnival rides, fun run. On scenic Rock Cove. skamaniacounty.org

SUP Salmon Classic. Cottonwood Beach, Captain William Clark Park, Washougal. Pro and recreational athletes. 2-mile youth and novice course; 4-mile recreational course; 8-mile competitive course. Bring your board or arrange ahead to rent from Gorge Performance, Portland or Big Winds, Hood River. supsalmonclassic.com

September

Aluminum Man Triathlon and Duathlon. The Dalles. Swim in the Columbia, bike the hills and run along the river. Sprint and Olympic triathlons; Olympic duathlon. nwprd.org

Bigfoot Bash and Bounty Festival. Home Valley Park. Hunt for the big guy, drink and eat at the Yeti Yard beer gardens. Local music, a carnival, talks by Bigfoot experts and camping along the river. bigfootbashandbounty.com

Crush Kickoff Weekend/Labor Day Open House.
Many participating wineries: tastings, guided tours and live music. columbiagorgewine.com.

Hood River Fly-In. Hundreds of antique planes aloft and on the ground; opportunities for rides. Food and drink. waaamuseum.org

Hood River Hops Fest. Downtown Hood River. Food vendors and 40 breweries. All ages. hoodriver.org

Hoptoberfest. Walking Man Brewing, Stevenson. Washington's craft beers, music and bratwurst. walkingmanbeer.com

Huckleberry Festival. Daubenspeck Park, Bingen. Bratwurst, beer, vendors and huckleberry treats. huckleberry-fest.com

Maryhill Museum of Art Free Museum Day. Goldendale (off SR 14). Download the free ticket, part of the Smithsonian Museum Day Live program. maryhillmuseum.org

Maryhill Winery Summer Concert Series. SR 14 east of Lyle. Seating for 4,000 on a lawn amphitheater overlooking the Columbia River. maryhillwinery.com

Pacific Crest Trail Days. Marine Park, Cascade Locks. Recreation gear from vendors, hikes and bike rides, camping on Thunder Island. pctdays.com

Roy Webster Cross-Channel Swim. Hood River. Every Labor Day, a 500-person, 1-mile recreational swim across the Columbia. hoodriver.org

Spring Creek National Fish Hatchery Open House.
Near White Salmon. Fish are spawning. Call for this year's date. 509 493 2037

October

Columbia River Gorge Quilt Show. Hood River Armory, Hood River. Quilt art on display and for sale. gorgequiltersguild.org/quiltshow.html

Fall Festival of the Arts. Events from Troutdale to Cascade Locks. fallfestivalofthearts.com

Gorge Fruit and Craft Fair. Hood River County Fairgrounds. Part of the Harvest Fest weekend. Local foods only. hoodriverfair.org

Gorge Green Home Tour. Hood River. Stops at about 12 homes. gorgeowned.org

Hood River Valley Harvest Fest. Event Site, Hood River. On the river, 125 vendors of food, drink, arts and crafts. Buy boxes of produce, local smoked salmon, chocolate-covered cherries and more. hoodriver.org

Maryhill Arts Festival. Maryhill Museum of Art, Goldendale (on SR 14). Northwest artists in all media, food vendors, plus the Concours de Maryhill, a show of classic, sport and custom cars. Maryhill Loops are open to driving for modern cars and also for a vintage car hill climb. maryhillmuseum.org

Pumpkin Patch. Skamania County Fairgrounds, Stevenson. Fun and pumpkins for kids ages 2 to 9. skamaniacounty.org

Riverside Apple Festival. Washougal. School fundraiser with horse rides, apple and food vendors, and famous pies. riversidesch.com

November

Columbia Gorge Fiber Festival. The Dalles. Yarn, fiber, hand-crafted goods, artisan cheese and fiber-related crafts. Workshops too. columbiagorgefiberfestival.com

Columbia Gorge Model Railroad Club Open House. Portland. Basketball-court size train layout of railroading in Portland and through the gorge in the 1950s. The Union Station model was built using the original blueprints. Watch trains run at weekend open houses. columbiagorgemodelrailroadclub.com

Mount Hood Independent Film Festival. Columbia Center for the Arts, Hood River. columbiaarts.org

Starlight Parade and Community Tree-Lighting. Downtown The Dalles. Lighted parade kicks off the holiday season the night after Thanksgiving. thedalleschamber.com

Thanksgiving Wine Weekend. Throughout the gorge. For offerings by specific vineyards see columbiagorgewine.com

December

Christmas in the Gorge. Skamania County Fairgrounds and downtown sites, Stevenson. Art and craft bazaar, parade, specials in restaurants and stores. cityofstevenson.com

Festival of Trees. The Dalles Civic Auditorium. Decorated trees auctioned for charity with visits from Santa. thedalleschamber.com

Hood River Holidays. Month-long events downtown and at local stores. hoodriver.org

Last Chance Holiday Bazaar. Hood River County Fairgrounds. hoodriverfair.org

OUTFITTERS, GUIDES, LESSONS, CRUISES, EXCURSIONS AND ONLINE RESOURCES

Some of these activities I have done; some services I have used. Others I have not. I make no warranty about the quality and safety record of businesses named here other than to say that, based on my research or experiences, they are businesses I would patronize. Use your own discretion and research to determine if their qualifications and certifications, if applicable, meet your needs.

Aerial scenic tours

Classic Wings Aero Services. 30- to 90-minute tours from the Hood River airport with FAA-certified flight instructors. 541-386-1133. flythegorge.com

Bike tours, rentals and guides

Discover Bicycles. Road and mountain bike rentals. 210 State St., Hood River. 541-386-4820. discoverbicycles.com

Dalles City Cyclery. Call to confirm availability. 121 E Second St., The Dalles. 541-769-0771

Hood River Adventures. Shuttle service to the top of Hood River's Post Canyon area. 541-400-1216. hoodriveradventures.com

Hood River Mountain Bike Adventures. Owner Greg Galliano will guide you on the best trails, tailored to your skills. 503-705-3592. hoodrivermountainbikeadventures.com

Mountain View Cycles. Road, mountain and hybrid bike rentals. Advance reservations recommended. 205 Oak St., Hood River. 541-386-2453. mtviewcycles.com

Pedal Bike Tours. One-way touring of a 9-mile segment of the Historic Columbia River Highway, with short waterfall hikes.

The van starts in Portland and drives you to Latourell Falls. Begin riding east and get picked up at Horsetail Falls for the drive back to Portland. 5 hours, rolling terrain. 503-243-2453. pedalbiketours.com

Buy the Hood River mountain bike trail map by adventuremaps.net at Dirty Fingers Bikes, 1235 State St., Hood River. dirtyfingersbikes. com. More on Hood River trails at Oregon Mountain Biking: ormtb.com

Birding

Portland Audubon. Free outings in the gorge and elsewhere. 503-292-6855. audubonportland.org

Vancouver Audubon. Its Steigerwald Lake and Columbia River Gorge web pages offer a great overview of birds you may see and where to see them. vancouveraudubon.org

Bus and van tours, charter

America's Hub Tours. Multnomah Falls, Gorge Waterfalls and Gorge Wine Tasting tours. Year-round. 503-896-2464. americashubworldtours.com

Grayline Tours. Daily in summer; less often during shoulder season. No tours Thanksgiving to late April. Half-day tour starts at Portland's Pioneer Courthouse Square and travels the Historic Columbia River Highway to Crown Point, Multnomah Falls and Bonneville Dam. 503-241-7373. grayline.com

Wildwood Adventures. Year-round. 3.5-hour tours starting from Portland's Director Park with stops for short walks at waterfalls on the Historic Columbia River Highway and Bonneville Dam. 503-396-3929. wildwoodtours.com

For other tours, see also Hikes: guided, and Wine tours.

Conservancies, friends and advocacy groups in the gorge

If you enjoy spending time in the gorge, consider joining one of these organizations:

Columbia Gorge Refuge Stewards. Since 2006. Volunteers work with the U.S. Fish and Wildlife Service to preserve and maintain three wildlife refuges on Washington's side of the gorge. refugestewards.org

Friends of Multnomah Falls. Since 1990. Preserves and enhances Oregon's number one visitor attraction. friendsofmultnomahfalls.org

Friends of the Columbia Gorge. Since 1980. Hikes, advocacy and land conservation. 5,000 members. gorgefriends.org

Friends of the Historic Columbia River Highway. Since 2006. Promotes the "King of Roads" via the Gorge Ride and the Antique Car Tour. hcrh.org

Friends of Vista House. Since 1982. Supports this gorge treasure and the visitors who come to see it. vistahouse.com

Klickitat Trail Conservancy. Since 2003. Preserves and promotes public use of this 31-mile trail along a former rail line. See its page for tips on biking the trail. klickitat-trail.org

Nature Conservancy. Owns and manages the Tom McCall Preserve at Rowena, Oregon and Pierce Island in the river near Beacon Rock State Park. nature.org

Cruising on the Columbia and Deschutes rivers

Oregon and Washington-based operators

Columbia Gorge Sternwheeler. May to October. Board in Cascade Locks. Ride downstream to Bonneville Dam, then upstream toward Hood River. 503-224-3900. portlandspirit.com

Deschutes River Jet Boat Tours. May and June. From the mouth of the Deschutes 25 miles to Mack's Canyon and back. 4 hours. Captain Brad Staples, bswfa@aol.com or 503-250-0558. deschutesriverjetboats.com

Explorer Jet Boat. June to September. Portland to Cascade Locks on a 35-passenger boat. See page 209 for a boat-and-bike option. 503-224-3900. portlandspirit.com

USA River Cruises. March to November. Eight-day cruises on eight vessels, from a 6-passenger yacht to a 210-passenger paddle wheeler. 800-578-1479. usarivercruises.com

Other cruise ship operators

AdventureSmith Explorations. Eight-day cruises. 88 passengers. 877-620-2875. adventuresmithexplorations.com

American Cruise Line. Seven-day cruises. 120 passengers. 800-460-4518. americancruiselines.com

American Queen Steamboat Company.
Nine day cruise on a huge steamboat. 888-749-5280
americanqueensteamboatcompany.com

Lindblad Expeditions/National Geographic. Seven-day cruise
on 62-passenger ship. 800-397-3348. expeditions.com (see also
nationalgeographicexpeditions.com)

Smithsonian Journeys. Seven-day cruise on 62-passenger ship.
855-330-1542. smithsonianjourneys.org

Un-Cruise Adventures. Eight-day cruise, 88 passengers.
888-862-8881. un-cruise.com

Hikes: guided

Friends of the Columbia Gorge. Approximately 100 guided hikes
each year. Reserve your space early. At gorgefriends.org, go to
"Hike the Gorge/Hike with Friends."

Martin's Gorge Tours. Owner Martin Hecht is a longtime gorge
explorer and guide. March through June: weekend morning
wildflower hikes. Year-round: midweek waterfall tours. July to
February: weekend waterfall tours. 503-349-1323. See
martinsgorgetours.com for waterfalls featured.

Mazamas. Founded in 1894, this Portland hiking and climbing
club leads 700 hikes year-round. Nominal fee charged. Carpool.
mazamas.org

Oregon Wild. Formerly the Oregon Natural Resources Council.
Free hikes (donations encouraged). oregonwild.org

Volcano Lands Nature Tours. Year-round. Owner/guide Ivan
Phillipsen has a PhD in zoology and is a certified Interpretive
Guide, focusing on helping visitors connect with nature. Full-day
van tours include hikes and lunch. 503-610-0571.
volcanolands.com

Hikes: online resources

Friends of the Columbia Gorge. Hike directions and histories.
gorgefriends.org/hikethe gorge/planyourowngorgehike

Northwest Waterfall Survey. Detailed info on gorge waterfalls.
waterfallsnorthwest.com

Scott Cook's Blog. Author of *Curious Gorge* expands on his
book's hike info at curiousgorgeblog.wordpress.com

Trailkeepers of Oregon. Comprehensive info for hikes on the
Washington and Oregon sides of the gorge. oregonhikers.org

Washington Trails Association. Trail info for gorge hikes in
Washington and Oregon is listed in the Southwest Washington
region. wta.org

Hikes: books

100 Hikes in Northwest Oregon and Southwest Washington by William L. Sullivan. One of the many meticulously researched guides by the godfather of Oregon hiking. (Navillus Press, 4th ed. 2013)

Afoot and Afield Portland/Vancouver by Douglas Lorain. Another classic local guide; 56 gorge hikes plus many more around the region. (Wilderness Press, 2nd. ed. 2008)

Curious Gorge: Over 100 Hikes and Explorations in the Columbia River Gorge by Scott Cook. It will take you there and make you laugh along the way. Comprehensive hike details plus enthusiastic storytelling and interesting historic info from a gorge resident. (Self-published, 3rd ed. 2010)

Sixty Hikes within Sixty Miles: Portland by Paul Gerald. Covers the gorge and other areas in a guide that's a good read on the trail and from the armchair. (Menasha Ridge Press, 5th ed. 2014)

Horseback riding

Double Mountain Horse Ranch. Year-round. Rescued and former show horses live out the next chapter of their lives here. First-time riders and riders with disabilities or special needs are welcome. 3995 Portland Drive, Hood River. 541-513-1152. ridinginhoodriver.com

Northwestern Lake Riding Stables. April 1 to October 31: morning, afternoon and evening rides. Other months: they'll take you out when conditions are fine. 1262 Little Buck Creek Rd., White Salmon. 509-493-1905 or 509-281-0093. nwstables.com

Jet Ski rentals

Hood River WaterPlay. Spring to September. 1- to 8-hour rentals. Ages 18 and older. On the beach at the Best Western Plus Hood River Inn. 541-386-9463. hoodriverwaterplay.com

Kayaks: rentals and lessons

Gorge Paddling Center. Whitewater and flatwater rentals, guided trips and lessons. At the Nichols Boat Basin, 101 N First St., Hood River. 541-806-4190. gorgekayaker.com

Hood River WaterPlay. Summer months when the water is flat: lessons and rentals on sit-on-top kayaks—good for beginners, wildlife watching, photography. On the beach at the Best Western Plus Hood River Inn. 541-386-9463. hoodriverwaterplay.com

Sweetwater SUP Rentals. Mid-June to mid-September. Call for rentals on other dates. Lacamas Lake Heritage Park, Camas. Lessons too. Reservations recommended. 360-609-1212. sweetwatersuprentals.com

Kiteboarding

See Windsurfing and kiteboarding

Paragliding: tandem rides and lessons

Drop 1,500 feet from Burdoin Mountain to Sailboard Park in Bingen. Flights last 15 to 50 minutes, depending on conditions. See cascadeparaglidingclub.org. On its "About CPC" page is a list of certified tandem instructors.

Public transportation, bus

Gorge TransLink. When planning a gorge trip by bus and/or bike, this is a good place to start. As an alliance of gorge public transit agencies with connections to the Portland-Vancouver area, it can help you plan a trip between counties. gorgetranslink.com

Specific providers are:

Greyhound. The Portland station is at 550 NW Sixth Ave. Buses run between Portland, Hood River and The Dalles. Reservations: 800-231-2222. greyhound.com

TriMet. Its bus, light rail and commuter rail services serve the Portland metro area (Oregon only) including the west end of the gorge at Troutdale. 503-238-7433. trimet.org

C-TRAN. Serving the Vancouver area east to Washougal, it also runs buses from Portland to Vancouver locations where you can connect with gorge transit agencies. 360-695-0123. c-tran.com

Columbia Area Transit. This Hood River County, Oregon, transportation district offers weekday buses between Hood River and The Dalles. On Tuesday and Thursday buses with bike racks connect those towns to four Portland-area stops. 541-386-4202. community.gorge.net/hrctd/

Skamania County Transit Services. Its WET (West End Transit) buses run from Vancouver's Fisher's Landing to Stevenson and Carson, Washington. On weekdays year-round buses run twice daily (three times on Friday). From early May to mid October, buses stop on weekends at trailheads for Cape Horn, Sams Walker Day Use Area, Beacon Rock State Park and Dog Mountain. Buses have bike racks. 509-427-3990. gorgetranslink.com

Mt. Adams Transportation Services (MATS). This Klickitat County, Washington, provider serves the gorge's east end, including White Salmon, Bingen, Dallesport, Wishram and Goldendale. If you're traveling via Amtrak to Bingen or Wishram, you can catch a MATS bus from the train station. Buses run weekdays. MATS also has Oregon stops in The Dalles and Hood River, making it the cheapest way for a walker or biker to cross the Hood River Bridge (where bikes and pedestrians are not allowed). Buses with bike racks cross the bridge three times a day, Monday, Wednesday and Friday, $1 each way. Call 509-493-4662 to ensure space is available for your bike. For Goldendale area info, call 509-733-3060.

Rafting: guides

Deschutes River: Class II and III+

RiverDrifters. Ages 4 and older. Half-day or full-day trips. 800-972-0430. riverdrifters.net

Hood River: Class IV to V

Wet Planet Whitewater Rafting and Kayaking. April to May. Previous experience required. Ages 16 and older. 877-390-9445 or 509-493-8989. wetplanetwhitewater.com

Klickitat River: Class III+

RiverDrifters. Ages 10 and older. Late April to June. 800-972-0430. riverdrifters.net

Wet Planet Whitewater Rafting and Kayaking. April to June. Ages 10 and older. 877-390-9445 or 509-493-8989. wetplanetwhitewater.com

Zoller's Outdoor Odysseys. April to June. Ages 7 and older. 509-493-2641. zooraft.com

White Salmon River: Class III and IV

All Adventures Rafting. Year-round. Ages 7 and older. 800-743-5628 or 509-998-8545. alladventuresrafting.com

Blue Sky Outfitters. May to October. Ages 10 and older. 800-228-7238. blueskyoutfitters.com

RiverDrifters. March to November. From March to May: ages 10 and older; from May to August: ages 6 and older. 800-972-0430. riverdrifters.net

Wet Planet Whitewater Rafting and Kayaking. April to October: ages 10 and older. 877-390-9445 or 509-493-8989. wetplanetwhitewater.com

Zoller's Outdoor Odysseys. Year-round: ages 7 and older. 509-493-2641. zooraft.com

Wind River: Class IV and V

RiverDrifters. April to mid-May. Class IV experience required. Ages 16 and older. 800-972-0430. riverdrifters.net

Wet Planet Whitewater Rafting and Kayaking. April to June. Previous experience required. Ages 18 and older. 877-390-9445 or 509-493-8989. wetplanetwhitewater.com

Sailboat rentals

Hood River WaterPlay. Spring to September. Ages 18 and older. Hobie-cat catamaran sailing. Three hour lessons, half- and full-day rentals. On the beach at the Best Western Plus Hood River Inn. 541-386-9463. hoodriverwaterplay.com

Standup paddling: lessons and rentals

Big Winds. Summer months. Event Site, Hood River for lessons and rentals. Also standup paddle yoga class, guided 8-mile downwind paddling trip or downwind shuttle from Viento State Park to the Event Site. Downwind season: May to September. 207 Front St., Hood River. 888-509-4210. bigwinds.com

Gorge Paddling Center. May 15 to October 15. Nichols Boat Basin, Hood River. 541-806-4190. gorgekayaker.com

Hood River WaterPlay. Spring to September. On the beach at the Best Western Plus Hood River Inn. 541-386-9463. hoodriverwaterplay.com

Sweetwater SUP Rentals. Mid-June to mid-September. Call for rentals on other dates. Lacamas Lake Heritage Park, 341 NW Lake Road, Camas. Lessons too. Reservations recommended. 360-609-1212. sweetwatersuprentals.com

Trains

Amtrak's Empire Builder. Leaves Portland every afternoon, crosses the Columbia and follows a waterfront route along the Washington side, with stops in the gorge at Bingen (a 90-minute trip) and Wishram (a little over 2 hours). In Bingen, walk or bike the short uphill to White Salmon to lodging at Inn of the White Salmon. With them, arrange a wine/bike tour or a wine tour. I don't recommend taking Amtrak back to Portland as it can be hours late by this point in its westbound trip from Chicago. See page 248 for public transportation options for the return. amtrak.com

Mount Hood Railroad. Excursions from Hood River on a 22-mile route past vineyards and orchards up the Hood River Valley to Parkdale. June to October: weekdays only except for special event trains. Dates vary with the month. Trains leave the Hood River station at 11 a.m., lay over 45 minutes in Parkdale, and return to Hood River at 3:15 p.m. Dinner and murder mystery trains too. 110 Railroad Ave., Hood River. 800-872-4661. mthoodrr.com

Windsurfing and kiteboarding

These Hood River-based businesses are permitted (at August 2015) by the Port of Hood River; they're required to use certified instructors and have liability insurance. For updates on authorized concessions for windsurfing and kiteboarding instruction visit portofhoodriver.com.

Big Winds. Windsurfing lessons, rentals at the Hook. Kiteboard rentals (but not sails). 207 Front St. 888-509-4210 or 541-386-6086. bigwinds.com

Brian's Windsurfing. Summer: Kiteboarding and windsurfing lessons and rentals at the Event Site. 541-377-9463. brianswindsurfing.com

Gorge Kiteboard School. April to early October: Lessons and rentals at the Event Site and the Spit. 503-577-3578. gorgekiteboardschool.com

Hood River WaterPlay. Spring to September. Lessons include all gear. Windsurfing only. On the beach at the Best Western Plus Hood River Inn. 541-386-9463. hoodriverwaterplay.com

Kite the Gorge. Kiteboarding lessons at the Spit. 541-490-9426. kitethegorge.com

New Wind Kite School. Summer at the Event Site. 541-387-2440. newwindkiteboarding.com

Also, for rentals only: **Windance Boardshop.** 108 Hwy 35, Hood River. 800-574-4020. windance.com

Columbia Gorge Windsurfing Association. Founded in 1987, this is a great resource for anyone curious about the sport. As part of its windsurfing advocacy work, the association has created and improved sites at Blackberry Beach, Doug's Beach, Viento, Rowena and Luhr Jensen. See the map of windsurfing sites at gorgewindsurfing.org.

Wine tours

Aspen Limo and Tours. Wine and limo, and other gorge tours. 503-274-9505. aspenlimotours.com

Evergreen Escapes. Its 6-hour Wine and Waterfalls tour travels the Historic Columbia River Highway past waterfalls to Hood River wineries. 503-252-1931. evergreenescapes.com

Hood River Mountain Bike Adventures. Owner Greg Galliano will guide you on a route to wineries, tailored to your skills. 503-705-3592. hoodrivermountainbikeadventures.com

Martin's Gorge Tours. Year-round, 4- to 6-hour tours. Tasting fees included in tour price. 503-349-1323. martinsgorgetours.com

Wine Dirt. Owner/guide Mary Alfieri Studt is an expert in enology (the study of wine-making) and the third generation of her family in the wine business. Full-day tours include stops at three to four wineries, lunch and info about the region's terroir. Begin in Portland or at gorge locations. 503-583-4391. winedirt.com

BUYING LOCAL FISH

May to July and late August to September are generally the months when Indian fishers sell their catch. To find fresh salmon buying tips, visit Columbia River Inter-Tribal Fish Commission at critfc.org and click "Buy Salmon." Or call 888-289-1855 or 503-238-0667.

Buy fresh fish:

East of North Bonneville, Washington:
Fort Raines fishing access site, about 1 mile west of the Bridge of the Gods, off SR 14.

Cascade Locks, Oregon: Seasonal sales in the parking area east of the Bridge of the Gods. Year-round sales at Brigham Fish Market, 681 WaNaPa St. 541-374-9340

The Dalles, Oregon: Lone Pine sales area. I-84, exit 87; look for signs.

ACKNOWLEDGMENTS

Thank you to Debbie Asakawa, board member of Friends of the Columbia Gorge, for giving me the idea to write a book about the connections between gorge towns and trails, and for being the inspiring gorge dynamo that she is. Renee Tkach of Friends' Towns to Trails program has been immensely helpful, especially in educating me about the Washington side of the gorge. Thanks also to Kevin Gorman and Maegan Jossy of Friends. Skamania County Chamber of Commerce's grant was a much-appreciated kickstart to this project, and Casey Roeder, executive director of the chamber, offered welcome advice and review. I so appreciate the friendship and collegiately of fellow guidebook writers Scott Cook, Bill Sullivan and Paul Gerald, whose books I have, use and love. Thank you also for your time and helpful counsel: Kristen Stallman, Columbia River Gorge National Scenic Area coordinator for ODOT; Len Otto, Troutdale Historical Society president; Lisa Farquharson, The Dalles Area Chamber of Commerce president; Ben Shumaker, City of Stevenson planning director; James Day of Washington State Parks; and Tom Kloster for his incredibly interesting WyEast blog. Thanks to Bryan Swan for his fascinating waterfallsnorthwest.com.

And huge thanks to the team who made this book with me: designers Brad Smith and Etah Chen of Hot Pepper Studios, mapmaker Matthew Hampton of Cascade Cartography, editor Jenefer Angell of Passionfruit Projects and book guru Bob Smith of BookPrinters Network. I learned from you all. Your ideas and work enhanced this project, and I'm grateful for your expertise and enthusiasm.

INDEX

advocacy, conservancy and education groups, 244-245
Aldrich Butte, 42
Amtrak, 10, 249, 250
apple orchards. *See* orchards and farm stands
Army Corps of Engineers, 39, 47, 107, 122, 204, 210
Army Corps of Engineers parks, 107, 120-122, 138-139, 203-205
auto courts, vintage, 79, 213
Balfour-Klickitat Day Use Area, 18, 118-119
beaches, 28, 46, 57, 108, 138, 157, 160, 180, 181, 225, 226, 228, 238
Beacon Rock State Park, 21, 36-39, 50
bike rentals, 128, 146, 171, 190, 243-244
bike tours, Cascade Locks, 196-203, 206-208
bike tour, Hood River, 171, 180-184
bike tour, Maryhill, 104-107
bike tours, Mosier, 152-158, 158-159
bike tour, North Bonneville, 42-47
bike tour, Stevenson, 55-59, 59-60
bike tours, The Dalles, 128-135, 136-138
bike tours, Troutdale, 228-230
bike tour, Washougal, 27-32
biking, car-free paths, 28-29, 42-47, 58-59, 61, 100, 136, 142, 158-159, 180-182, 196-203
biking, tours and guides. *See* bike rentals
Bingen, WA, 83-86
bird-watching sites, 28-29, 38, 46, 118-119, 244
boat and bike tour, 209-210
Bonneville Hot Springs, 39-42, 50
Bonneville Landslide, 16, 36, 42, 46, 56, 60, 201
Bonneville Lock and Dam, Oregon side, 12, 201-202, 209-210, 212
Bonneville Lock and Dam, Washington side, 46-47, 49
Boring Lava domes, 26
brew pubs. *See* "Eat and Drink" listings in tours
Bridal Veil State Park and Scenic Viewpoint, 221
Bridge of the Gods, 16, 53, 59-60, 196
bridges, noteworthy, 59-60, 67, 70, 76, 127, 129, 150, 153, 156, 157, 196, 197, 200, 203, 221, 223,
     229-230
bus routes. *See* public transportation
C-TRAN bus service, 248
Cabin Creek Falls, 184
campgrounds, 35, 50, 64, 79, 97, 112, 124, 147, 162, 192, 213
Cape Horn, 26-27
Captain William Clark Park, 28
Carson, WA, 66-79
Cascade Locks Historical Museum, 205, 212
Cascade Locks Marine Park, 16, 59, 134, 203-205
Cascade Locks, OR, 194-213
Cascade Mountains, name, 204
Cascade Volcanic Arc, 75
Cascades Massacre, 46, 59
Cascades of the Columbia, 5, 60, 201, 204
Catherine Creek, 86, 115, 119
Celilo Bridge, 127, 143
Celilo Falls, 5, 107, 120, 129, 138-139, 143

cemeteries, 42, 43, 55, 59, 92, 118, 121, 134
Centerville, WA, 101, 104
chambers of commerce. *See* "Discover and Learn" listings in tours
cherry orchards. *See* orchards and farm stands
Civilian Conservation Corps sites, 71, 74, 200, 201, 213
climate. *See* weather
Columbia Area Transit bus service, 248
Columbia Gorge Discovery Center and Museum, 136, 146
Columbia Gorge Interpretive Center Museum, 60, 63
Columbia Gorge Refuge Stewards, 245
Columbia Gorge sternwheeler, 181, 195, 201, 205, 238, 245
Columbia Hills State Park, 18, 120-122
Columbia River Gorge National Scenic Area, 1, 3, 5, 9, 26, 47, 71, 86, 119, 183, 189, 216, 217
Columbia River Highway. *See* Historic Columbia River Highway
Condit Dam, 93-94
Confluence Project art installations, 139, 225
Cook Hill, 184
Corbett, OR, 28, 217
Cottonwood Beach, 28-29
courthouses, 57, 63, 104, 113, 128, 145
Coyote Wall, 86, 120, 158-159
Crate's Point, 136
Crawford Oaks, 122
Crown Point, 12, 217, 220
cruise ships and tours, 245-246
Dalles-Celilo Canal and Locks, 143
Dalles Mountain Ranch, 19, 122
Depot Rail Museum, 228, 234
Deschutes River, 139, 142-143, 249
Deschutes River Railbed Trail, 142
Deschutes River State Recreation Area, 142-143
Dike Trail, Washougal, 28-29
Dining. *See* "Eat" listings in tours
Discover Pass, 8-9, 26, 27, 36, 38, 52, 86-87, 100, 105, 108, 114
distilleries, 63, 190, 233
Doetsch Ranch, 39
Dog Mountain, 77, 184
Doug's Beach State Park, 108
Dougan Creek Falls, 27
Dougan Falls, 27
Drano Lake, 90-91
driving tours, scenic, Oregon, 138-143, 152-158, 173-179, 206-208, 216-226
driving tours, scenic, Washington, 12-21, 26-27, 87-92, 101-104, 105-108, 118-120
Dry Creek Falls, Oregon, 208
Dry Creek Falls, Washington, 74
Eagle Creek and waterfalls, 12, 197, 200, 208
Eagle Creek Overlook, 201
eagles, viewing, 118-119
Easy CLIMB trail, 208
Elowah Falls, 203
Event Site, Hood River, 181
Falls Creek Falls, 75
ferries, historic, 57, 142, 157
festivals by month, 236-242
fish, buying local, 203, 253

fish counts, daily recording, 210,
fishing, guides, 33
Fort Cascades National Historic Site, 46, 49
Fort Dalles, 132-133, 146
Franz Lake National Wildlife Refuge, 38
Friends of Multnomah Falls, 234, 245
Friends of the Columbia Gorge, 1, 26-27, 117-118, 150, 152, 245, 246
Friends of the Historic Columbia River Highway, 245
Friends of Vista House, 234, 245
galleries. *See* "Shop" listings in tours
Gifford Pinchot National Forest, 66-76
Glenn Otto Park, 216, 226, 228-229
Goldendale Observatory State Park, 98, 104, 111
Goldendale, WA, 101, 104
Good Roads movement, 105-107, 220
Gorge Heritage Museum, 96
Gorge TransLink, 248
Gorton Creek Falls, 206-207
Government Mineral Springs, 66, 71-74, 79
Government Rock, 206
Greyhound bus service, 248
guides to hire. *See* Appendix B
Guy Talbot State Park, 221
Hamilton Island, 46, 202
Hamilton Mountain, 36, 38, 42, 46
Hardy Falls, 39
Harlow House Museum, 228, 234
hatcheries. *See* salmon hatcheries
Heaven and Hell Falls, 61
High Bridge, Carson, WA, 67, 70
highlights of the gorge, 12-21
hiking guidebooks, 246-247
hikes, guided, 246
Hill, Sam, 03, 105-107, 220
Historic Columbia River Highway, 3-4, 9-10, 12, 106, 129, 152-157, 173, 216-224, 229-270
Historic Columbia River Highway State Trail, 10, 149, 158-159, 183, 184, 196-203, 230
History Museum of Hood River, 184, 190
Hole in the Wall Falls, 184
Hood River Bridge, 180, 191, 249
Hood River Heights, 171, 179, 186
Hood River, OR, 164-193
Hood River (the river), 175-178, 180-181, 193, 249
the Hook, Hood River, 181
horseback riding, 82, 118, 172, 247
Horsetail Falls, 223
Horsethief Butte, 122, 125
Horsethief Lake, 121-122, 125
hostels, 97, 235
hot spring resorts, 39, 42, 49, 76, 79,
hotels. *See* "Stay" listings in tours
I-84, 3, 9
Ice Age Floods, 4, 39, 117-118, 153, 216
Indian Creek Trail, 167-170
industries, 1, 4-5, 70-71, 86, 87, 90-91, 136, 150, 174, 179, 180-183, 202-203, 221
in-lieu fishing sites, 5, 92, 139, 160, 253

Ives Island, 46

Jet Ski rentals, 247

Kanaka Creek, 57

kayaks, lessons and rentals, 247

King of Roads exhibit, 228, 234

kiteboarding, lessons and rentals, 251

Klickitat County Courthouse, 104, 113

Klickitat Mineral Springs, 101

Klickitat River, 101, 109, 249

Klickitat Trail, 18, 100, 101, 109

Klickitat Trail Conservancy, 245

Klickitat, WA, 101, 120

Koberg Beach State Recreation Site, 160, 180

Labyrinth, 86

Lacamas Lake, 33

Lancaster, Samuel, 106, 220-221

Larch Mountain, 217

Latourell Falls, 220-221

lessons, windsurfing and other water sports, 247-251

Lewis and Clark Expedition, 28, 46, 136, 142, 180, 225

Lewis and Clark Festival Park, 136-138

Lewis and Clark State Park, 228

Little White Salmon National Fish Hatchery, 90-91

Little White Salmon River, 90-92

locks, past and present, 139, 201, 203-205, 209, 212

Lodging. *See* "Stay" listings in tours

log flumes, 79, 90-91, 221

logging and mills, 1, 5, 70-71, 79, 86, 87, 90-91, 202-203, 221

Long Narrows, 5, 129, 139

Luhr Jensen Beach, 181

Lyle Cherry Orchard, 117-118

Lyle Twin Bridges Historical Museum, 111, 123

Lyle, WA, 98, 100, 117

Mark O. Hatfield Visitor Center, 161

Maryhill Loops Road, 105-106

Maryhill Museum of Art, 18, 19, 106-107, 111

Maryhill, WA, 105-107

Mayer State Park, 152-153, 156-157

McCord Creek, 203

Memaloose Overlook, 153

Menucha, 217

Mill A, WA, 91

missionaries, 132-133, 136

Missoula Floods. *See* Ice Age Floods

Moffett Creek, 203

Mosier Creek, 150

Mosier Plateau, 150-152

Mosier twin tunnels, 159

Mosier, OR, 148-163

motels. *See* "Stay" listings in tours

Mt. Adams Transportation Services, 249

Multnomah Falls, 12, 223, 234

Munra Falls, 202

museums. *See* "Discover and Learn" listings in tours or specific names

Native Americans, 4-5, 38, 42-43, 46-47, 51, 60, 81, 91, 100, 120, 129, 139, 180, 183, 206

Nature Conservancy properties, 39, 153, 245
Nichols Boat Basin, 181
North Bonneville, WA, 36-51
Northwest Forest Pass, 9, 47, 48, 70, 77, 206, 208, 217
Northwestern Park, 93
Observation Peak, 75
Odell, OR, 174-175
Old St. Peter's Landmark, 129, 146
Oneonta Creek, 223
Oneonta Gorge, 223-224
orchards and farm stands, 105, 150, 152, 158, 161-163, 173-174
Oregon Department of Transportation, 10, 220
Oregon State Parks pass, 9, 158
Oregon Trail sites, 136, 142-143
Pacific Crest Trail, 60, 208
Panorama Point, 173
paragliding, rides and lessons, 248
passes, 8-9
Pendleton Woolen Mills, 21, 32, 34
petroglyphs, 28, 114, 121
Pierce Island, 39
Pine Grove, OR, 165, 174
Point Vancouver, 29
Ponytail Falls, 223
pools, public, 128
poor farm, converted, 226
Port of Camas-Washougal, 27, 35
portage routes, historic, 46, 60, 204-205
Portland Women's Forum overlook, 217
Post Canyon mountain biking, 171
Presby Museum, 111
public transportation, 10, 248
Puff Falls, 74-75
Punchbowl Falls, Hood River, 170, 179
rafting, guides and outfitters, 249-250
rail lines in the gorge. *See* trains
rainfall. *See* weather
Reed Island State Park, 28
rentals, bikes. *See* bike rentals
river sport lessons and rentals, 247-251
river temperature, daily recording, 210
Riverfront Park, The Dalles, 138
Riverfront Trail, The Dalles, 136-138
Rock Cove, 58-59
Rock Creek Falls, 55-56
rodeos, 239-240
Rodney Falls, 39
Rooster Rock State Park, 217, 225
Rowena Crest Overlook, 16, 17, 153
Ruckel Creek, 197
Russell, Nancy, 26-27, 117, 150
Ruthton County Park, 13, 182, 183
sailboat rentals, 250
salmon hatcheries, 87, 90, 91, 197
salmon, buying fresh, 253

salmon spawning sites, 12, 197, 200
Sams Walker Day Use/Picnic Area, 47
sandbars, 118, 179, 181
Sandy River, 216, 225-226, 228-229
Sandy River Delta, 215, 225
scenic touring routes. *See* driving tours, scenic
Schreiner Farms, 108, 111
settlement, Euro-American, 5
Seven Mile Hill, 158
Shepperd's Dell State Natural Area, 221
shopping. *See* "Shop" listings in tours
Short Narrows, 5, 129, 139
Skamania County Courthouse, 57, 63
Skamania County Fairgrounds, 58
Skamania County Transit Services, 248
Skamania Landing, 47-48
Skamania Lodge, 21, 59, 61, 64, 65
Skamania, WA, 37, 47-48
soda springs, 71, 74, 101
Sorosis Park, 134
the Spit, 181
Spring Creek National Fish Hatchery, 20, 81, 87
Springdale, OR, 216
SR 14, 10
St. Cloud Ranch Day Use/Picnic Area, 48
standup paddling rentals and lessons, 250
Stark Street, historic infrastructure, 229
Starvation Creek Falls, 184
Steamboat Landing Park, 28
steamboats
Steigerwald Lake National Wildlife Refuge, 23, 28, 32
Stevenson, WA, 52-63
Stonehenge replica, 99, 105-106
Straight's Point, 120
sturgeon, 29, 210
swimming, 27, 28, 46, 128, 173, 225, 226
Syncline. *See* Coyote Wall
Table Mountain, 56, 203
Tanner Creek, 202
taxes, lodging, 11
taxes, sales, 11
The Dalles Dam Visitor Center, 132, 146
The Dalles, OR, 126-147, 157
Thunder Island, 204
Tom McCall Point, 153
Toothrock Tunnel, 201
tours, aerial, 172, 243
tours, astronomical, 104, 111
tours, bike, 243
tours, breweries, 183, 185
tours, bronze foundry, 211
tours, bus and van, 244
tours, cruise ships, 245-246
tours, dams, 12, 49, 93-94, 146, 212
tours, guided hikes, 246

tours, jet boat, 142, 209-210, 245
tours, organic juice manufacturer, 175
tours, petroglyphs, 114, 121
tours, wine, 171, 252
tours, woolen mill, 34
Towns to Trails hikes and program, 117-118, 150-152,
Trail of the Gods, 59-60
Trailkeepers of Oregon, 246
trains, excursions and routes, 10, 164, 250-251
TriMet bus and rail service, 248
Triple Falls, 223
Troutdale, OR, 214-216, 225-230
Trust for Public Land, 47-48
tuberculosis sanatoriums, historic, 134
Tucker County Park, 178
tunnels, historic, 90, 159, 201
Two Rivers Heritage Museum, 32, 34
U-pick farms. *See* orchards and farm stands
U.S. Army Corps of Engineers. *See* Army Corps of Engineers
U.S. Army forts, 46, 49, 57, 132-133, 146
Underwood Mountain, 90-91, 118
Upper McCord Creek Falls, 203
Viento State Park, 184
vineyards and tasting rooms, 63, 96, 111, 123, 145, 161, 190
visitor centers. *See* "Discover and Learn" listings in tours and 236
Vista House, 12, 13, 217, 220, 222, 234
volcanoes, 75, 91
Wahclella Falls, 202
Wah Gwin Gwin Falls, 183
Wahkeena Falls, 221, 223
walking tour, Cascade Locks, 203-206
walking tour, Hood River, 166-171
walking tour, Stevenson, 55-59, 59-60
walking tour, The Dalles, 128-135
walking tour, Troutdale, 226-229
walking tour, Washougal, 27-32
walking tour, White Salmon, 82-83, 84-85
Washougal River, 27, 29
Washougal, WA, 22-35
Waterfall Alley, 220-224
waterfalls, Oregon, 12, 150, 175, 178, 183, 184, 197, 202, 203, 206, 208-209, 216, 220-223, 230
waterfalls, Washington, 27, 39, 55, 61, 74-75, 93
waterfall touring, 214-224
Waterfront Park, Washougal, 27
Waterfront Park and Trail, Hood River, 181
weather, 7-8
Wells Island, 181-182
Western Antique Aeroplane and Automobile Museum, 16, 17, 178, 190
White Salmon River, 18, 82, 93-94, 249
White Salmon, WA, 80-83
wildflower season, 7
Wind Mountain, 77
Wind River, 70-71, 77, 250
Wind River Canopy Crane, 71
windsurfing viewing sites, 20, 87, 157, 181

windsurfing, lessons and rentals, 251
wine tours, 171, 252
wineries. *See* vineyards and tasting rooms
Wishram, WA, 127
wooden water pipes, 170
Works Progress Administration sites, 132, 201-202, 209, 229
Wyeth Campground, 206
ziplining, 59

ABOUT THE AUTHOR

Laura O. Foster writes about Portland and the Pacific Northwest. Her books take readers on explorations of a city's or region's geology, architecture, neighborhoods, parklands and human and natural history.

Born and raised in Aurora, Illinois, Foster moved to Portland in 1989 and began a career in contract writing and editing. She later pivoted to nonfiction manuscript development and writing for Metro, the Portland-area regional government, on topics such as the Oregon Zoo, recycling, natural gardening, transportation alternatives, and the histories and conservation practices at parks and natural areas. Since 2009 she has led urban explorations for Portland's Multnomah Athletic Club and occasionally for nonprofits and municipalities.

Other books by Laura O. Foster

Portland Hill Walks: 24 Explorations in Parks and Neighborhoods (Timber Press, 2005, rev. ed. 2013)

Portland City Walks: 20 Explorations in and around Town (Timber Press, 2008)

Walk There! 50 Treks in and around Portland and Vancouver (Metro, 2008, 2009)

Lake Oswego: Images of America (Arcadia Publishing, 2009)

The Portland Stairs Book (Timber Press, 2010)

Boys Who Rocked the World (Co-author. Beyond Words, 2001; rev. ed. Aladdin/Beyond Words, 2012)

Walking with Ramona: Exploring Beverly Cleary's Portland (Microcosm Publishing, 2016)

Reach her on Facebook, at LauraOFoster.com or at GorgeGetaways.com.